everybody
lies

everybody lies

What the Internet Can Tell Us About Who We Really Are

Seth Stephens-Davidowitz

BLOOMSBURY

LONDON · OXFORD · NEW YORK · NEW DELHI · SYDNEY

Bloomsbury Publishing
An imprint of Bloomsbury Publishing Plc

50 Bedford Square   1385 Broadway
London   New York
WC1B 3DP   NY 10018
UK   USA

www.bloomsbury.com

BLOOMSBURY and the Diana logo are trademarks of Bloomsbury Publishing Plc

First published in 2017 in the United States by HarperCollins Publishers, New York

First published in Great Britain 2017

Designed by Suet Yee Chong

British Library Cataloguing-in-Publication Data
A catalogue record for this book is available from the British Library.

ISBN: HB: 978-1-4088-9471-2
       TPB: 978-1-4088-9470-5
       ePub: 978-1-4088-9469-9

2 4 6 8 10 9 7 5 3 1

Printed and bound in Great Britain by CPI Group (UK) Ltd, Croydon CR0 4YY

To find out more about our authors and books visit www.bloomsbury.com.
Here you will find extracts, author interviews, details of forthcoming
events and the option to sign up for our newsletters.

To Mom and Dad

CONTENTS

PART III **BIG DATA: HANDLE WITH CARE**

FOREWORD

Ever since philosophers speculated about a "cerebroscope," a mythical device that would display a person's thoughts on a screen, social scientists have been looking for tools to expose the workings of human nature. During my career as an experimental psychologist, different ones have gone in and out of fashion, and I've tried them all—rating scales, reaction times, pupil dilation, functional neuroimaging, even epilepsy patients with implanted electrodes who were happy to while away the hours in a language experiment while waiting to have a seizure.

Yet none of these methods provides an unobstructed view into the mind. The problem is a savage tradeoff. Human thoughts are complex propositions; unlike Woody Allen speed-reading *War and Peace*, we don't just think "It was about some Russians." But propositions in all their tangled multidimensional glory are difficult for a scientist to analyze. Sure, when people pour their hearts out, we apprehend the richness of their stream of consciousness, but monologues are not an ideal dataset for testing hypotheses. On the other hand, if we concentrate on measures that are easily quantifiable, like people's reaction time to words, or their skin response to pictures, we can do the statistics, but we've pureed the complex texture of cognition into a single number. Even the most sophisticated neuroimaging methodologies can tell us how a thought is splayed out in 3-D space, but not what the thought consists of.

As if the tradeoff between tractability and richness weren't bad enough, scientists of human nature are vexed by the Law of Small Numbers—Amos Tversky and Daniel Kahneman's name for the fallacy of thinking that the traits of a population will be reflected in any sample, no matter how small. Even the most numerate scientists have woefully defective intuitions about how many subjects one really needs in a study before one can abstract away from the random quirks and bumps and generalize to all Americans, to say nothing of *Homo sapiens*. It's all the iffier when the sample is gathered by convenience, such as by offering beer money to the sophomores in our courses.

This book is about a whole new way of studying the mind. Big Data from internet searches and other online responses are not a cerebroscope, but Seth Stephens-Davidowitz shows that they offer an unprecedented peek into people's psyches. At the privacy of their keyboards, people confess the strangest things, sometimes (as in dating sites or searches for professional advice) because they have real-life consequences, at other times precisely because they *don't* have consequences: people can unburden themselves of some wish or fear without a real person reacting in dismay or worse. Either way, the people are not just pressing a button or turning a knob, but keying in any of trillions of sequences of characters to spell out their thoughts in all their explosive, combinatorial vastness. Better still, they lay down these digital traces in a form that is easy to aggregate and analyze. They come from all walks of life. They can take part in unobtrusive experiments which vary the stimuli and tabulate the responses in real time. And they happily supply these data in gargantuan numbers.

Everybody Lies is more than a proof of concept. Time and again my preconceptions about my country and my species were turned upside-down by Stephens-Davidowitz's discoveries. Where did Donald Trump's unexpected support come from? When Ann Landers asked her readers in 1976 whether they regretted having children and was shocked to find that a majority did, was she misled by an unrepresentative, self-selected sample? Is the internet to blame for that redundantly named crisis of the late 2010s, the "filter bubble"? What triggers hate crimes? Do people seek jokes to cheer themselves up? And though I like to think that nothing can shock me, I was shocked aplenty by what the internet reveals about human sexuality—including the discovery that every month a certain number of women search for "humping stuffed animals." No experiment using reaction time or pupil dilation or functional neuroimaging could ever have turned up that fact.

Everybody will enjoy *Everybody Lies*. With unflagging curiosity and an endearing wit, Stephens-Davidowitz points to a new path for social science in the twenty-first century. With this endlessly fascinating window into human obsessions, who needs a cerebroscope?

—Steven Pinker, 2017

EVERYBODY LIES

INTRODUCTION

THE OUTLINES OF A REVOLUTION

Surely he would lose, they said.

In the 2016 Republican primaries, polling experts concluded that Donald Trump didn't stand a chance. After all, Trump had insulted a variety of minority groups. The polls and their interpreters told us few Americans approved of such outrages.

Most polling experts at the time thought that Trump would lose in the general election. Too many likely voters said they were put off by his manner and views.

But there were some clues that Trump might actually win both the primaries and the general election—on the internet.

I am an internet data expert. Every day, I track the digital trails that people leave as they make their way across the web. From the buttons or keys we click or tap, I try to understand what we really want, what we will really do, and who we really are. Let me explain how I got started on this unusual path.

The story begins—and this seems like ages ago—with the 2008 presidential election and a long-debated question in social science: How significant is racial prejudice in America?

Barack Obama was running as the first African-American presidential nominee of a major party. He won—rather easily. And the polls suggested that race was not a factor in how Americans voted. Gallup, for example, conducted numerous polls before and after Obama's first election. Their conclusion? American voters largely did not care that Barack Obama was black. Shortly after the election, two well-known professors at the University of California, Berkeley pored through other survey-based data, using more sophisticated data-mining techniques. They reached a similar conclusion.

And so, during Obama's presidency, this became the conventional wisdom in many parts of the media and in large swaths of the academy. The sources that the media and social scientists have used for eighty-plus years to understand the world told us that the overwhelming majority of Americans did not care that Obama was black when judging whether he should be their president.

This country, long soiled by slavery and Jim Crow laws, seemed finally to have stopped judging people by the color of their skin. This seemed to suggest that racism was on its last legs in America. In fact, some pundits even declared that we lived in a post-racial society.

In 2012, I was a graduate student in economics, lost in life, burnt-out in my field, and confident, even cocky, that I had a pretty good understanding of how the world worked, of what people thought and cared about in the twenty-first century. And when it came to this issue of prejudice, I allowed myself to believe, based on everything I had read in psychology and political science, that explicit racism was limited to a small percentage of Americans—the majority of them conservative Republicans, most of them living in the deep South.

Then, I found Google Trends.

Google Trends, a tool that was released with little fanfare in 2009, tells users how frequently any word or phrase has been searched in different locations at different times. It was advertised as a fun tool—perhaps enabling friends to discuss which celebrity was most popular or what fashion was suddenly hot. The earliest versions included a playful admonishment that people "wouldn't want to write your PhD dissertation" with the data, which immediately motivated me to write my dissertation with it.*

At the time, Google search data didn't seem to be a proper source of information for "serious" academic research. Unlike

---

* Google Trends has been a source of much of my data. However, since it only allows you to compare the relative frequency of different searches but does not report the absolute number of any particular search, I have usually supplemented it with Google AdWords, which reports exactly how frequently every search is made. In most cases I have also been able to sharpen the picture with the help of my own Trends-based algorithm, which I describe in my dissertation, "Essays Using Google Data," and in my *Journal of Public Economics* paper, "The Cost of Racial Animus on a Black Candidate: Evidence Using Google Search Data." The dissertation, a link to the paper, and a complete explanation of the data and code used in all the original research presented in this book are available on my website, sethsd.com.

surveys, Google search data wasn't created as a way to help us understand the human psyche. Google was invented so that people could learn about the world, not so researchers could learn about people. But it turns out the trails we leave as we seek knowledge on the internet are tremendously revealing.

In other words, people's search for information is, in itself, information. When and where they search for facts, quotes, jokes, places, persons, things, or help, it turns out, can tell us a lot more about what they really think, really desire, really fear, and really do than anyone might have guessed. This is especially true since people sometimes don't so much query Google as confide in it: "I hate my boss." "I am drunk." "My dad hit me."

The everyday act of typing a word or phrase into a compact, rectangular white box leaves a small trace of truth that, when multiplied by millions, eventually reveals profound realities. The first word I typed in Google Trends was "God." I learned that the states that make the most Google searches mentioning "God" were Alabama, Mississippi, and Arkansas—the Bible Belt. And those searches are most frequently on Sundays. None of which was surprising, but it was intriguing that search data could reveal such a clear pattern. I tried "Knicks," which it turns out is Googled most in New York City. Another no-brainer. Then I typed in my name. "We're sorry," Google Trends informed me. "There is not enough search volume" to show these results. Google Trends, I learned, will provide data only when lots of people make the same search.

But the power of Google searches is not that they can tell us that God is popular down South, the Knicks are popular in New York City, or that I'm not popular anywhere. Any survey could tell you that. The power in Google data is that people tell the giant search engine things they might not tell anyone else.

Take, for example, sex (a subject I will investigate in much greater detail later in this book). Surveys cannot be trusted to tell us the truth about our sex lives. I analyzed data from the General Social Survey, which is considered one of the most influential and authoritative sources for information on Americans' behaviors. According to that survey, when it comes to heterosexual sex, women say they have sex, on average, fifty-five times per year, using a condom 16 percent of the time. This adds up to about 1.1 billion condoms used per year. But heterosexual men say they use 1.6 billion condoms every year. Those numbers, by definition, would have to be the same. So who is telling the truth, men or women?

Neither, it turns out. According to Nielsen, the global information and measurement company that tracks consumer behavior, fewer than 600 million condoms are sold every year. So everyone is lying; the only difference is by how much.

The lying is in fact widespread. Men who have never been married claim to use on average twenty-nine condoms per year. This would add up to more than the total number of condoms sold in the United States to married and single people combined. Married people probably exaggerate how much sex they have, too. On average, married men under sixty-five tell surveys they have sex once a week. Only 1 percent say they have gone the past year without sex. Married women report having a little less sex but not much less.

Google searches give a far less lively—and, I argue, far more accurate—picture of sex during marriage. On Google, the top complaint about a marriage is not having sex. Searches for "sexless marriage" are three and a half times more common than "unhappy marriage" and eight times more common than "loveless marriage." Even unmarried couples complain somewhat frequently about not having sex. Google searches for "sexless relationship" are second only to searches for "abusive relationship." (This data, I should emphasize, is all presented anonymously. Google, of course, does not report data about any particular individual's searches.)

And Google searches presented a picture of America that was strikingly different from that post-racial utopia sketched out by the surveys. I remember when I first typed "nigger" into Google Trends. Call me naïve. But given how toxic the word is, I fully expected this to be a low-volume search. Boy, was I wrong. In the United States, the word "nigger"—or its plural, "niggers"—was included in roughly the same number of searches as the word "migraine(s)," "economist," and "Lakers." I wondered if searches for rap lyrics were skewing the results? Nope. The word used in rap songs is almost always "nigga(s)." So what was the motivation of Americans searching for "nigger"? Frequently, they were looking for jokes mocking African-Americans. In fact, 20 percent of searches with the word "nigger" also included the word "jokes." Other common searches included "stupid niggers" and "I hate niggers."

There were millions of these searches every year. A large number of Americans were, in the privacy of their own homes, making shockingly racist inquiries. The more I researched, the more disturbing the information got.

On Obama's first election night, when most of the commentary focused on praise of Obama and acknowledgment of the historic nature of his election, roughly one in every hun-

dred Google searches that included the word "Obama" also included "kkk" or "nigger(s)." Maybe that doesn't sound so high,
but think of the thousands of nonracist reasons to Google this
young outsider with a charming family about to take over the
world's most powerful job. On election night, searches and sign-
ups for Stormfront, a white nationalist site with surprisingly
high popularity in the United States, were more than ten times
higher than normal. In some states, there were more searches
for "nigger president" than "first black president."

There was a darkness and hatred that was hidden from the
traditional sources but was quite apparent in the searches that
people made.

Those searches are hard to reconcile with a society in which
racism is a small factor. In 2012 I knew of Donald J. Trump
mostly as a businessman and reality show performer. I had no
more idea than anyone else that he would, four years later, be a
serious presidential candidate. But those ugly searches are not
hard to reconcile with the success of a candidate who—in his
attacks on immigrants, in his angers and resentments—often
played to people's worst inclinations.

The Google searches also told us that much of what we thought
about the location of racism was wrong. Surveys and conventional wisdom placed modern racism predominantly in the
South and mostly among Republicans. But the places with the
highest racist search rates included upstate New York, western
Pennsylvania, eastern Ohio, industrial Michigan and rural Illinois, along with West Virginia, southern Louisiana, and Mississippi. The true divide, Google search data suggested, was not

South versus North; it was East versus West. You don't get this sort of thing much west of the Mississippi. And racism was not limited to Republicans. In fact, racist searches were no higher in places with a high percentage of Republicans than in places with a high percentage of Democrats. Google searches, in other words, helped draw a new map of racism in the United States—and this map looked very different from what you may have guessed. Republicans in the South may be more likely to admit to racism. But plenty of Democrats in the North have similar attitudes.

Four years later, this map would prove quite significant in explaining the political success of Trump.

In 2012, I was using this map of racism I had developed using Google searches to reevaluate exactly the role that Obama's race played. The data was clear. In parts of the country with a high number of racist searches, Obama did substantially worse than John Kerry, the white Democratic presidential candidate, had four years earlier. The relationship was not explained by any other factor about these areas, including education levels, age, church attendance, or gun ownership. Racist searches did not predict poor performance for any other Democratic candidate. Only for Obama.

And the results implied a large effect. Obama lost roughly 4 percentage points nationwide just from explicit racism. This was far higher than might have been expected based on any surveys. Barack Obama, of course, was elected and reelected president, helped by some very favorable conditions for Democrats, but he had to overcome quite a bit more than anyone who was relying on traditional data sources—and that was just about everyone—had realized. There were enough racists to help win a primary or tip a general election in a year not so favorable to Democrats.

My study was initially rejected by five academic journals. Many of the peer reviewers, if you will forgive a little disgruntlement, said that it was impossible to believe that so many Americans harbored such vicious racism. This simply did not fit what people had been saying. Besides, Google searches seemed like such a bizarre dataset.

Now that we have witnessed the inauguration of President Donald J. Trump, my finding seems more plausible.

The more I have studied, the more I have learned that Google has lots of information that is missed by the polls that can be helpful in understanding—among many, many other subjects—an election.

There is information on who will actually turn out to vote. More than half of citizens who don't vote tell surveys immediately before an election that they intend to, skewing our estimation of turnout, whereas Google searches for "how to vote" or "where to vote" weeks before an election can accurately predict which parts of the country are going to have a big showing at the polls.

There might even be information on who they will vote for. Can we really predict which candidate people will vote for just based on what they search? Clearly, we can't just study which candidates are searched for most frequently. Many people search for a candidate because they love him. A similar number of people search for a candidate because they hate him. That said, Stuart Gabriel, a professor of finance at the University of California, Los Angeles, and I have found a surprising clue about which way people are planning to vote. A large percentage of election-related searches contain queries with both candidates' names. During the 2016 election between Trump and Hillary Clinton, some people searched for "Trump Clinton polls." Others looked for highlights from the "Clinton Trump debate." In fact, 12 percent of search queries with "Trump" also included the word "Clinton." More than one-quarter of search queries with "Clinton" also included the word "Trump."

We have found that these seemingly neutral searches may actually give us some clues to which candidate a person supports.

How? The order in which the candidates appear. Our research suggests that a person is significantly more likely to put the candidate they support first in a search that includes both candidates' names.

In the previous three elections, the candidate who appeared first in more searches received the most votes. More interesting, the order the candidates were searched was predictive of which way a particular state would go.

The order in which candidates are searched also seems to contain information that the polls can miss. In the 2012 election between Obama and Republican Mitt Romney, Nate Silver, the virtuoso statistician and journalist, accurately predicted the result in all fifty states. However, we found that in states that listed Romney before Obama in searches most frequently, Romney actually did better than Silver had predicted. In states that most frequently listed Obama before Romney, Obama did better than Silver had predicted.

This indicator could contain information that polls miss

because voters are either lying to themselves or uncomfortable revealing their true preferences to pollsters. Perhaps if they claimed that they were undecided in 2012, but were consistently searching for "Romney Obama polls," "Romney Obama debate," and "Romney Obama election," they were planning to vote for Romney all along.

So did Google predict Trump? Well, we still have a lot of work to do—and I'll have to be joined by lots more researchers—before we know how best to use Google data to predict election results. This is a new science, and we only have a few elections for which this data exists. I am certainly not saying we are at the point—or ever will be at the point—where we can throw out public opinion polls completely as a tool for helping us predict elections.

But there were definitely portents, at many points, on the internet that Trump might do better than the polls were predicting.

During the general election, there were clues that the electorate might be a favorable one for Trump. Black Americans told polls they would turn out in large numbers to oppose Trump. But Google searches for information on voting in heavily black areas were way down. On election day, Clinton would be hurt by low black turnout.

There were even signs that supposedly undecided voters were going Trump's way. Gabriel and I found that there were more searches for "Trump Clinton" than "Clinton Trump" in key states in the Midwest that Clinton was expected to win. Indeed, Trump owed his election to the fact that he sharply outperformed his polls there.

But the major clue, I would argue, that Trump might prove a successful candidate—in the primaries, to begin with—was all that secret racism that my Obama study had uncovered. The Google searches revealed a darkness and hatred among a meaningful number of Americans that pundits, for many years, missed. Search data revealed that we lived in a very different society from the one academics and journalists, relying on polls, thought that we lived in. It revealed a nasty, scary, and widespread rage that was waiting for a candidate to give voice to it.

People frequently lie—to themselves and to others. In 2008, Americans told surveys that they no longer cared about race. Eight years later, they elected as president Donald J. Trump, a man who retweeted a false claim that black people are responsible for the majority of murders of white Americans, defended his supporters for roughing up a Black Lives Matters protester at one of his rallies, and hesitated in repudiating support from a former leader of the Ku Klux Klan. The same hidden racism that hurt Barack Obama helped Donald Trump.

Early in the primaries, Nate Silver famously claimed that there was virtually no chance that Trump would win. As the primaries progressed and it became increasingly clear that Trump had widespread support, Silver decided to look at the data to see if he could understand what was going on. How could Trump possibly be doing so well?

Silver noticed that the areas where Trump performed best made for an odd map. Trump performed well in parts of the Northeast and industrial Midwest, as well as the South. He performed notably worse out West. Silver looked for variables to try to explain this map. Was it unemployment? Was it religion? Was it gun ownership? Was it rates of immigration? Was it opposition to Obama?

Silver found that the single factor that best correlated with Donald Trump's support in the Republican primaries was that

Racist Search Rate

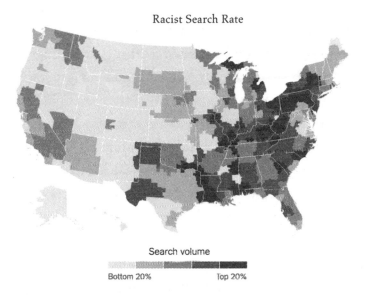

Search volume

Bottom 20%   Top 20%

Donald Trump Support in Republican Primary

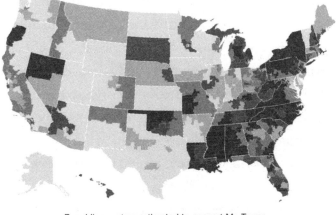

Republican voters estimated to support Mr. Trump

28%   31%   34%   37%

measure I had discovered four years earlier. Areas that supported Trump in the largest numbers were those that made the most Google searches for "nigger."

I have spent just about every day of the past four years analyzing Google data. This included a stint as a data scientist at Google, which hired me after learning about my racism research. And I continue to explore this data as an opinion writer and data journalist for the *New York Times*. The revelations have kept coming. Mental illness; human sexuality; child abuse; abortion; advertising; religion; health. Not exactly small topics, and this dataset, which didn't exist a couple of decades ago, offered surprising new perspectives on all of them. Economists and other social scientists are always hunting for new sources of data, so let me be blunt: I am now convinced that Google searches are the most important dataset ever collected on the human psyche.

This dataset, however, is not the only tool the internet has delivered for understanding our world. I soon realized there are other digital gold mines as well. I downloaded all of Wikipedia, pored through Facebook profiles, and scraped Stormfront. In addition, PornHub, one of the largest pornographic sites on the internet, gave me its complete data on the searches and video views of anonymous people around the world. In other words, I have taken a very deep dive into what is now called Big Data. Further, I have interviewed dozens of others—academics, data journalists, and entrepreneurs—who are also exploring these new realms. Many of their studies will be discussed here.

But first, a confession: I am not going to give a precise definition of what Big Data is. Why? Because it's an inherently vague concept. How big is big? Are 18,462 observations Small Data and 18,463 observations Big Data? I prefer to take an inclusive view of what qualifies: while most of the data I fiddle with is from the internet, I will discuss other sources, too. We are living through an explosion in the amount and quality of all kinds of available information. Much of the new information flows from Google and social media. Some of it is a product of digitization of information that was previously hidden away in cabinets and files. Some of it is from increased resources devoted to market research. Some of the studies discussed in this book don't use huge datasets at all but instead just employ a new and creative approach to data—approaches that are crucial in an era overflowing with information.

So why exactly is Big Data so powerful? Think of all the information that is scattered online on a given day—we have a number, in fact, for just how much information there is. On an average day in the early part of the twenty-first century, human beings generate 2.5 million trillion bytes of data.

And these bytes are clues.

A woman is bored on a Thursday afternoon. She Googles for some more "funny clean jokes." She checks her email. She signs on to Twitter. She Googles "nigger jokes."

A man is feeling blue. He Googles for "depression symptoms" and "depression stories." He plays a game of solitaire.

A woman sees the announcement of her friend getting engaged on Facebook. The woman, who is single, blocks the friend.

A man takes a break from Googling about the NFL and rap music to ask the search engine a question: "Is it normal to have dreams about kissing men?"

A woman clicks on a BuzzFeed story showing the "15 cutest cats."

A man sees the same story about cats. But on his screen it is called "15 most adorable cats." He doesn't click.

A woman Googles "Is my son a genius?"

A man Googles "how to get my daughter to lose weight."

A woman is on a vacation with her six best female friends. All her friends keep saying how much fun they're having. She sneaks off to Google "loneliness when away from husband."

A man, the previous woman's husband, is on a vacation with his six best male friends. He sneaks off to Google to type "signs your wife is cheating."

Some of this data will include information that would otherwise never be admitted to anybody. If we aggregate it all, keep it anonymous to make sure we never know about the fears, desires, and behaviors of any specific individuals, and add some data science, we start to get a new look at human beings—their behaviors, their desires, their natures. In fact, at the risk of sounding grandiose, I have come to believe that the new data increasingly available in our digital age will radically expand our understanding of humankind. The microscope showed us there is more to a drop of pond water than we think we see. The telescope showed us there is more to the night sky than we think we see. And new, digital data now shows us there is more to human society than we think we see. It may be our era's microscope or telescope—making possible important, even revolutionary insights.

There is another risk in making such declarations—not just sounding grandiose but also trendy. Many people have been making big claims about the power of Big Data. But they have been short on evidence.

This has inspired Big Data skeptics, of whom there are also many, to dismiss the search for bigger datasets. "I am not saying here that there is no information in Big Data," essayist and statistician Nassim Taleb has written. "There is plenty of information. The problem—the central issue—is that the needle comes in an increasingly larger haystack."

One of the primary goals of this book, then, is to provide the missing evidence of what can be done with Big Data—how we can find the needles, if you will, in those larger and larger haystacks. I hope to provide enough examples of Big Data offering new insights into human psychology and behavior so that you will begin to see the outlines of something truly revolutionary.

"Hold on, Seth," you might be saying right about now. "You're promising a revolution. You're waxing poetic about these big, new datasets. But thus far, you have used all of this amazing, remarkable, breathtaking, groundbreaking data to tell me basically two things: there are plenty of racists in America, and people, particularly men, exaggerate how much sex they have."

I admit sometimes the new data does just confirm the obvious. If you think these findings were obvious, wait until you get to Chapter 4, where I show you clear, unimpeachable evidence from Google searches that men have tremendous concern and insecurity around—wait for it—their penis size.

There is, I would claim, some value in proving things you may have already suspected but had otherwise little evidence for. Suspecting something is one thing. Proving it is another. But if all Big Data could do is confirm your suspicions, it would not be revolutionary. Thankfully, Big Data can do a lot more than that. Time and again, data shows me the world works in precisely the opposite way as I would have guessed. Here are some examples you might find more surprising.

You might think that a major cause of racism is economic insecurity and vulnerability. You might naturally suspect, then, that when people lose their jobs, racism increases. But, actually, neither racist searches nor membership in Stormfront rises when unemployment does.

You might think that anxiety is highest in overeducated big cities. The urban neurotic is a famous stereotype. But Google searches reflecting anxiety—such as "anxiety symptoms" or "anxiety help"—tend to be higher in places with lower levels of education, lower median incomes, and where a larger portion of the population lives in rural areas. There are higher search rates for anxiety in rural, upstate New York than New York City.

You might think that a terrorist attack that kills dozens or hundreds of people would automatically be followed by massive, widespread anxiety. Terrorism, by definition, is supposed to instill a sense of terror. I looked at Google searches reflecting anxiety. I tested how much these searches rose in a country in the days, weeks, and months following every major European or American terrorist attack since 2004. So, on average, how much did anxiety-related searches rise? They didn't. At all.

You might think that people search for jokes more often when they are sad. Many of history's greatest thinkers have claimed that we turn to humor as a release from pain. Humor has long been thought of as a way to cope with the frustrations, the pain, the inevitable disappointments of life. As Charlie Chaplin put it, "Laughter is the tonic, the relief, the surcease from pain."

However, searches for jokes are lowest on Mondays, the day when people report they are most unhappy. They are lowest on cloudy and rainy days. And they plummet after a major tragedy, such as when two bombs killed three and injured hundreds during the 2013 Boston Marathon. People are actually more likely to seek out jokes when things are going well in life than when they aren't.

Sometimes a new dataset reveals a behavior, desire, or concern that I would have never even considered. There are numerous sexual proclivities that fall into this category. For example, did you know that in India the number one search beginning "my husband wants . . ." is "my husband wants me to breastfeed him"? This comment is far more common in India than in other countries. Moreover, porn searches for depictions of women breastfeeding men are four times higher in India and Bangladesh than in any other country in the world. I certainly never would have suspected that before I saw the data.

Further, while the fact that men are obsessed with their penis size may not be too surprising, the biggest bodily insecurity for women, as expressed on Google, is surprising indeed. Based on this new data, the female equivalent of worrying about the size of your penis may be—pausing to build suspense— worrying about whether your vagina smells. Women make nearly as many searches expressing concern about their genitals as men do worrying about theirs. And the top concern women express is its odor—and how they might improve it. I certainly didn't know that before I saw the data.

Sometimes new data reveals cultural differences I had never even contemplated. One example: the very different ways that men around the world respond to their wives being pregnant. In Mexico, the top searches about "my pregnant wife" include "frases de amor para mi esposa embarazada" (words of love to my pregnant wife) and "poemas para mi esposa embarazada" (poems for my pregnant wife). In the United States, the top searches include "my wife is pregnant now what" and "my wife is pregnant what do I do."

But this book is more than a collection of odd facts or one-off studies, though there will be plenty of those. Because these methodologies are so new and are only going to get more powerful, I will lay out some ideas on how they work and what makes them groundbreaking. I will also acknowledge Big Data's limitations.

Some of the enthusiasm for the data revolution's potential has been misplaced. Most of those enamored with Big Data gush about how immense these datasets can get. This obsession with dataset size is not new. Before Google, Amazon, and Facebook, before the phrase "Big Data" existed, a conference was held in Dallas, Texas, on "Large and Complex Datasets." Jerry Friedman, a statistics professor at Stanford who was a colleague of mine when I worked at Google, recalls that 1977 conference. One distinguished statistician would get up to talk. He would explain that he had accumulated an amazing, astonishing five gigabytes of data. The next distinguished statistician would get up to talk. He would begin, "The last speaker had gigabytes. That's nothing. I've got terabytes." The emphasis of the talk, in other words, was on how much information you could accumulate, not what you hoped to do with it, or what questions you planned to answer. "I found it amusing, at the time," Friedman says, that "the thing that you were supposed to be impressed with was how large their dataset is. It still happens."

Too many data scientists today are accumulating massive sets of data and telling us very little of importance—e.g., that the Knicks are popular in New York. Too many businesses are drowning in data. They have lots of terabytes but few major insights. The size of a dataset, I believe, is frequently overrated. There is a subtle, but important, explanation for this. The bigger an effect, the fewer the number of observations necessary to see it. You only need to touch a hot stove once to realize that it's dangerous. You may need to drink coffee thousands of times to determine whether it tends to give you a headache. Which lesson is more important? Clearly, the hot stove, which, because of the intensity of its impact, shows up so quickly, with so little data.

In fact, the smartest Big Data companies are often cutting down their data. At Google, major decisions are based on only a tiny sampling of all their data. You don't always need a ton of data to find important insights. You need the right data. A major reason that Google searches are so valuable is not that there are so many of them; it is that people are so honest in them. People lie to friends, lovers, doctors, surveys, and themselves. But on Google they might share embarrassing information, about, among other things, their sexless marriages, their mental health issues, their insecurities, and their animosity toward black people.

Most important, to squeeze insights out of Big Data, you have to ask the right questions. Just as you can't point a telescope randomly at the night sky and have it discover Pluto for you, you can't download a whole bunch of data and have it discover the secrets of human nature for you. You must look in promising places—Google searches that begin "my husband wants . . ." in India, for example.

This book is going to show how Big Data is best used and explain in detail why it can be so powerful. And along the way, you'll also learn about what I and others have already discovered with it, including:

> › How many men are gay?
> › Does advertising work?
> › Why was American Pharoah a great racehorse?
> › Is the media biased?
> › Are Freudian slips real?
> › Who cheats on their taxes?
> › Does it matter where you go to college?
> › Can you beat the stock market?
> › What's the best place to raise kids?
> › What makes a story go viral?
> › What should you talk about on a first date if you want a second?

. . . and much, much more.

But before we get to all that, we need to discuss a more basic question: why do we need data at all? And for that, I am going to introduce my grandmother.

PART I

DATA, BIG AND SMALL

1

YOUR FAULTY GUT

If you're thirty-three years old and have attended a few Thanksgivings in a row without a date, the topic of mate choice is likely to arise. And just about everybody will have an opinion.

"Seth needs a crazy girl, like him," my sister says.

"You're crazy! He needs a normal girl, to balance him out," my brother says.

"Seth's not crazy," my mother says.

"You're crazy! Of course, Seth is crazy," my father says.

All of a sudden, my shy, soft-spoken grandmother, quiet through the dinner, speaks. The loud, aggressive New York voices go silent, and all eyes focus on the small old lady with short yellow hair and still a trace of an Eastern European accent. "Seth, you need a nice girl. Not too pretty. Very smart. Good with people. Social, so you will do things. Sense of humor, because you have a good sense of humor."

Why does this old woman's advice command such

attention and respect in my family? Well, my eighty-eight-year-old grandmother has seen more than everybody else at the table. She's observed more marriages, many that worked and many that didn't. And over the decades, she has cataloged the qualities that make for successful relationships. At that Thanksgiving table, for that question, my grandmother has access to the largest number of data points. My grandmother is Big Data.

In this book, I want to demystify data science. Like it or not, data is playing an increasingly important role in all of our lives—and its role is going to get larger. Newspapers now have full sections devoted to data. Companies have teams with the exclusive task of analyzing their data. Investors give start-ups tens of millions of dollars if they can store more data. Even if you never learn how to run a regression or calculate a confidence interval, you are going to encounter a lot of data—in the pages you read, the business meetings you attend, the gossip you hear next to the watercoolers you drink from.

Many people are anxious over this development. They are intimidated by data, easily lost and confused in a world of numbers. They think that a quantitative understanding of the world is for a select few left-brained prodigies, not for them. As soon as they encounter numbers, they are ready to turn the page, end the meeting, or change the conversation.

But I have spent ten years in the data analysis business and have been fortunate to work with many of the top people in the field. And one of the most important lessons I have learned is this: Good data science is less complicated than people think. The best data science, in fact, is surprisingly intuitive.

What makes data science intuitive? At its core, data science is about spotting patterns and predicting how one variable will affect another. People do this all the time.

Just think how my grandmother gave me relationship advice. She utilized the large database of relationships that her brain has uploaded over a near century of life—in the stories she has heard from her family, her friends, her acquaintances. She limited her analysis to a sample of relationships in which the man had many qualities that I have—a sensitive temperament, a tendency to isolate himself, a sense of humor. She zeroed in on key qualities of the woman—how kind she was, how smart she was, how pretty she was. She correlated these key qualities of the woman with a key quality of the relationship—whether it was a good one. Finally, she reported her results. In other words, she spotted patterns and predicted how one variable will affect another. Grandma is a data scientist.

You are a data scientist, too. When you were a kid, you noticed that when you cried, your mom gave you attention. That is data science. When you reached adulthood, you noticed that if you complain too much, people want to hang out with you less. That is data science, too. When people hang out with you less, you noticed, you are less happy. When you are less happy, you are less friendly. When you are less friendly, people want to hang out with you even less. Data science. Data science. Data science.

Because data science is so natural, the best Big Data studies, I have found, can be understood by just about any smart person. If you can't understand a study, the problem is probably with the study, not with you.

Want proof that great data science tends to be intuitive? I recently came across a study that may be one of the most important conducted in the past few years. It is also one of the most intuitive studies I've ever seen. I want you to think not just about the importance of the study—but how natural and grandma-like it is.

The study was by a team of researchers from Columbia University and Microsoft. The team wanted to find what symptoms predict pancreatic cancer. This disease has a low five-year survival rate—only about 3 percent—but early detection can double a patient's chances.

The researchers' method? They utilized data from tens of thousands of anonymous users of Bing, Microsoft's search engine. They coded a user as having recently been given a diagnosis of pancreatic cancer based on unmistakable searches, such as "just diagnosed with pancreatic cancer" or "I was told I have pancreatic cancer, what to expect."

Next, the researchers looked at searches for health symptoms. They compared that small number of users who later reported a pancreatic cancer diagnosis with those who didn't. What symptoms, in other words, predicted that, in a few weeks or months, a user will be reporting a diagnosis?

The results were striking. Searching for back pain and then yellowing skin turned out to be a sign of pancreatic cancer; searching for just back pain alone made it unlikely someone had pancreatic cancer. Similarly, searching for indigestion and then abdominal pain was evidence of pancreatic cancer, while searching for just indigestion without abdominal pain meant a person was unlikely to have it. The researchers could identify 5 to 15 percent of cases with almost no false positives. Now, this may not sound like a great rate; but if you have pancreatic cancer, even a 10 percent chance of possibly doubling your chances of survival would feel like a windfall.

The paper detailing this study would be difficult for non-experts to fully make sense of. It includes a lot of technical jargon, such as the Kolmogorov-Smirnov test, the meaning of which, I have to admit, I had forgotten. (It's a way to determine whether a model correctly fits data.)

However, note how natural and intuitive this remarkable study is at its most fundamental level. The researchers looked at a wide array of medical cases and tried to connect symptoms to a particular illness. You know who else uses this methodology in trying to figure out whether someone has a disease? Husbands and wives, mothers and fathers, and nurses and doctors. Based on experience and knowledge, they try to connect fevers, headaches, runny noses, and stomach pains to various diseases. In other words, the Columbia and Microsoft researchers wrote a groundbreaking study by utilizing the natural, obvious methodology that everybody uses to make health diagnoses.

But wait. Let's slow down here. If the methodology of the best data science is frequently natural and intuitive, as I claim, this raises a fundamental question about the value of Big Data. If humans are naturally data scientists, if data science is intuitive, why do we need computers and statistical software? Why do we need the Kolmogorov-Smirnov test? Can't we just use our gut? Can't we do it like Grandma does, like nurses and doctors do?

This gets to an argument intensified after the release of Malcolm Gladwell's bestselling book *Blink*, which extols the magic of people's gut instincts. Gladwell tells the stories of people who, relying solely on their guts, can tell whether a statue is fake; whether a tennis player will fault before he hits the ball; how much a customer is willing to pay. The heroes in *Blink* do not run regressions; they do not calculate confidence intervals; they do not run Kolmogorov-Smirnov tests. But they generally make remarkable predictions. Many people have intuitively supported Gladwell's defense of intuition: they trust their guts and feelings. Fans of *Blink* might celebrate the wisdom of my grandmother giving relationship advice without the aid of computers. Fans of *Blink* may be less apt to celebrate my studies or the other studies profiled in this book, which use computers. If Big Data—of the computer type, rather than the grandma type—is a revolution, it has to prove that it's more powerful than our unaided intuition, which, as Gladwell has pointed out, can often be remarkable.

The Columbia and Microsoft study offers a clear example of rigorous data science and computers teaching us things our gut alone could never find. This is also one case where the size of the dataset matters. Sometimes there is insufficient experience for our unaided gut to draw upon. It is unlikely that you—or your close friends or family members—have seen enough cases of pancreatic cancer to tease out the difference between indigestion followed by abdominal pain compared to indigestion alone. Indeed, it is inevitable, as the Bing dataset gets bigger, that the researchers will pick up many more subtle patterns in the timing of symptoms—for this and other illnesses—that even doctors might miss.

Moreover, while our gut may usually give us a good general sense of how the world works, it is frequently not precise.

We need data to sharpen the picture. Consider, for example, the effects of weather on mood. You would probably guess that people are more likely to feel more gloomy on a 10-degree day than on a 70-degree day. Indeed, this is correct. But you might not guess how big an impact this temperature difference can make. I looked for correlations between an area's Google searches for depression and a wide range of factors, including economic conditions, education levels, and church attendance. Winter climate swamped all the rest. In winter months, warm climates, such as that of Honolulu, Hawaii, have 40 percent fewer depression searches than cold climates, such as that of Chicago, Illinois. Just how significant is this effect? An optimistic read of the effectiveness of antidepressants would find that the most effective drugs decrease the incidence of depression by only about 20 percent. To judge from the Google numbers, a Chicago-to-Honolulu move would be at least twice as effective as medication for your winter blues.*

Sometimes our gut, when not guided by careful computer analysis, can be dead wrong. We can get blinded by our own experiences and prejudices. Indeed, even though my grandmother is able to utilize her decades of experience to give better relationship advice than the rest of my family, she still has some dubious views on what makes a relationship last. For example, she has frequently emphasized to me the importance of having common friends. She believes that this was a key factor in her marriage's success: she spent most warm evenings

---

* Full disclosure: Shortly after I completed this study, I moved from California to New York. Using data to learn what you should do is often easy. Actually doing it is tough.

with her husband, my grandfather, in their small backyard in Queens, New York, sitting on lawn chairs and gossiping with their tight group of neighbors.

However, at the risk of throwing my own grandmother under the bus, data science suggests that Grandma's theory is wrong. A team of computer scientists recently analyzed the biggest dataset ever assembled on human relationships—Facebook. They looked at a large number of couples who were, at some point, "in a relationship." Some of these couples stayed "in a relationship." Others switched their status to "single." Having a common core group of friends, the researchers found, is a strong predictor that a relationship will *not* last. Perhaps hanging out every night with your partner and the same small group of people is not such a good thing; separate social circles may help make relationships stronger.

As you can see, our intuition alone, when we stay away from the computers and go with our gut, can sometimes amaze. But it can make big mistakes. Grandma may have fallen into one cognitive trap: we tend to exaggerate the relevance of our own experience. In the parlance of data scientists, we *weight* our data, and we give far too much weight to one particular data point: ourselves.

Grandma was so focused on her evening schmoozes with Grandpa and their friends that she did not think enough about other couples. She forgot to fully consider her brother-in-law and his wife, who chitchatted most nights with a small, consistent group of friends but fought frequently and divorced. She forgot to fully consider my parents, her daughter and son-in-law. My parents go their separate ways many nights—my dad to a jazz club or ball game with his friends, my mom to a restaurant or the theater with her friends; yet they remain happily married.

When relying on our gut, we can also be thrown off by the basic human fascination with the dramatic. We tend to overestimate the prevalence of anything that makes for a memorable story. For example, when asked in a survey, people consistently rank tornadoes as a more common cause of death than asthma. In fact, asthma causes about seventy times more deaths. Deaths by asthma don't stand out—and don't make the news. Deaths by tornadoes do.

We are often wrong, in other words, about how the world works when we rely just on what we hear or personally experience. While the methodology of good data science is often intuitive, the results are frequently counterintuitive. Data science takes a natural and intuitive human process—spotting patterns and making sense of them—and injects it with steroids, potentially showing us that the world works in a completely different way from how we thought it did. That's what happened when I studied the predictors of basketball success.

When I was a little boy, I had one dream and one dream only: I wanted to grow up to be an economist and data scientist. No. I'm just kidding. I wanted desperately to be a professional basketball player, to follow in the footsteps of my hero, Patrick Ewing, all-star center for the New York Knicks.

I sometimes suspect that inside every data scientist is a kid trying to figure out why his childhood dreams didn't come true. So it is not surprising that I recently investigated what it takes to make the NBA. The results of the investigation were surprising. In fact, they demonstrate once again how good data science can change your view of the world, and how counterintuitive the numbers can be.

The particular question I looked at is this: are you more likely to make it in the NBA if you grow up poor or middle-class?

Most people would guess the former. Conventional wisdom says that growing up in difficult circumstances, perhaps in the projects with a single, teenage mom, helps foster the drive necessary to reach the top levels of this intensely competitive sport.

This view was expressed by William Ellerbee, a high school basketball coach in Philadelphia, in an interview with *Sports Illustrated.* "Suburban kids tend to play for the fun of it," Ellerbee said. "Inner-city kids look at basketball as a matter of life or death." I, alas, was raised by married parents in the New Jersey suburbs. LeBron James, the best player of my generation, was born poor to a sixteen-year-old single mother in Akron, Ohio.

Indeed, an internet survey I conducted suggested that the majority of Americans think the same thing Coach Ellerbee and I thought: that most NBA players grow up in poverty.

Is this conventional wisdom correct?

Let's look at the data. There is no comprehensive data source on the socioeconomics of NBA players. But by being data detectives, by utilizing data from a whole bunch of sources—basketball-reference.com, ancestry.com, the U.S. Census, and others—we can figure out what family background is actually most conducive to making the NBA. This study, you will note, uses a variety of data sources, some of them bigger, some of them smaller, some of them online, and some of them offline. As exciting as some of the new digital sources are, a good data scientist is not above consulting old-fashioned sources if they can help. The best way to get the right answer to a question is to combine all available data.

The first relevant data is the birthplace of every player. For every county in the United States, I recorded how many black and white men were born in the 1980s. I then recorded how many of them reached the NBA. I compared this to a county's average household income. I also controlled for the racial demographics of a county, since—and this is a subject for a whole other book—black men are about forty times more likely than white men to reach the NBA.

The data tells us that a man has a substantially better chance of reaching the NBA if he was born in a wealthy county. A black kid born in one of the wealthiest counties in the United States, for example, is more than twice as likely to make the NBA than a black kid born in one of the poorest counties. For a white kid, the advantage of being born in one of the wealthiest counties compared to being born in one of the poorest is 60 percent.

This suggests, contrary to conventional wisdom, that poor men are actually underrepresented in the NBA. However, this data is not perfect, since many wealthy counties in the United States, such as New York County (Manhattan), also include poor neighborhoods, such as Harlem. So it's still possible that a difficult childhood helps you make the NBA. We still need more clues, more data.

So I investigated the family backgrounds of NBA players. This information was found in news stories and on social networks. This methodology was quite time-consuming, so I limited the analysis to the one hundred African-American NBA players born in the 1980s who scored the most points. Compared to the average black man in the United States, NBA superstars were about 30 percent less likely to have been born to a teenage mother or an unwed mother. In other words, the family backgrounds of the best black NBA players also suggest that a comfortable background is a big advantage for achieving success.

That said, neither the county-level birth data nor the family background of a limited sample of players gives perfect information on the childhoods of all NBA players. So I was still not entirely convinced that two-parent, middle-class families produce more NBA stars than single-parent, poor families. The more data we can throw at this question, the better.

Then I remembered one more data point that can provide telling clues to a man's background. It was suggested in a paper by two economists, Roland Fryer and Steven Levitt, that a black person's first name is an indication of his socioeconomic background. Fryer and Levitt studied birth certificates in California in the 1980s and found that, among African-Americans, poor, uneducated, and single moms tend to give their kids different names than do middle-class, educated, and married parents.

Kids from better-off backgrounds are more likely to be given common names, such as Kevin, Chris, and John. Kids from difficult homes in the projects are more likely to be given unique names, such as Knowshon, Uneek, and Breionshay. African-American kids born into poverty are nearly twice as likely to have a name that is given to no other child born in that same year.

So what about the first names of black NBA players? Do

they sound more like middle-class or poor blacks? Looking at the same time period, California-born NBA players were half as likely to have unique names as the average black male, a statistically significant difference.

Know someone who thinks the NBA is a league for kids from the ghetto? Tell him to just listen closely to the next game on the radio. Tell him to note how frequently Russell dribbles past Dwight and then tries to slip the ball past the outstretched arms of Josh and into the waiting hands of Kevin. If the NBA really were a league filled with poor black men, it would sound quite different. There would be a lot more men with names like LeBron.

Now, we have gathered three different pieces of evidence— the county of birth, the marital status of the mothers of the top scorers, and the first names of players. No source is perfect. But all three support the same story. Better socioeconomic status means a higher chance of making the NBA. The conventional wisdom, in other words, is wrong.

Among all African-Americans born in the 1980s, about 60 percent had unmarried parents. But I estimate that among African-Americans born in that decade who reached the NBA, a significant majority had married parents. In other words, the NBA is not composed primarily of men with backgrounds like that of LeBron James. There are more men like Chris Bosh, raised by two parents in Texas who cultivated his interest in electronic gadgets, or Chris Paul, the second son of middle-class parents in Lewisville, North Carolina, whose family joined him on an episode of *Family Feud* in 2011.

The goal of a data scientist is to understand the world. Once we find the counterintuitive result, we can use more data science to help us explain why the world is not as it seems. Why, for example, do middle-class men have an edge in basketball relative to poor men? There are at least two explanations.

First, because poor men tend to end up shorter. Scholars have long known that childhood health care and nutrition play a large role in adult health. This is why the average man in the developed world is now four inches taller than a century and a half ago. Data suggests that Americans from poor backgrounds, due to weaker early-life health care and nutrition, are shorter.

Data can also tell us the effect of height on reaching the NBA. You undoubtedly intuited that being tall can be of assistance to an aspiring basketball player. Just contrast the height of the typical ballplayer on the court to the typical fan in the stands. (The average NBA player is 6'7"; the average American man is 5'9".)

How much does height matter? NBA players sometimes fib a little about their height, and there is no listing of the complete height distribution of American males. But working with a rough mathematical estimate of what this distribution might look like and the NBA's own numbers, it is easy to confirm that the effects of height are enormous—maybe even more than we might have suspected. I estimate that each additional inch roughly doubles your odds of making it to the NBA. And this is true throughout the height distribution. A 5'11" man has twice the odds of reaching the NBA as a 5'10" man. A 6'11" man has twice the odds of reaching the NBA as a 6'10" man. It appears that, among men less than six feet tall, only about one in two million reach the NBA. Among those over seven feet tall, I and others have estimated, something like one in five reach the NBA.

Data, you will note, clarifies why my dream of basketball stardom was derailed. It was not because I was brought up in the suburbs. It was because I am 5'9" and white (not to mention slow). Also, I am lazy. And I have poor stamina, awful shooting form, and occasionally a panic attack when the ball gets in my hand.

A second reason that boys from tough backgrounds may struggle to make the NBA is that they sometimes lack certain social skills. Using data on thousands of schoolchildren, economists have found that middle-class, two-parent families are on average substantially better at raising kids who are trusting, disciplined, persistent, focused, and organized.

So how do poor social skills derail an otherwise promising basketball career?

Let's look at the story of Doug Wrenn, one of the most talented basketball prospects in the 1990s. His college coach, Jim Calhoun at the University of Connecticut, who has trained future NBA all-stars, claimed Wrenn jumped the highest of any man he had ever worked with. But Wrenn had a challenging upbringing. He was raised by a single mother in Blood Alley, one of the roughest neighborhoods in Seattle. In Connecticut, he consistently clashed with those around him. He would taunt players, question coaches, and wear loose-fitting clothes in violation of team rules. He also had legal troubles—he stole shoes from a store and snapped at police officers. Calhoun finally had enough and kicked him off the team.

Wrenn got a second chance at the University of

Washington. But there, too, an inability to get along with people derailed him. He fought with his coach over playing time and shot selection and was kicked off this team as well. Wrenn went undrafted by the NBA, bounced around lower leagues, moved in with his mother, and was eventually imprisoned for assault. "My career is over," Wrenn told the *Seattle Times* in 2009. "My dreams, my aspirations are over. Doug Wrenn is dead. That basketball player, that dude is dead. It's over." Wrenn had the talent not just to be an NBA player, but to be a great, even a legendary player. But he never developed the temperament to even stay on a college team. Perhaps if he'd had a stable early life, he could have been the next Michael Jordan.

Michael Jordan, of course, also had an impressive vertical leap. Plus a large ego and intense competitiveness—a personality at times that was not unlike Wrenn's. Jordan could be a difficult kid. At the age of twelve, he was kicked out of school for fighting. But he had at least one thing that Wrenn lacked: a stable, middle-class upbringing. His father was an equipment supervisor for General Electric, his mother a banker. And they helped him navigate his career.

In fact, Jordan's life is filled with stories of his family guiding him away from the traps that a great, competitive talent can fall into. After Jordan was kicked out of school, his mother responded by taking him with her to work. He was not allowed to leave the car and instead had to sit there in the parking lot reading books. After he was drafted by the Chicago Bulls, his parents and siblings took turns visiting him to make sure he avoided the temptations that come with fame and money.

Jordan's career did not end like Wrenn's, with a little-read

quote in the *Seattle Times*. It ended with a speech upon induction into the Basketball Hall of Fame that was watched by
millions of people. In his speech, Jordan said he tried to stay
"focused on the good things about life—you know how people
perceive you, how you respect them . . . how you are perceived
publicly. Take a pause and think about the things that you do.
And that all came from my parents."

The data tells us Jordan is absolutely right to thank his
middle-class, married parents. The data tells us that in worse-
off families, in worse-off communities, there are NBA-level
talents who are not in the NBA. These men had the genes, had
the ambition, but never developed the temperament to become
basketball superstars.

And no—whatever we might intuit—being in circumstances so desperate that basketball seems "a matter of life or
death" does not help. Stories like that of Doug Wrenn can help
illustrate this. And data proves it.

In June 2013, LeBron James was interviewed on television
after winning his second NBA championship. (He has since
won a third.) "I'm LeBron James," he announced. "From Akron, Ohio. From the inner city. I am not even supposed to be
here." Twitter and other social networks erupted with criticism.
How could such a supremely gifted person, identified from an
absurdly young age as the future of basketball, claim to be an
underdog? In fact, anyone from a difficult environment, no
matter his athletic prowess, has the odds stacked against him.
James's accomplishments, in other words, are even more ex-
ceptional than they appear to be at first. Data proves that, too.

PART II

THE POWERS OF BIG DATA

2

WAS FREUD RIGHT?

I recently saw a person walking down a street described as a "penistrian." You caught that, right? A "penistrian" instead of a "pedestrian." I saw it in a large dataset of typos people make. A person sees someone walking and writes the word "penis." Has to mean something, right?

I recently learned of a man who dreamed of eating a banana while walking to the altar to marry his wife. I saw it in a large dataset of dreams people record on an app. A man imagines marrying a woman while eating a phallic-shaped food. That also has to mean something, right?

Was Sigmund Freud right? Since his theories first came to public attention, the most honest answer to this question would be a shrug. It was Karl Popper, the Austrian-British philosopher, who made this point clearest. Popper famously claimed that Freud's theories were not falsifiable. There was no way to test whether they were true or false.

Freud could say the person writing of a "penistrian" was revealing a possibly repressed sexual desire. The person could respond that she wasn't revealing anything; that she could have just as easily made an innocent typo, such as "pedaltrian." It would be a he-said, she-said situation. Freud could say the gentleman dreaming of eating a banana on his wedding day was secretly thinking of a penis, revealing his desire to really marry a man rather than a woman. The gentleman could say he just happened to be dreaming of a banana. He could have just as easily been dreaming of eating an apple as he walked to the altar. It would be he-said, he-said. There was no way to put Freud's theory to a real test.

Until now, that is.

Data science makes many parts of Freud falsifiable—it puts many of his famous theories to the test. Let's start with phallic symbols in dreams. Using a huge dataset of recorded dreams, we can readily note how frequently phallic-shaped objects appear. Food is a good place to focus this study. It shows up in many dreams, and many foods are shaped like phalluses—bananas, cucumbers, hot dogs, etc. We can then measure the factors that might make us dream more about certain foods than others—how frequently they are eaten, how tasty most people find them, and, yes, whether they are phallic in nature.

We can test whether two foods, both of which are equally popular, but one of which is shaped like a phallus, appear in dreams in different amounts. If phallus-shaped foods are no more likely to be dreamed about than other foods, then phallic symbols are not a significant factor in our dreams. Thanks to Big Data, this part of Freud's theory may indeed be falsifiable.

I received data from Shadow, an app that asks users to record their dreams. I coded the foods included in tens of thousands of dreams.

Overall, what makes us dream of foods? The main predictor is how frequently we consume them. The substance that is most dreamed about is water. The top twenty foods include chicken, bread, sandwiches, and rice—all notably un-Freudian.

The second predictor of how frequently a food appears in dreams is how tasty people find it. The two foods we dream about most often are the notably un-Freudian but famously tasty chocolate and pizza.

So what about phallic-shaped foods? Do they sneak into our dreams with unexpected frequency? Nope.

Bananas are the second most common fruit to appear in dreams. But they are also the second most commonly consumed fruit. So we don't need Freud to explain how often we dream about bananas. Cucumbers are the seventh most common vegetable to appear in dreams. They are the seventh most consumed vegetable. So again their shape isn't necessary to explain their presence in our minds as we sleep. Hot dogs are dreamed of far less frequently than hamburgers. This is true even controlling for the fact that people eat more burgers than dogs.

Overall, using a regression analysis (a method that allows social scientists to tease apart the impact of multiple factors) across all fruits and vegetables, I found that a food's being shaped like a phallus did not give it more likelihood of appearing in dreams than would be expected by its popularity. This theory of Freud's is falsifiable—and, at least according to my look at the data, false.

Next, consider Freudian slips. The psychologist hypothesized that we use our errors—the ways we misspeak or miswrite—to reveal our subconscious desires, frequently sexual. Can we use Big Data to test this? Here's one way: see if our errors—our slips—lean in the direction of the naughty. If our buried sexual desires sneak out in our slips, there should be a disproportionate number of errors that include words like "penis," "cock," and "sex."

This is why I studied a dataset of more than 40,000 typing errors collected by Microsoft researchers. The dataset included mistakes that people make but then immediately correct. In these tens of thousands of errors, there were plenty of individuals committing errors of a sexual sort. There was the aforementioned "penistrian." There was also someone who typed "sexurity" instead of "security" and "cocks" instead of "rocks." But there were also plenty of innocent slips. People wrote of "pindows" and "fegetables," "aftermoons" and "refriderators."

So was the number of sexual slips unusual?

To test this, I first used the Microsoft dataset to model how frequently people mistakenly switch particular letters. I calculated how often they replace a *t* with an *s*, a *g* with an *h*. I then created a computer program that made mistakes in the way that people do. We might call it Error Bot. Error Bot replaced a *t* with an *s* with the same frequency that humans in the Microsoft study did. It replaced a *g* with an *h* as often as they did. And so on. I ran the program on the same words people had gotten wrong in the Microsoft study. In other words, the bot tried to spell "pedestrian" and "rocks," "windows" and "refrigerator." But it switched an *r* with a *t* as often as people do and wrote, for example, "tocks." It switched an *r* with a *c* as often as humans do and wrote "cocks."

So what do we learn from comparing Error Bot with normally careless humans? After making a few million errors, just from misplacing letters in the ways that humans do, Error Bot had made numerous mistakes of a Freudian nature. It misspelled "seashell" as "sexshell," "lipstick" as "lipsdick," and "luckiest" as "fuckiest," along with many other similar mistakes. And—here's the key point—Error Bot, which of course does not have a subconscious, was just as likely to make errors that could be perceived as sexual as real people were. With the caveat, as we social scientists like to say, that there needs to be more research, this means that sexually oriented errors are no more likely for humans to make than can be expected by chance.

In other words, for people to make errors such as "penistrian," "sexurity," and "cocks," it is not necessary to have some connection between mistakes and the forbidden, some theory of the mind where people reveal their secret desires via their errors. These slips of the fingers can be explained entirely by the typical frequency of typos. People make lots of mistakes. And if you make enough mistakes, eventually you start saying things like "lipsdick," "fuckiest," and "penistrian." If a monkey types long enough, he will eventually write "to be or not to be." If a person types long enough, she will eventually write "penistrian."

Freud's theory that errors reveal our subconscious wants is indeed falsifiable—and, according to my analysis of the data, false.

Big Data tells us a banana is always just a banana and a "penistrian" just a misspelled "pedestrian."

So was Freud totally off-target in all his theories? Not quite. When I first got access to PornHub data, I found a revelation there that struck me as at least somewhat Freudian. In fact, this is among the most surprising things I have found yet during my data investigations: a shocking number of people visiting mainstream porn sites are looking for portrayals of incest.

Of the top hundred searches by men on PornHub, one of the most popular porn sites, sixteen are looking for incest-themed videos. Fair warning—this is going to get a little graphic: they include "brother and sister," "step mom fucks son," "mom and son," "mom fucks son," and "real brother and sister." The plurality of male incestuous searches are for scenes featuring mothers and sons. And women? Nine of the top hundred searches by women on PornHub are for incest-themed videos, and they feature similar imagery—though with the gender of any parent and child who is mentioned usually reversed. Thus the plurality of incestuous searches made by women are for scenes featuring fathers and daughters.

It's not hard to locate in this data at least a faint echo of Freud's Oedipal complex. He hypothesized a near-universal desire in childhood, which is later repressed, for sexual involvement with opposite-sex parents. If only the Viennese psychologist had lived long enough to turn his analytic skills to

PornHub data, where interest in opposite-sex parents seems to be borne out by adults—with great explicitness—and little is repressed.

Of course, PornHub data can't tell us for certain who people are fantasizing about when watching such videos. Are they actually imagining having sex with their own parents? Google searches can give some more clues that there are plenty of people with such desires.

Consider all searches of the form "I want to have sex with my . . ." The number one way to complete this search is "mom." Overall, more than three-fourths of searches of this form are incestuous. And this is not due to the particular phrasing. Searches of the form "I am attracted to . . . ," for example, are even more dominated by admissions of incestuous desires. Now I concede—at the risk of disappointing Herr Freud—that these are not particularly common searches: a few thousand people every year in the United States admitting an attraction to their mother. Someone would also have to break the news to Freud that Google searches, as will be discussed later in this book, sometimes skew toward the forbidden.

But still. There are plenty of inappropriate attractions that people have that I would have expected to have been mentioned more frequently in searches. Boss? Employee? Student? Therapist? Patient? Wife's best friend? Daughter's best friend? Wife's sister? Best friend's wife? None of these confessed desires can compete with mom. Maybe, combined with the PornHub data, that really does mean something.

And Freud's general assertion that sexuality can be shaped by childhood experiences is supported elsewhere in Google and PornHub data, which reveals that men, at least, retain an inordinate number of fantasies related to childhood. According to searches from wives about their husbands, some of the top fetishes of adult men are the desire to wear diapers and wanting to be breastfed, particularly, as discussed earlier, in India. Moreover, cartoon porn—animated explicit sex scenes featuring characters from shows popular among adolescent boys—has achieved a high degree of popularity. Or consider the occupations of women most frequently searched for in porn by men. Men who are 18–24 years old search most frequently for women who are babysitters. As do 25–64-year-old men. And men 65 years and older. And for men in every age group, teacher and cheerleader are both in the top four. Clearly, the early years of life seem to play an outsize role in men's adult fantasies.

I have not yet been able to use all this unprecedented data on adult sexuality to figure out precisely how sexual preferences form. Over the next few decades, other social scientists and I will be able to create new, falsifiable theories on adult sexuality and test them with actual data.

Already I can predict some basic themes that will undoubtedly be part of a data-based theory of adult sexuality. It is clearly not going to be the identical story to the one Freud told, with his particular, well-defined, universal stages of childhood and repression. But, based on my first look at PornHub data, I am absolutely certain the final verdict on adult sexuality will feature some key themes that Freud emphasized. Childhood will play a major role. So will mothers.

It likely would have been impossible to analyze Freud in this way ten years ago. It certainly would have been impossible eighty years ago, when Freud was still alive. So let's think through why these data sources helped. This exercise can help us understand why Big Data is so powerful.

Remember, we have said that just having mounds and mounds of data by itself doesn't automatically generate insights. Data size, by itself, is overrated. Why, then, is Big Data so powerful? Why will it create a revolution in how we see ourselves? There are, I claim, four unique powers of Big Data. This analysis of Freud provides a good illustration of them.

You may have noticed, to begin with, that we're taking pornography seriously in this discussion of Freud. And we are going to utilize data from pornography frequently in this book. Somewhat surprisingly, porn data is rarely utilized by sociologists, most of whom are comfortable relying on the traditional survey datasets they have built their careers on. But a moment's reflection shows that the widespread use of porn— and the search and views data that comes with it—is the most important development in our ability to understand human sexuality in, well . . . Actually, it's probably the most important ever. It is data that Schopenhauer, Nietzsche, Freud, and Foucault would have drooled over. This data did not exist when they were alive. It did not exist a couple decades ago. It exists now. There are many unique data sources, on a range of topics, that give us windows into areas about which we could previously just guess. *Offering up new types of data is the first power of Big Data.*

The porn data and the Google search data are not just new;

they are honest. In the pre-digital age, people hid their embarrassing thoughts from other people. In the digital age, they still hide them from other people, but not from the internet and in particular sites such as Google and PornHub, which protect their anonymity. These sites function as a sort of digital truth serum—hence our ability to uncover a widespread fascination with incest. Big Data allows us to finally see what people really want and really do, not what they say they want and say they do. *Providing honest data is the second power of Big Data.*

Because there is now so much data, there is meaningful information on even tiny slices of a population. We can compare, say, the number of people who dream of cucumbers versus those who dream of tomatoes. *Allowing us to zoom in on small subsets of people is the third power of Big Data.*

Big Data has one more impressive power—one that was not utilized in my quick study of Freud but could be in a future one: it allows us to undertake rapid, controlled experiments. This allows us to test for causality, not merely correlations. These kinds of tests are mostly used by businesses now, but they will prove a powerful tool for social scientists. *Allowing us to do many causal experiments is the fourth power of Big Data.*

Now it is time to unpack each of these powers and explore exactly why Big Data matters.

3

DATA REIMAGINED

At 6 A.M. on a particular Friday of every month, the streets of most of Manhattan will be largely desolate. The stores lining these streets will be closed, their façades covered by steel security gates, the apartments above dark and silent.

The floors of Goldman Sachs, the global investment banking institution in lower Manhattan, on the other hand, will be brightly lit, its elevators taking thousands of workers to their desks. By 7 A.M. most of these desks will be occupied.

It would not be unfair on any other day to describe this hour in this part of town as sleepy. On this Friday morning, however, there will be a buzz of energy and excitement. On this day, information that will massively impact the stock market is set to arrive.

Minutes after its release, this information will be reported by news sites. Seconds after its release, this information will be discussed, debated, and dissected, loudly, at Goldman and hundreds of other financial firms. But much of the real action in finance these days happens in milliseconds. Goldman and other financial firms paid tens of millions of dollars to get access to fiber-optic cables that reduced the time information travels from Chicago to New Jersey by just four milliseconds (from 17 to 13). Financial firms have algorithms in place to read the information and trade based on it—all in a matter of milliseconds. After this crucial information is released, the market will move in less time than it takes you to blink your eye.

So what is this crucial data that is so valuable to Goldman and numerous other financial institutions?

The monthly unemployment rate.

The rate, however—which has such a profound impact on the stock market that financial institutions have done whatever it takes to maximize the speed with which they receive, analyze, and act upon it—is from a phone survey that the Bureau of Labor Statistics conducts and the information is some three weeks—or 2 billion milliseconds—old by the time it is released.

When firms are spending millions of dollars to chip a millisecond off the flow of information, it might strike you as more than a bit strange that the government takes so long to calculate the unemployment rate.

Indeed, getting these critical numbers out sooner was one of Alan Krueger's primary agendas when he took over as President Obama's chairman of the Council of Economic Advisors in 2011. He was unsuccessful. "Either the BLS doesn't have the resources," he concluded. "Or they are stuck in twentieth-century thinking."

With the government clearly not picking up the pace anytime soon, is there a way to get at least a rough measure of the unemployment statistics at a faster rate? In this high-tech era—when nearly every click any human makes on the internet is recorded somewhere—do we really have to wait weeks to find out how many people are out of work?

One potential solution was inspired by the work of a former Google engineer, Jeremy Ginsberg. Ginsberg noticed that health data, like unemployment data, was released with a delay by the government. The Centers for Disease Control and Prevention takes one week to release influenza data, even though doctors and hospitals would benefit from having the data much sooner.

Ginsberg suspected that people sick with the flu are likely to make flu-related searches. In essence, they would report their symptoms to Google. These searches, he thought, could give a reasonably accurate measure of the current influenza rate. Indeed, searches such as "flu symptoms" and "muscle aches" have proven important indicators of how fast the flu is spreading.*

Meanwhile, Google engineers created a service, Google Correlate, that gives outside researchers the means to experiment with the same type of analyses across a wide range of fields, not just health. Researchers can take any data series that they are tracking over time and see what Google searches correlate most with that dataset.

For example, using Google Correlate, Hal Varian, chief

---

* While the initial version of Google Flu had significant flaws, researchers have recently recalibrated the model, with more success.

economist at Google, and I were able to show which searches most closely track housing prices. When housing prices are rising, Americans tend to search for such phrases as "80/20 mortgage," "new home builder," and "appreciation rate." When housing prices are falling, Americans tend to search for such phrases as "short sale process," "underwater mortgage," and "mortgage forgiveness debt relief."

So can Google searches be used as a litmus test for unemployment in the same way they can for housing prices or influenza? Can we tell, simply by what people are Googling, how many people are unemployed, and can we do so well before the government collates its survey results?

One day, I put the United States unemployment rate from 2004 through 2011 into Google Correlate.

Of the trillions of Google searches during that time, what do you think turned out to be most tightly connected to unemployment? You might imagine "unemployment office"—or something similar. That was high but not at the very top. "New jobs"? Also high but also not at the very top.

The highest during the period I searched—and these terms do shift—was "Slutload." That's right, the most frequent search was for a pornographic site. This may seem strange at first blush, but unemployed people presumably have a lot of time on their hands. Many are stuck at home, alone and bored. Another of the highly correlated searches—this one in the PG realm—is "Spider Solitaire." Again, not surprising for a group of people who presumably have a lot of time on their hands.

Now, I am not arguing, based on this one analysis, that tracking "Slutload" or "Spider Solitaire" is the best way to predict the unemployment rate. The specific diversions that unemployed people use can change over time (at one point, "Rawtube," a different porn site, was among the strongest correlations) and none of these particular terms by itself attracts anything approaching a plurality of the unemployed. But I have generally found that a mix of diversion-related searches can track the unemployment rate—and would be a part of the best model predicting it.

This example illustrates the first power of Big Data, the reimagining of what qualifies as data. Frequently, the value of Big Data is not its size; it's that it can offer you new kinds of information to study—information that had never previously been collected.

Before Google there was information available on certain leisure activities—movie ticket sales, for example—that could yield some clues as to how much time people have on their hands. But the opportunity to know how much solitaire is being played or porn is being watched is new—and powerful. In this instance this data might help us more quickly measure how the economy is doing—at least until the government learns to conduct and collate a survey more quickly.

Life on Google's campus in Mountain View, California, is very different from that in Goldman Sachs's Manhattan headquarters. At 9 A.M. Google's offices are nearly empty. If any workers are around, it is probably to eat breakfast for free—banana-blueberry pancakes, scrambled egg whites, filtered cucumber water. Some employees might be out of town: at an off-site meeting in Boulder or Las Vegas or perhaps on a free ski trip to Lake Tahoe. Around lunchtime, the sand volleyball courts and grass soccer fields will be filled. The best burrito I've ever eaten was at Google's Mexican restaurant.

How can one of the biggest and most competitive tech companies in the world seemingly be so relaxed and generous? Google harnessed Big Data in a way that no other company ever has to build an automated money stream. The company plays a crucial role in this book since Google searches are by far the dominant source of Big Data. But it is important to remember that Google's success is itself built on the collection of a new kind of data.

If you are old enough to have used the internet in the twentieth century, you might remember the various search engines that existed back then—MetaCrawler, Lycos, AltaVista, to name a few. And you might remember that these search engines were, at best, mildly reliable. Sometimes, if you were lucky, they managed to find what you wanted. Often, they would not. If you typed "Bill Clinton" into the most popular search engines in the late 1990s, the top results included a random site that just proclaimed "Bill Clinton Sucks" or a site that featured a bad Clinton joke. Hardly the most relevant information about the then president of the United States.

In 1998, Google showed up. And its search results were undeniably better those that of every one of its competitors. If you typed "Bill Clinton" into Google in 1998, you were given his website, the White House email address, and the best biographies of the man that existed on the internet. Google seemed to be magic.

What had Google's founders, Sergey Brin and Larry Page, done differently?

Other search engines located for their users the websites that most frequently included the phrase for which they searched. If you were looking for information on "Bill Clinton," those search engines would find, across the entire internet, the websites that had the most references to Bill Clinton. There were many reasons this ranking system was imperfect and one of them was that it was easy to game the system. A joke site with the text "Bill Clinton Bill Clinton Bill Clinton Bill Clinton Bill Clinton" hidden somewhere on its page would score higher than the White House's official website.*

What Brin and Page did was find a way to record a new type of information that was far more valuable than a simple count of words. Websites often would, when discussing a subject, link to the sites they thought were most helpful in understanding that subject. For example, the *New York Times*, if it mentioned Bill Clinton, might allow readers who clicked on his name to be sent to the White House's official website.

Every website creating one of these links was, in a sense, giving its opinion of the best information on Bill Clinton. Brin and Page could aggregate all these opinions on every topic. It could crowdsource the opinions of the *New York Times*, millions of Listservs, hundreds of bloggers, and everyone else on the internet. If a whole slew of people thought that the most

---

* In 1998, if you searched "cars" on a popular pre-Google search engine, you were inundated with porn sites. These porn sites had written the word "cars" frequently in white letters on a white background to trick the search engine. They then got a few extra clicks from people who meant to buy a car but got distracted by the porn.

important link for "Bill Clinton" was his official website, this was probably the website that most people searching for "Bill Clinton" would want to see.

These kinds of links were data that other search engines didn't even consider, and they were incredibly predictive of the most useful information on a given topic. The point here is that Google didn't dominate search merely by collecting more data than everyone else. They did it by finding a *better* type of data. Fewer than two years after its launch, Google, powered by its link analysis, grew to be the internet's most popular search engine. Today, Brin and Page are together worth more than $60 billion.

As with Google, so with everyone else trying to use data to understand the world. The Big Data revolution is less about collecting more and more data. It is about collecting the right data.

But the internet isn't the only place where you can collect new data and where getting the right data can have profoundly disruptive results. This book is largely about how the data on the web can help us better understand people. The next section, however, doesn't have anything to do with web data. In fact, it doesn't have anything to do with people. But it does help illustrate the main point of this chapter: the outsize value of new, unconventional data. And the principles it teaches us are helpful in understanding the digital-based data revolution.

BODIES AS DATA

In the summer of 2013, a reddish-brown horse, of above-average size, with a black mane, sat in a small barn in upstate

New York. He was one of 152 one-year-old horses at August's Fasig-Tipton Select Yearling Sale in Saratoga Springs, and one of ten thousand one-year-old horses being auctioned off that year.

Wealthy men and women, when they shell out a lot of money on a racehorse, want the honor of choosing the horse's name. Thus the reddish-brown horse did not yet have a name and, like most horses at the auction, was instead referred to by his barn number, 85.

There was little that made No. 85 stand out at this auction. His pedigree was good but not great. His sire (father), Pioneerof [sic] the Nile, was a top racehorse, but other kids of Pioneerof the Nile had not had much racing success. There were also doubts based on how No. 85 looked. He had a scratch on his ankle, for example, which some buyers worried might be evidence of an injury.

The current owner of No. 85 was an Egyptian beer magnate, Ahmed Zayat, who had come to upstate New York looking to sell the horse and buy a few others.

Like almost all owners, Zayat hired a team of experts to help him choose which horses to buy. But his experts were a bit different than those used by nearly every other owner. The typical horse experts you'd see at an event like this were middle-aged men, many from Kentucky or rural Florida with little education but with a family background in the horse business. Zayat's experts, however, came from a small firm called EQB. The head of EQB was not an old-school horse man. The head of EQB, instead, was Jeff Seder, an eccentric, Philadelphia-born man with a pile of degrees from Harvard.

Zayat had worked with EQB before, so the process was

familiar. After a few days of evaluating horses, Seder's team would come back to Zayat with five or so horses they recommended buying to replace No. 85.

This time, though, was different. Seder's team came back to Zayat and told him they were unable to fulfill his request. They simply could not recommend that he buy any of the 151 other horses offered up for sale that day. Instead, they offered an unexpected and near-desperate plea. Zayat absolutely, positively could not sell horse No. 85. This horse, EQB declared, was not just the best horse in the auction; he was the best horse of the year and, quite possibly, the decade. "Sell your house," the team implored him. "Do not sell this horse."

The next day, with little fanfare, horse No. 85 was bought for $300,000 by a man calling himself Incardo Bloodstock. Bloodstock, it was later revealed, was a pseudonym used by Ahmed Zayat. In response to the pleas of Seder, Zayat had bought back his own horse, an almost unprecedented action. (The rules of the auction prevented Zayat from simply removing the horse from the auction, thus necessitating the pseudonymous transaction.) Sixty-two horses at the auction sold for a higher price than horse No. 85, with two fetching more than $1 million each.

Three months later, Zayat finally chose a name for No. 85: American Pharoah. And eighteen months later, on a 75-degree Saturday evening in the suburbs of New York City, American Pharoah became the first horse in more than three decades to win the Triple Crown.

What did Jeff Seder know about horse No. 85 that apparently nobody else knew? How did this Harvard man get so good at evaluating horses?

I first met up with Seder, who was then sixty-four, on a scorching June afternoon in Ocala, Florida, more than a year after American Pharoah's Triple Crown. The event was a week-long showcase for two-year-old horses, culminating in an auction, not dissimilar to the 2013 event where Zayat bought his own horse back.

Seder has a booming, Mel Brooks–like voice, a full head of hair, and a discernable bounce in his step. He was wearing suspenders, khakis, a black shirt with his company's logo on it, and a hearing aid.

Over the next three days, he told me his life story—and how he became so good at predicting horses. It was hardly a direct route. After graduating magna cum laude and Phi Beta Kappa from Harvard, Seder went on to get, also from Harvard, a law degree and a business degree. At age twenty-six, he was working as an analyst for Citigroup in New York City but felt unhappy and burnt-out. One day, sitting in the atrium at the firm's new offices on Lexington Avenue, he found himself studying a large mural of an open field. The painting reminded him of his love of the countryside and his love of horses. He went home and looked at himself in the mirror with his three-piece suit on. He knew then that he was not meant to be a banker and he was not meant to live in New York City. The next morning, he quit his job.

Seder moved to rural Pennsylvania and ambled through a variety of jobs in textiles and sports medicine before devoting his life full-time to his passion: predicting the success of racehorses. The numbers in horse racing are rough. Of the one thousand two-year-old horses showcased at Ocala's auction, one of the nation's most prestigious, perhaps five will end up winning a race with a significant purse. What will happen to the other 995 horses? Roughly one-third will prove too slow. Another one-third will get injured—most because their limbs can't withstand the enormous pressure of galloping at full speed. (Every year, hundreds of horses die on American racetracks, mostly due to broken legs.) And the remaining one-third will have what you might call Bartleby syndrome. Bartleby, the scrivener in Herman Melville's extraordinary short story, stops working and answers every request his employer makes with "I would prefer not to." Many horses, early in their racing careers, apparently come to realize that they don't need to run if they don't feel like it. They may start a race running fast, but, at some point, they'll simply slow down or stop running altogether. Why run around an oval as fast as you can, especially when your hooves and hocks ache? "I would prefer not to," they decide. (I have a soft spot for Bartlebys, horse or human.)

With the odds stacked against them, how can owners pick a profitable horse? Historically, people have believed that the best way to predict whether a horse will succeed has been to analyze his or her pedigree. Being a horse expert means being able to rattle off everything anybody could possibly want to know about a horse's father, mother, grandfathers, grandmothers, brothers, and sisters. Agents announce, for instance, that a big horse "came to her size legitimately" if her mother's line has lots of big horses.

There is one problem, however. While pedigree does matter, it can still only explain a small part of a racing horse's success. Consider the track record of full siblings of all the horses named Horse of the Year, racing's most prestigious annual award. These horses have the best possible pedigrees—the identical family history as world-historical horses. Still, more than three-fourths do not win a major race. The traditional way of predicting horse success, the data tells us, leaves plenty of room for improvement.

It's actually not that surprising that pedigree is not that predictive. Think of humans. Imagine an NBA owner who bought his future team, as ten-year-olds, based on their pedigrees. He would have hired an agent to examine Earvin Johnson III, son of "Magic" Johnson. "He's got nice size, thus far," an agent might say. "It's legitimate size, from the Johnson line. He should have great vision, selflessness, size, and speed. He seems to be outgoing, great personality. Confident walk. Personable. This is a great bet." Unfortunately, fourteen years later, this owner would have a 6'2" (short for a pro ball player) fashion blogger for *E!* Earvin Johnson III might be of great assistance in designing the uniforms, but he would probably offer little help on the court.

Along with the fashion blogger, an NBA owner who chose a team as many owners choose horses would likely snap up Jeffrey and Marcus Jordan, both sons of Michael Jordan, and both of whom proved mediocre college players. Good luck against the Cleveland Cavaliers. They are led by LeBron James, whose mom is 5'5". Or imagine a country that elected its leaders based on their pedigrees. We'd be led by people like George W. Bush. (Sorry, couldn't resist.)

Horse agents do use other information besides pedigree. For example, they analyze the gaits of two-year-olds and examine horses visually. In Ocala, I spent hours chatting with various agents, which was long enough to determine that there was little agreement on what in fact they were looking for.

Add to these rampant contradictions and uncertainties the fact that some horse buyers have what seems like infinite funds, and you get a market with rather large inefficiencies. Ten years ago, Horse No. 153 was a two-year-old who ran faster than every other horse, looked beautiful to most agents, and had a wonderful pedigree—a descendant of Northern Dancer and Secretariat, two of the greatest racehorses of all time. An Irish billionaire and a Dubai sheik both wanted to purchase him. They got into a bidding war that quickly turned into a contest of pride. As hundreds of stunned horse men and women looked on, the bids kept getting higher and higher, until the two-year-old horse finally sold for $16 million, by far the highest price ever paid for a horse. Horse No. 153, who was given the name The Green Monkey, ran three races, earned just $10,000, and was retired.

Seder never had any interest in the traditional methods of evaluating horses. He was interested only in data. He planned to measure various attributes of racehorses and see which of them correlated with their performance. It's important to note that Seder worked out his plan half a decade before the World Wide Web was invented. But his strategy was very much based on data science. And the lessons from his story are applicable to anybody using Big Data.

For years, Seder's pursuit produced nothing but frustration. He measured the size of horses' nostrils, creating the world's first and largest dataset on horse nostril size and eventual earnings. Nostril size, he found, did not predict horse success. He gave horses EKGs to examine their hearts and cut the limbs off dead horses to measure the volume of their fast-twitch muscles. He once grabbed a shovel outside a barn to determine the size of horses' excrement, on the theory that shedding too much weight before an event can slow a horse down. None of this correlated with racing success.

Then, twelve years ago, he got his first big break. Seder decided to measure the size of the horses' internal organs. Since this was impossible with existing technology, he constructed his own portable ultrasound. The results were remarkable. He found that the size of the heart, and particularly the size of the left ventricle, was a massive predictor of a horse's success, the single most important variable. Another organ that mattered was the spleen: horses with small spleens earned virtually nothing.

Seder had a couple more hits. He digitized thousands of videos of horses galloping and found that certain gaits did correlate with racetrack success. He also discovered that some two-year-old horses wheeze after running one-eighth of a mile. Such horses sometimes sell for as much as a million dollars, but Seder's data told him that the wheezers virtually never pan out. He thus assigns an assistant to sit near the finish line and weed out the wheezers.

Of about a thousand horses at the Ocala auction, roughly ten will pass all of Seder's tests. He ignores pedigree entirely, except as it will influence the price a horse will sell for. "Pedigree tells us a horse might have a very small chance of being great," he says. "But if I can see he's great, what do I care how he got there?"

One night, Seder invited me to his room at the Hilton hotel in Ocala. In the room, he told me about his childhood, his family, and his career. He showed me pictures of his wife, daughter, and son. He told me he was one of three Jewish students in his Philadelphia high school, and that when he entered he was

4'10". (He grew in college to 5'9".) He told me about his favorite horse: Pinky Pizwaanski. Seder bought and named this horse after a gay rider. He felt that Pinky, the horse, always gave a great effort even if he wasn't the most successful.

Finally, he showed me the file that included all the data he had recorded on No. 85, the file that drove the biggest prediction of his career. Was he giving away his secret? Perhaps, but he said he didn't care. More important to him than protecting his secrets was being proven right, showing to the world that these twenty years of cracking limbs, shoveling poop, and jerry-rigging ultrasounds had been worth it.

Here's some of the data on horse No. 85:

NO. 85 (LATER AMERICAN PHAROAH) PERCENTILES AS A ONE-YEAR-OLD

	PERCENTILE
Height	56
Weight	61
Pedigree	70
Left Ventricle	*99.61*

There it was, stark and clear, the reason that Seder and his team had become so obsessed with No. 85. His left ventricle was in the 99.61st percentile!

Not only that, but all his other important organs, including the rest of his heart and spleen, were exceptionally large as well. Generally speaking, when it comes to racing, Seder had found, the bigger the left ventricle, the better. But a left ventricle as big as this can be a sign of illness if the other organs are tiny. In American Pharoah, all the key organs were bigger than average, and the left ventricle was enormous. The data screamed that No. 85 was a 1-in-100,000 or even a one-in-a-million horse.

What can data scientists learn from Seder's project?

First, and perhaps most important, if you are going to try to use new data to revolutionize a field, it is best to go into a field where old methods are lousy. The pedigree-obsessed horse agents whom Seder beat left plenty of room for improvement. So did the word-count-obsessed search engines that Google beat.

One weakness of Google's attempt to predict influenza using search data is that you can already predict influenza very well just using last week's data and a simple seasonal adjustment. There is still debate about how much search data adds to that simple, powerful model. In my opinion, Google searches have more promise measuring health conditions for which existing data is weaker and therefore something like Google STD may prove more valuable in the long haul than Google Flu.

The second lesson is that, when trying to make predictions, you needn't worry too much about why your models work. Seder could not fully explain to me why the left ventricle is so important in predicting a horse's success. Nor could he precisely account for the value of the spleen. Perhaps one day horse cardiologists and hematologists will solve these mysteries. But for now it doesn't matter. Seder is in the prediction business, not the explanation business. And, in the prediction business, you just need to know that something works, not why.

For example, Walmart uses data from sales in all their stores to know what products to shelve. Before Hurricane

Frances, a destructive storm that hit the Southeast in 2004, Walmart suspected—correctly—that people's shopping habits may change when a city is about to be pummeled by a storm. They pored through sales data from previous hurricanes to see what people might want to buy. A major answer? Strawberry Pop-Tarts. This product sells seven times faster than normal in the days leading up to a hurricane.

Based on their analysis, Walmart had trucks loaded with strawberry Pop-Tarts heading down Interstate 95 toward stores in the path of the hurricane. And indeed, these Pop-Tarts sold well.

Why Pop-Tarts? Probably because they don't require refrigeration or cooking. Why strawberry? No clue. But when hurricanes hit, people turn to strawberry Pop-Tarts apparently. So in the days before a hurricane, Walmart now regularly stocks its shelves with boxes upon boxes of strawberry Pop-Tarts. The reason for the relationship doesn't matter. But the relationship itself does. Maybe one day food scientists will figure out the association between hurricanes and toaster pastries filled with strawberry jam. But, while waiting for some such explanation, Walmart still needs to stock its shelves with strawberry Pop-Tarts when hurricanes are approaching and save the Rice Krispies treats for sunnier days.

This lesson is also clear in the story of Orley Ashenfelter. What Seder is to horses, Ashenfelter, an economist at Princeton, may be to wine.

A little over a decade ago, Ashenfelter was frustrated. He had been buying a lot of red wine from the Bordeaux region of France. Sometimes this wine was delicious, worthy of its high price. Many times, though, it was a letdown.

Why, Ashenfelter wondered, was he paying the same price for wine that turned out so differently?

One day, Ashenfelter received a tip from a journalist friend and wine connoisseur. There was indeed a way to figure out whether a wine would be good. The key, Ashenfelter's friend told him, was the weather during the growing season.

Ashenfelter's interest was piqued. He went on a quest to figure out if this was true and he could consistently purchase better wine. He downloaded thirty years of weather data on the Bordeaux region. He also collected auction prices of wines. The auctions, which occur many years after the wine was originally sold, would tell you how the wine turned out.

The result was amazing. A huge percentage of the quality of a wine could be explained simply by the weather during the growing season.

In fact, a wine's quality could be broken down to one simple formula, which we might call the First Law of Viticulture:

Price = 12.145 + 0.00117 winter rainfall + 0.0614 average growing season temperature – 0.00386 harvest rainfall.

So why does wine quality in the Bordeaux region work like this? What explains the First Law of Viticulture? There is some explanation for Ashenfelter's wine formula—heat and early irrigation are necessary for grapes to properly ripen.

But the precise details of his predictive formula go well beyond any theory and will likely never be fully understood even by experts in the field.

Why does a centimeter of winter rain add, on average, exactly 0.1 cents to the price of a fully matured bottle of red wine? Why not 0.2 cents? Why not 0.05? Nobody can answer these questions. But if there are 1,000 centimeters of additional rain in a winter, you should be willing to pay an additional $1 for a bottle of wine.

Indeed, Ashenfelter, despite not knowing exactly why his regression worked exactly as it did, used it to purchase wines. According to him, "It worked out great." The quality of the wines he drank noticeably improved.

If your goal is to predict the future—what wine will taste good, what products will sell, which horses will run fast—you do not need to worry too much about why your model works exactly as it does. Just get the numbers right. That is the second lesson of Jeff Seder's horse story.

The final lesson to be learned from Seder's successful attempt to predict a potential Triple Crown winner is that you have to be open and flexible in determining what counts as data. It is not as if the old-time horse agents were oblivious to data before Seder came along. They scrutinized race times and pedigree charts. Seder's genius was to look for data where others hadn't looked before, to consider nontraditional sources of data. For a data scientist, a fresh and original perspective can pay off.

WORDS AS DATA

One day in 2004, two young economists with an expertise in media, then Ph.D. students at Harvard, were reading about a recent court decision in Massachusetts legalizing gay marriage.

The economists, Matt Gentzkow and Jesse Shapiro, noticed

something interesting: two newspapers employed strikingly different language to report the same story. The *Washington Times*, which has a reputation for being conservative, head-lined the story: "Homosexuals 'Marry' in Massachusetts." The *Washington Post*, which has a reputation for being liberal, re-ported that there had been a victory for "same-sex couples."

It's no surprise that different news organizations can tilt in different directions, that newspapers can cover the same story with a different focus. For years, in fact, Gentzkow and Shapiro had been pondering if they might use their economics training to help understand media bias. Why do some news organiza-tions seem to take a more liberal view and others a more con-servative one?

But Gentzkow and Shapiro didn't really have any ideas on how they might tackle this question; they couldn't figure out how they could systematically and objectively measure media subjectivity.

What Gentzkow and Shapiro found interesting, then, about the gay marriage story was not that news organizations differed in their coverage; it was *how* the newspapers' coverage differed—it came down to a distinct shift in word choice. In 2004, "homosexuals," as used by the *Washington Times*, was an old-fashioned and disparaging way to describe gay people, whereas "same-sex couples," as used by the *Washington Post*, emphasized that gay relationships were just another form of romance.

The scholars wondered whether language might be the key to understanding bias. Did liberals and conservatives consis-tently use different phrases? Could the words that newspapers use in stories be turned into data? What might this reveal about the American press? Could we figure out whether the press was liberal or conservative? And could we figure out why? In 2004, these weren't idle questions. The billions of words in American newspapers were no longer trapped on newsprint or microfilm. Certain websites now recorded every word included in every story for nearly every newspaper in the United States. Gentzkow and Shapiro could scrape these sites and quickly test the extent to which language could measure newspaper bias. And, by doing this, they could sharpen our understanding of how the news media works.

But, before describing what they found, let's leave for a moment the story of Gentzkow and Shapiro and their attempt to quantify the language in newspapers, and discuss how scholars, across a wide range of fields, have utilized this new type of data—words—to better understand human nature.

Language has, of course, always been a topic of interest to social scientists. However, studying language generally required the close reading of texts, and turning huge swaths of text into data wasn't feasible. Now, with computers and digitization, tabulating words across massive sets of documents is easy. Language has thus become subject to Big Data analysis. The links that Google utilized were composed of words. So are the Google searches that I study. Words feature frequently in this book. But language is so important to the Big Data revolution, it deserves its own section. In fact, it is being used so much now that there is an entire field devoted to it: "text as data."

A major development in this field is Google Ngrams. A few years ago, two young biologists, Erez Aiden and Jean-Baptiste

Michel, had their research assistants counting words one by one in old, dusty texts to try to find new insights on how certain usages of words spread. One day, Aiden and Michel heard about a new project by Google to digitize a large portion of the world's books. Almost immediately, the biologists grasped that this would be a much easier way to understand the history of language.

"We realized our methods were so hopelessly obsolete," Aiden told *Discover* magazine. "It was clear that you couldn't compete with this juggernaut of digitization." So they decided to collaborate with the search company. With the help of Google engineers, they created a service that searches through the millions of digitized books for a particular word or phrase. It then will tell researchers how frequently that word or phrase appeared in every year, from 1800 to 2010.

So what can we learn from the frequency with which words or phrases appear in books in different years? For one thing, we learn about the slow growth in popularity of sausage and the relatively recent and rapid growth in popularity of pizza.

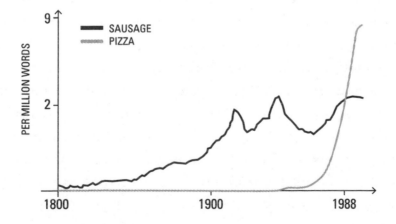

But there are lessons far more profound than that. For instance, Google Ngrams can teach us how national identity formed. One fascinating example is presented in Aiden and Michel's book, *Uncharted*.

First, a quick question. Do you think the United States is currently a united or a divided country? If you are like most people, you would say the United States is divided these days due to the high level of political polarization. You might even say the country is about as divided as it has ever been. America, after all, is now color-coded: red states are Republican; blue states are Democratic. But, in *Uncharted*, Aiden and Michel note one fascinating data point that reveals just how much more divided the United States once was. The data point is the language people use to talk about the country.

Note the words I used in the previous paragraph when I discussed how divided the country is. I wrote, "The United States *is* divided." I referred to the United States as a singular noun. This is natural; it is proper grammar and standard usage. I am sure you didn't even notice.

However, Americans didn't always speak this way. In the early days of the country, Americans referred to the United States using the plural form. For example, John Adams, in his 1799 State of the Union address, referred to "the United States in *their* treaties with his Britanic Majesty." If my book were written in 1800, I would have said, "The United States *are* divided." This little usage difference has long been a fascination for historians, since it suggests there was a point when America stopped thinking of itself as a collection of states and started thinking of itself as one nation.

So when did this happen? Historians, *Uncharted* informs us, have never been sure, as there has been no systematic way to test it. But many have long suspected the cause was the Civil War. In fact, James McPherson, former president of the American Historical Association and a Pulitzer Prize winner, noted bluntly: "The war marked a transition of the United States to a singular noun."

But it turns out McPherson was wrong. Google Ngrams gave Aiden and Michel a systematic way to check this. They could see how frequently American books used the phrase "The United States are . . ." versus "The United States is . . ." for every year in the country's history. The transformation was more gradual and didn't accelerate until well after the Civil War ended.

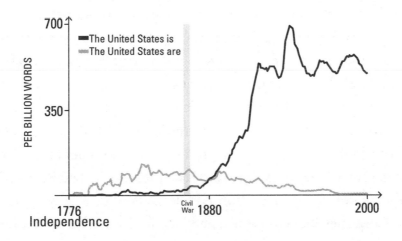

Fifteen years after the Civil War, there were still more uses of "The United States are . . ." than "The United States is . . . ," showing the country was still divided linguistically. Military victories happen quicker than changes in mindsets.

So much for how a country unites. How do a man and woman unite? Words can help here, too.

For example, we can predict whether a man and woman will go on a second date based on how they speak on the first date.

This was shown by an interdisciplinary team of Stanford and Northwestern scientists: Daniel McFarland, Dan Jurafsky, and Craig Rawlings. They studied hundreds of heterosexual speed daters and tried to determine what predicts whether they will feel a connection and want a second date.

They first used traditional data. They asked daters for their height, weight, and hobbies and tested how these factors correlated with someone reporting a spark of romantic interest. Women, on average, prefer men who are taller and share their hobbies; men, on average, prefer women who are skinnier and share their hobbies. Nothing new there.

But the scientists also collected a new type of data. They instructed the daters to take tape recorders with them. The recordings of the dates were then digitized. The scientists were thus able to code the words used, the presence of laughter, and the tone of voice. They could test both how men and women signaled they were interested and how partners earned that interest.

So what did the linguistic data tell us? First, how a man or woman conveys that he or she is interested. One of the ways a man signals that he is attracted is obvious: he laughs at a woman's jokes. Another is less obvious: when speaking, he limits the range of his pitch. There is research that suggests a monotone voice is often seen by women as masculine, which implies that men, perhaps subconsciously, exaggerate their masculinity when they like a woman.

The scientists found that a woman signals her interest by varying her pitch, speaking more softly, and taking shorter turns talking. There are also major clues about a woman's interest based on the particular words she uses. A woman is unlikely to be interested when she uses hedge words and phrases such as "probably" or "I guess."

Fellas, if a woman is hedging her statements on any topic— if she "sorta" likes her drink or "kinda" feels chilly or "probably" will have another hors d'oeuvre—you can bet that she is "sorta" "kinda" "probably" not into you.

A woman *is* likely to be interested when she talks about herself. It turns out that, for a man looking to connect, the most beautiful word you can hear from a woman's mouth may be "I": it's a sign she is feeling comfortable. A woman also is likely to be interested if she uses self-marking phrases such as "Ya know?" and "I mean." Why? The scientists noted that these phrases invite the listener's attention. They are friendly and warm and suggest a person is looking to connect, ya know what I mean?

Now, how can men and women communicate in order to get a date interested in them? The data tells us that there are plenty of ways a man can talk to raise the chances a woman likes him. Women like men who follow their lead. Perhaps not surprisingly, a woman is more likely to report a connection if a man laughs at her jokes and keeps the conversation on topics she introduces rather than constantly changing the subject to those he wants to talk about.* Women also like men who express support and sympathy. If a man says, "That's awesome!" or "That's really cool," a woman is significantly more likely to report a connection. Likewise if he uses phrases such as "That's tough" or "You must be sad."

For women, there is some bad news here, as the data seems to confirm a distasteful truth about men. Conversation plays only a small role in how they respond to women. Physical appearance trumps all else in predicting whether a man reports a connection. That said, there is one word that a woman can use to at least slightly improve the odds a man likes her and it's one we've already discussed: "I." Men are more likely to report clicking with a woman who talks about herself. And as previously noted, a woman is also more likely to report a connection after a date where she talks about herself. Thus it is a great sign, on a first date, if there is substantial discussion about the woman. The woman signals her comfort and probably appreciates that the man is not hogging the conversation. And the man likes that the woman is opening up. A second date is likely.

Finally, there is one clear indicator of trouble in a date transcript: a question mark. If there are lots of questions asked on a date, it is less likely that both the man and the woman will report a connection. This seems counterintuitive; you might

---

* One theory I am working on: Big Data just confirms everything the late Leonard Cohen ever said. For example, Leonard Cohen once gave his nephew the following advice for wooing women: "Listen well. Then listen some more. And when you think you are done listening, listen some more." That seems to be roughly similar to what these scientists found.

think that questions are a sign of interest. But not so on a first date. On a first date, most questions are signs of boredom. "What are your hobbies?" "How many brothers and sisters do you have?" These are the kinds of things people say when the conversation stalls. A great first date may include a single question at the end: "Will you go out with me again?" If this is the only question on the date, the answer is likely to be "Yes."

And men and women don't just talk differently when they're trying to woo each other. They talk differently in general.

A team of psychologists analyzed the words used in hundreds of thousands of Facebook posts. They measured how frequently every word is used by men and women. They could then declare which are the most masculine and most feminine words in the English language.

Many of these word preferences, alas, were obvious. For example, women talk about "shopping" and "my hair" much more frequently than men do. Men talk about "football" and "Xbox" much more frequently than women do. You probably didn't need a team of psychologists analyzing Big Data to tell you that.

Some of the findings, however, were more interesting. Women use the word "tomorrow" far more often than men do, perhaps because men aren't so great at thinking ahead. Adding the letter "o" to the word "so" is one of the most feminine linguistic traits. Among the words most disproportionately used by women are "soo," "sooo," "soooo," "sooooo," and "soooooo."

Maybe it was my childhood exposure to women who weren't afraid to throw the occasional f-bomb. But I always thought cursing was an equal-opportunity trait. Not so. Among the words used much more frequently by men than women are "fuck," "shit," "fucks," "bullshit," "fucking," and "fuckers."

Here are word clouds showing words used mostly by men and those used mostly by women. The larger a word appears, the more that word's use tilts toward that gender.

Males

Females

What I like about this study is the new data informs us of patterns that have long existed but we hadn't necessarily been aware of. Men and women have always spoken in different ways. But, for tens of thousands of years, this data disappeared as soon as the sound waves faded in space. Now this data is preserved on computers and can be analyzed by computers.

Or perhaps what I should have said, given my gender: "The words used to fucking disappear. Now we can take a break from watching football and playing Xbox and learn this shit. That is, if anyone gives a fuck."

It isn't just men and women who speak differently. People use different words as they age. This might even give us some clues as to how the aging process plays out. Here, from the same study, are the words most disproportionately used by people of different ages on Facebook. I call this graphic

DRINK. WORK. PRAY.

19- to 22-year-olds

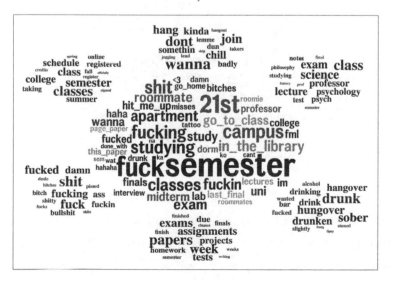

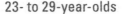

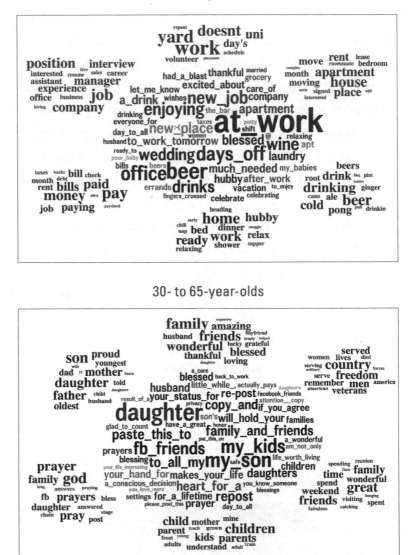

"Drink. Work. Pray." In people's teens, they're drinking. In their twenties, they are working. In their thirties and onward, they are praying.

A powerful new tool for analyzing text is something called sentiment analysis. Scientists can now estimate how happy or sad a particular passage of text is.

How? Teams of scientists have asked large numbers of people to code tens of thousands of words in the English language as positive or negative. The most positive words, according to this methodology, include "happy," "love," and "awesome." The most negative words include "sad," "death," and "depression." They thus have built an index of the mood of a huge set of words.

Using this index, they can measure the average mood of words in a passage of text. If someone writes "I am happy and in love and feeling awesome," sentiment analysis would code that as extremely happy text. If someone writes "I am sad thinking about all the world's death and depression," sentiment analysis would code that as extremely sad text. Other pieces of text would be somewhere in between.

So what can you learn when you code the mood of text? Facebook data scientists have shown one exciting possibility. They can estimate a country's Gross National Happiness every day. If people's status messages tend to be positive, the country is assumed happy for the day. If they tend to be negative, the country is assumed sad for the day.

Among the Facebook data scientists' findings: Christmas is one of the happiest days of the year. Now, I was skeptical of this analysis—and am a bit skeptical of this whole project. Generally, I think many people are secretly sad on Christmas because they are lonely or fighting with their family. More generally, I tend not to trust Facebook status updates, for reasons that I will discuss in the next chapter—namely, our propensity to lie about our lives on social media.

If you are alone and miserable on Christmas, do you really want to bother all of your friends by posting about how unhappy you are? I suspect there are many people spending a joyless Christmas who still post on Facebook about how grateful they are for their "wonderful, awesome, amazing, happy life." They then get coded as substantially raising America's Gross National Happiness. If we are going to really code Gross National Happiness, we should use more sources than just Facebook status updates.

That said, the finding that Christmas is, on balance, a joyous occasion does seem legitimately to be true. Google searches for depression and Gallup surveys also tell us that Christmas is among the happiest days of the year. And, contrary to an urban myth, suicides drop around the holidays. Even if there are some sad and lonely people on Christmas, there are many more merry ones.

These days, when people sit down to read, most of the time it is to peruse status updates on Facebook. But, once upon a time, not so long ago, human beings read stories, sometimes in books. Sentiment analysis can teach us a lot here, too.

A team of scientists, led by Andy Reagan, now at the University of California at Berkeley School of Information, downloaded the text of thousands of books and movie scripts. They could then code how happy or sad each point of the story was.

Consider, for example, the book *Harry Potter and the Deathly Hallows*. Here, from that team of scientists, is how the mood of the story changes, along with a description of key plot points.

Harry Potter and the Deathly Hallows
by J.K. Rowling

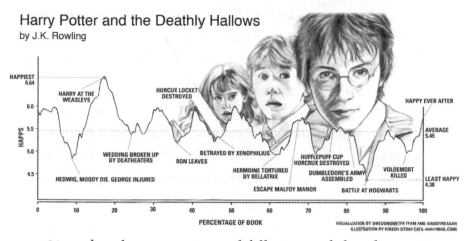

Note that the many rises and falls in mood that the sentiment analysis detects correspond to key events.

Most stories have simpler structures. Take, for example, Shakespeare's tragedy *King John*. In this play, nothing goes right. King John of England is asked to renounce his throne. He is excommunicated for disobeying the pope. War breaks out. His nephew dies, perhaps by suicide. Other people die. Finally, John is poisoned by a disgruntled monk.

And here is the sentiment analysis as the play progresses.

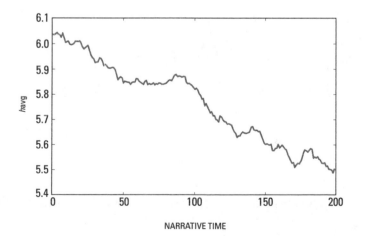

In other words, just from the words, the computer was able to detect that things go from bad to worse to worst.

Or consider the movie *127 Hours*. A basic plot summary of this movie is as follows:

A mountaineer goes to Utah's Canyonlands National Park to hike. He befriends other hikers but then parts ways with them. Suddenly, he slips and knocks loose a boulder, which traps his hand and wrist. He attempts various escapes, but each one fails. He becomes depressed. Finally, he amputates his arm and escapes. He gets married, starts a family, and continues climbing, although now he makes sure to leave a note whenever he goes off.

And here is the sentiment analysis as the movie progresses, again by Reagan's team of scientists.

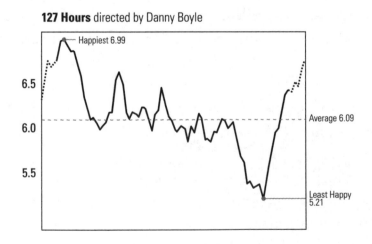

127 Hours directed by Danny Boyle

So what do we learn from the mood of thousands of these stories?

The computer scientists found that a huge percentage of stories fit into one of six relatively simple structures. They are, borrowing a chart from Reagan's team:

Rags to Riches (rise)
Riches to Rags (fall)
Man in a Hole (fall, then rise)
Icarus (rise, then fall)
Cinderella (rise, then fall, then rise)
Oedipus (fall, then rise, then fall)

There might be small twists and turns not captured by this simple scheme. For example, *127 Hours* ranks as a Man in a Hole story, even though there are moments along the way down when sentiments temporarily improve. The large, overarching structure of most stories fits into one of the six categories. *Harry Potter and the Deathly Hallows* is an exception.

There are a lot of additional questions we might answer. For example, how has the structure of stories changed through time? Have stories gotten more complicated through the years? Do cultures differ in the types of stories they tell? What types of stories do people like most? Do different story structures appeal to men and women? What about people in different countries?

Ultimately, text as data may give us unprecedented insights into what audiences actually want, which may be different from what authors or executives think they want. Already there are some clues that point in this direction.

Consider a study by two Wharton School professors, Jonah Berger and Katherine L. Milkman, on what types of stories get shared. They tested whether positive stories or negative stories were more likely to make the *New York Times'* most-emailed list. They downloaded every *Times* article over a three-month period. Using sentiment analysis, the professors coded the mood of articles. Examples of positive stories included "Wide-Eyed New Arrivals Falling in Love with the City" and "Tony Award for Philanthropy." Stories such as "Web Rumors Tied to Korean Actress' Suicide" and "Germany: Baby Polar Bear's Feeder Dies" proved, not surprisingly, to be negative.

The professors also had information about where the story was placed. Was it on the home page? On the top right? The top left? And they had information about when the story came out. Late Tuesday night? Monday morning?

They could compare two articles—one of them positive, one of them negative—that appeared in a similar place on the *Times* site and came out at a similar time and see which one was more likely to be emailed.

So what gets shared, positive or negative articles?

Positive articles. As the authors conclude, "Content is more likely to become viral the more positive it is."

Note this would seem to contrast with the conventional journalistic wisdom that people are attracted to violent and catastrophic stories. It may be true that news media give people plenty of dark stories. There is something to the newsroom adage, "If it bleeds, it leads." The Wharton professors' study, however, suggests that people may actually want more cheery stories. It may suggest a new adage: "If it smiles, it's emailed," though that doesn't really rhyme.

So much for sad and happy text. How do you figure out what words are liberal or conservative? And what does that tell us about the modern news media? This is a bit more complicated, which brings us back to Gentzkow and Shapiro. Remember, they were the economists who saw gay marriage described different ways in two different newspapers and wondered if they could use language to uncover political bias.

The first thing these two ambitious young scholars did was examine transcripts of the *Congressional Record*. Since this record was already digitized, they could download every word used by every Democratic congressperson in 2005 and every word used by every Republican congressperson in 2005. They could then see if certain phrases were significantly more likely to be used by Democrats or Republicans.

Some were indeed. Here are a few examples in each category.

PHRASES USED FAR MORE BY DEMOCRATS	PHRASES USED FAR MORE BY REPUBLICANS
Estate tax	Death tax
Privatize social security	Reform social security
Rosa Parks	Saddam Hussein
Workers' rights	Private property rights
Poor people	Government spending

What explains these differences in language?

Sometimes Democrats and Republicans use different phrasing to describe the same concept. In 2005, Republicans tried to cut the federal inheritance tax. They tended to describe it as a "death tax" (which sounds like an imposition upon the newly deceased). Democrats described it as an "estate tax" (which sounds like a tax on the wealthy). Similarly, Republicans tried to move Social Security into individual retirement accounts. To Republicans, this was a "reform." To Democrats, this was a more dangerous-sounding "privatization."

Sometimes differences in language are a question of emphasis. Republicans and Democrats presumably both have great respect for Rosa Parks, the civil rights hero. But Democrats talked about her more frequently. Likewise, Democrats and Republicans presumably both think that Saddam Hussein, the former leader of Iraq, was an evil dictator. But Republicans repeatedly mentioned him in their attempt to justify the Iraq War. Similarly, "workers' rights" and concern for "poor people" are core principles of the Democratic Party. "Private property rights" and cutting "government spending" are core principles of Republicans.

And these differences in language use are substantial. For example, in 2005, congressional Republicans used the phrase "death tax" 365 times and "estate tax" only 46 times. For congressional Democrats, the pattern was reversed. They used the phrase "death tax" only 35 times and "estate tax" 195 times.

And if these words can tell us whether a congressperson is a Democrat or a Republican, the scholars realized, they could also tell us whether a newspaper tilts left or right. Just as Republican congresspeople might be more likely to use the phrase "death tax" to persuade people to oppose it, conservative newspapers might do the same. The relatively liberal *Washington Post* used the phrase "estate tax" 13.7 times more frequently than they used the phrase "death tax." The conservative *Wash-*

ington Times used "death tax" and "estate tax" about the same amount.

Thanks to the wonders of the internet, Gentzkow and Shapiro could analyze the language used in a large number of the nation's newspapers. The scholars utilized two websites, newslibrary.com and proquest.com, which together had digitized 433 newspapers. They then counted how frequently one thousand such politically charged phrases were used in newspapers in order to measure the papers' political slant. The most liberal newspaper, by this measure, proved to be the *Philadelphia Daily News;* the most conservative: the *Billings* (Montana) *Gazette.*

When you have the first comprehensive measure of media bias for such a wide swath of outlets, you can answer perhaps the most important question about the press: why do some publications lean left and others right?

The economists quickly homed in on one key factor: the politics of a given area. If an area is generally liberal, as Philadelphia and Detroit are, the dominant newspaper there tends to be liberal. If an area is more conservative, as are Billings and Amarillo, Texas, the dominant paper there tends to be conservative. In other words, the evidence strongly suggests that newspapers are inclined to give their readers what they want.

You might think a paper's owner would have some influence on the slant of its coverage, but as a rule, who owns a paper has less effect than we might think upon its political bias. Note what happens when the same person or company owns papers in different markets. Consider the New York Times Company. It owns what Gentzkow and Shapiro find to be the liberal-leaning *New York Times,* based in New York City, where roughly 70 percent of the population is Democratic. It also owned, at the time of the study, the conservative-leaning, by their measure, *Spartanburg Herald-Journal,* in Spartanburg, South Carolina, where roughly 70 percent of the population is Republican. There are exceptions, of course: Rupert Murdoch's News Corporation owns what just about anyone would find to be the conservative *New York Post.* But, overall, the findings suggest that the market determines newspapers' slants far more than owners do.

The study has a profound impact on how we think about the news media. Many people, particularly Marxists, have viewed American journalism as controlled by rich people or corporations with the goal of influencing the masses, perhaps to push people toward their political views. Gentzkow and Shapiro's paper suggests, however, that this is not the predominant motivation of owners. The owners of the American press, instead, are primarily giving the masses what they want so that the owners can become even richer.

Oh, and one more question—a big, controversial, and perhaps even more provocative question. Do the American news media, on average, slant left or right? Are the media on average liberal or conservative?

Gentzkow and Shapiro found that newspapers slant left. The average newspaper is more similar, in the words it uses, to a Democratic congressperson than it is to a Republican congressperson.

"Aha!" conservative readers may be ready to scream, "I told you so!" Many conservatives have long suspected newspapers have been biased to try to manipulate the masses to support left-wing viewpoints.

Not so, say the authors. In fact, the liberal bias is well cali-brated to what newspaper readers want. Newspaper readership, on average, tilts a bit left. (They have data on that.) And news-papers, on average, tilt a bit left to give their readers the view-points they demand.

There is no grand conspiracy. There is just capitalism.

The news media, Gentzkow and Shapiro's results imply, often operate like every other industry on the planet. Just as supermarkets figure out what ice cream people want and fill their shelves with it, newspapers figure out what viewpoints people want and fill their pages with it. "It's just a business," Shapiro told me. That is what you can learn when you break down and quantify matters as convoluted as news, analysis, and opinion into their component parts: words.

PICTURES AS DATA

Traditionally, when academics or businesspeople wanted data, they conducted surveys. The data came neatly formed, drawn from numbers or checked boxes on questionnaires. This is no longer the case. The days of structured, clean, simple, survey-based data are over. In this new age, the messy traces we leave as we go through life are becoming the primary source of data.

As we've already seen, words are data. Clicks are data. Links are data. Typos are data. Bananas in dreams are data. Tone of voice is data. Wheezing is data. Heartbeats are data. Spleen size is data. Searches are, I argue, the most revelatory data.

Pictures, it turns out, are data, too.

Just as words, which were once confined to books and periodicals on dusty shelves, have now been digitized, pictures have been liberated from albums and cardboard boxes. They too have been transformed into bits and released into the cloud. And as text can give us history lessons—showing us, for example, the changing ways people have spoken—pictures can give us history lessons—showing us, for example, the changing ways people have posed.

Consider an ingenious study by a team of four computer scientists at Brown and Berkeley. They took advantage of a neat digital-era development: many high schools have scanned their historical yearbooks and made them available online. Across the internet, the researchers found 949 scanned yearbooks from American high schools spanning the years 1905–2013. This included tens of thousands of senior portraits. Using computer software, they were able to create an "average" face out of the pictures from every decade. In other words, they could figure out the average location and configuration of people's noses, eyes, lips, and hair. Here are the average faces from across the last century plus, broken down by gender:

Notice anything? Americans—and particularly women—started smiling. They went from nearly stone-faced at the start of the twentieth century to beaming by the end.

So why the change? Did Americans get happier?

Nope. Other scholars have helped answer this question. The reason is, at least to me, fascinating. When photographs were first invented, people thought of them like paintings. There was nothing else to compare them to. Thus, subjects in photos copied subjects in paintings. And since people sitting for portraits couldn't hold a smile for the many hours the painting took, they adopted a serious look. Subjects in photos adopted the same look.

What finally got them to change? Business, profit, and marketing, of course. In the mid-twentieth century, Kodak, the film and camera company, was frustrated by the limited number of pictures people were taking and devised a strategy to get them to take more. Kodak's advertising began associating photos with happiness. The goal was to get people in the habit of taking a picture whenever they wanted to show others what a good time they were having. All those smiling yearbook photos are a result of that successful campaign (as are most of the photos you see on Facebook and Instagram today).

But photos as data can tell us much more than when high school seniors began to say "cheese." Surprisingly, images may be able to tell us how the economy is doing.

Consider one provocatively titled academic paper: "Measuring Economic Growth from Outer Space." When a paper has a title like that, you can bet I'm going to read it. The authors of this paper—J. Vernon Henderson, Adam Storeygard, and David N. Weil—begin by noting that in many developing countries, existing measures of gross domestic product (GDP) are inefficient. This is because large portions of economic activity happen off the books, and the government agencies meant to measure economic output have limited resources.

The authors' rather unconventional idea? They could help measure GDP based on how much light there is in these countries at night. They got that information from photographs taken by a U.S. Air Force satellite that circles the earth fourteen times per day.

Why might light at night be a good measure of GDP? Well, in very poor parts of the world, people struggle to pay for electricity. And as a result, when economic conditions are bad, households and villages will dramatically reduce the amount of light they allow themselves at night.

Night light dropped sharply in Indonesia during the 1998 Asian financial crisis. In South Korea, night light increased 72 percent from 1992 to 2008, corresponding to a remarkably strong economic performance over this period. In North Korea, over the same time, night light actually fell, corresponding to a dismal economic performance during this time.

In 1998, in southern Madagascar, a large accumulation of rubies and sapphires was discovered. The town of Ilakaka went from little more than a truck stop to a major trading center. There was virtually no night light in Ilakaka prior to 1998. In the next five years, there was an explosion of light at night.

The authors admit their night light data is far from a perfect measure of economic output. You most definitely cannot know exactly how an economy is doing just from how much light satellites can pick up at night. The authors do not recommend using this measure at all for developed countries, such as the United States, where the existing economic data is more accurate. And to be fair, even in developing countries, they find that night light is only about as useful as the official measures. But combining both the flawed government data with the imperfect night light data gives a better estimate than either source alone could provide. You can, in other words, improve your understanding of developing economies using pictures taken from outer space.

Joseph Reisinger, a computer science Ph.D. with a soft voice, shares the night light authors' frustration with the existing datasets on the economies in developing countries. In April 2014, Reisinger notes, Nigeria updated its GDP estimate, taking into account new sectors they may have missed in previous estimates. Their estimated GDP was now 90 percent higher.

"They're the largest economy in Africa," Reisinger said, his voice slowly rising. "We don't even know the most basic thing we would want to know about that country."

He wanted to find a way to get a sharper look at economic performance. His solution is quite an example of how to reimagine what constitutes data and the value of doing so.

Reisinger founded a company, Premise, which employs a group of workers in developing countries, armed with smartphones. The employees' job? To take pictures of interesting goings-on that might have economic import.

The employees might get snapshots outside gas stations or of fruit bins in supermarkets. They take pictures of the same locations over and over again. The pictures are sent back to Premise, whose second group of employees—computer scientists—turn the photos into data. The company's analysts can code everything from the length of lines in gas stations to how many apples are available in a supermarket to the ripeness of these apples to the price listed on the apples' bin. Based on photographs of all sorts of activity, Premise can begin to put together estimates of economic output and inflation. In developing countries, long lines in gas stations are a leading indicator of economic trouble. So are unavailable or unripe apples. Premise's on-the-ground pictures of China helped them discover food inflation there in 2011 and food deflation in 2012, long before the official data came in.

Premise sells this information to banks or hedge funds and also collaborates with the World Bank.

Like many good ideas, Premise's is a gift that keeps on giving. The World Bank was recently interested in the size of the underground cigarette economy in the Philippines. In particular, they wanted to know the effects of the government's recent efforts, which included random raids, to crack down on manufacturers that produced cigarettes without paying a tax. Premise's clever idea? Take photos of cigarette boxes seen on the street. See how many of them have tax stamps, which all legitimate cigarettes do. They have found that this part of the underground economy, while large in 2015, got significantly smaller in 2016. The government's efforts worked, although seeing something usually so hidden—illegal cigarettes—required new data.

As we've seen, what constitutes data has been wildly reimagined in the digital age and a lot of insights have been found in this new information. Learning what drives media bias, what makes a good first date, and how developing economies are really doing is just the beginning.

Not incidentally, a lot of money has also been made from such new data, starting with Messrs. Brin's and Page's tens of billions. Joseph Reisinger hasn't done badly himself. Observers estimate that Premise is now making tens of millions of dollars in annual revenue. Investors recently poured $50 million into the company. This means some investors consider Premise among the most valuable enterprises in the world primarily in the business of taking and selling photos, in the same league as *Playboy*.

There is, in other words, outsize value, for scholars and entrepreneurs alike, in utilizing all the new types of data now available, in thinking broadly about what counts as data. These days, a data scientist must not limit herself to a narrow or traditional view of data. These days, photographs of supermarket lines are valuable data. The fullness of supermarket bins is data. The ripeness of apples is data. Photos from outer space are data. The curvature of lips is data. Everything is data!

And with all this new data, we can finally see through people's lies.

4

DIGITAL TRUTH SERUM

Everybody lies.

People lie about how many drinks they had on the way home. They lie about how often they go to the gym, how much those new shoes cost, whether they read that book. They call in sick when they're not. They say they'll be in touch when they won't. They say it's not about you when it is. They say they love you when they don't. They say they're happy while in the dumps. They say they like women when they really like men.

People lie to friends. They lie to bosses. They lie to kids. They lie to parents. They lie to doctors. They lie to husbands. They lie to wives. They lie to themselves.

And they damn sure lie to surveys.

Here's my brief survey for you:

Have you ever cheated on an exam? _____
Have you ever fantasized about killing someone? _____

Were you tempted to lie? Many people underreport embarrassing behaviors and thoughts on surveys. They want to look good, even though most surveys are anonymous. This is called social desirability bias.

An important paper in 1950 provided powerful evidence of how surveys can fall victim to such bias. Researchers collected data, from official sources, on the residents of Denver: what percentage of them voted, gave to charity, and owned a library card. They then surveyed the residents to see if the percentages would match. The results were, at the time, shocking. What the residents reported to the surveys was very different from the data the researchers had gathered. Even though nobody gave their names, people, in large numbers, exaggerated their voter registration status, voting behavior, and charitable giving.

	REPORTED ON SURVEY	OFFICIAL COUNT
Registered to vote	83%	69%
Voted in last presidential election	73%	61%
Voted in last mayoral election	63%	36%
Have a library card	20%	13%
Gave to a recent Community Chest charitable drive	67%	33%

Has anything changed in sixty-five years? In the age of the internet, not owning a library card is no longer embarrassing. But, while what's embarrassing or desirable may have changed, people's tendency to deceive pollsters remains strong.

A recent survey asked University of Maryland graduates

various questions about their college experience. The answers were compared to official records. People consistently gave wrong information, in ways that made them look good. Fewer than 2 percent reported that they graduated with lower than a 2.5 GPA. (In reality, about 11 percent did.) And 44 percent said they had donated to the university in the past year. (In reality, about 28 percent did.)

And it is certainly possible that lying played a role in the failure of the polls to predict Donald Trump's 2016 victory. Polls, on average, underestimated his support by about 2 percentage points. Some people may have been embarrassed to say they were planning to support him. Some may have claimed they were undecided when they were really going Trump's way all along.

Why do people misinform anonymous surveys? I asked Roger Tourangeau, a research professor emeritus at the University of Michigan and perhaps the world's foremost expert on social desirability bias. Our weakness for "white lies" is an important part of the problem, he explained. "About one-third of the time, people lie in real life," he suggests. "The habits carry over to surveys."

Then there's that odd habit we sometimes have of lying to ourselves. "There is an unwillingness to admit to yourself that, say, you were a screw-up as a student," says Tourangeau.

Lying to oneself may explain why so many people say they are above average. How big is this problem? More than 40 percent of one company's engineers said they are in the top 5 percent. More than 90 percent of college professors say they do above-average work. One-quarter of high school seniors think they are in the top 1 percent in their ability to get along with other people. If you are deluding yourself, you can't be honest in a survey.

Another factor that plays into our lying to surveys is our strong desire to make a good impression on the stranger conducting the interview, if there is someone conducting the interview, that is. As Tourangeau puts it, "A person who looks like your favorite aunt walks in. . . . Do you want to tell your favorite aunt you used marijuana last month?" * Do you want to admit that you didn't give money to your good old alma mater?

For this reason, the more impersonal the conditions, the more honest people will be. For eliciting truthful answers, internet surveys are better than phone surveys, which are better than in-person surveys. People will admit more if they are alone than if others are in the room with them.

However, on sensitive topics, every survey method will elicit substantial misreporting. Tourangeau here used a word that is often thrown around by economists: "incentive." People have no incentive to tell surveys the truth.

---

* Another reason for lying is simply to mess with surveys. This is a huge problem for any research regarding teenagers, fundamentally complicating our ability to understand this age group. Researchers originally found a correlation between a teenager's being adopted and a variety of negative behaviors, such as using drugs, drinking alcohol, and skipping school. In subsequent research, they found this correlation was entirely explained by the 19 percent of self-reported adopted teenagers who weren't actually adopted. Follow-up research has found that a meaningful percent of teenagers tell surveys they are more than seven feet tall, weigh more than four hundred pounds, or have three children. One survey found 99 percent of students who reported having an artificial limb to academic researchers were kidding.

How, therefore, can we learn what our fellow humans are really thinking and doing?

In some instances, there are official data sources we can reference to get the truth. Even if people lie about their charitable donations, for example, we can get real numbers about giving in an area from the charities themselves. But when we are trying to learn about behaviors that are not tabulated in official records or we are trying to learn what people are thinking—their true beliefs, feelings, and desires—there is no other source of information except what people may deign to tell surveys. Until now, that is.

This is the second power of Big Data: certain online sources get people to admit things they would not admit anywhere else. They serve as a digital truth serum. Think of Google searches. Remember the conditions that make people more honest. Online? Check. Alone? Check. No person administering a survey? Check.

And there's another huge advantage that Google searches have in getting people to tell the truth: incentives. If you enjoy racist jokes, you have zero incentive to share that un-PC fact with a survey. You do, however, have an incentive to search for the best new racist jokes online. If you think you may be suffering from depression, you don't have an incentive to admit this to a survey. You do have an incentive to ask Google for symptoms and potential treatments.

Even if you are lying to yourself, Google may nevertheless know the truth. A couple of days before the election, you and some of your neighbors may legitimately think you will drive to a polling place and cast ballots. But, if you and they haven't searched for any information on how to vote or where to vote, data scientists like me can figure out that turnout in your area will actually be low. Similarly, maybe you haven't admitted to yourself that you may suffer from depression, even as you're Googling about crying jags and difficulty getting out of bed. You would show up, however, in an area's depression-related searches that I analyzed earlier in this book.

Think of your own experience using Google. I am guessing you have upon occasion typed things into that search box that reveal a behavior or thought that you would hesitate to admit in polite company. In fact, the evidence is overwhelming that a large majority of Americans are telling Google some very personal things. Americans, for instance, search for "porn" more than they search for "weather." This is difficult, by the way, to reconcile with the survey data since only about 25 percent of men and 8 percent of women admit they watch pornography.

You may have also noticed a certain honesty in Google searches when looking at the way this search engine automatically tries to complete your queries. Its suggestions are based on the most common searches that other people have made. So auto-complete clues us in to what people are Googling. In fact, auto-complete can be a bit misleading. Google won't suggest certain words it deems inappropriate, such as "cock," "fuck," and "porn." This means auto-complete tells us that people's Google thoughts are less racy than they actually are. Even so, some sensitive stuff often still comes up.

If you type "Why is . . ." the first two Google auto-completes currently are "Why is the sky blue?" and "Why is there a leap day?" suggesting these are the two most common ways to complete this search. The third: "Why is my poop green?" And Google auto-complete can get disturbing. Today, if you type in "Is it normal to want to . . . ," the first suggestion is "kill." If you type in "Is it normal to want to kill . . . ," the first suggestion is "my family."

Need more evidence that Google searches can give a different picture of the world than the one we usually see? Consider searches related to regrets around the decision to have or not to have children. Before deciding, some people fear they might make the wrong choice. And, almost always, the question is whether they will regret *not having* kids. People are seven times more likely to ask Google whether they will regret not having children than whether they will regret having children.

After making their decision—either to reproduce (or adopt) or not—people sometimes confess to Google that they rue their choice. This may come as something of a shock but post-decision, the numbers are reversed. Adults with children are 3.6 times more likely to tell Google they regret their decision than are adults without children.

One caveat that should be kept in mind throughout this chapter: Google can display a bias toward unseemly thoughts, thoughts people feel they can't discuss with anyone else. Nonetheless, if we are trying to uncover hidden thoughts, Google's ability to ferret them out can be useful. And the large disparity between regrets on having versus not having kids seems to be telling us that the unseemly thought in this case is a significant one.

Let's pause for a moment to consider what it even means to make a search such as "I regret having children." Google presents itself as a source from which we can seek information directly, on topics like the weather, who won last night's game, or when the Statue of Liberty was erected. But sometimes we type our uncensored thoughts into Google, without much hope that it will be able to help us. In this case, the search window serves as a kind of confessional.

There are thousands of searches every year, for example, for "I hate cold weather," "People are annoying," and "I am sad." Of course, those thousands of Google searches for "I am sad" represent only a tiny of fraction of the hundreds of millions of people who feel sad in a given year. Searches expressing thoughts, rather than looking for information, my research has found, are only made by a small sample of everyone for whom that thought comes to mind. Similarly, my research suggests that the seven thousand searches by Americans every year for "I regret having children" represent a small sample of those who have had that thought.

Kids are obviously a huge joy for many, probably most, people. And, despite my mom's fear that "you and your stupid data analysis" are going to limit her number of grandchildren, this research has not changed my desire to have kids. But that unseemly regret is interesting—and another aspect of humanity that we tend not to see in the traditional datasets. Our culture is constantly flooding us with images of wonderful, happy families. Most people would never consider having children as something they might regret. But some do. They may admit this to no one—except Google.

THE TRUTH ABOUT SEX

How many American men are gay? This is a legendary question in sexuality research. Yet it has been among the toughest questions for social scientists to answer. Psychologists no longer believe Alfred Kinsey's famous estimate—based on surveys that oversampled prisoners and prostitutes—that 10 percent of American men are gay. Representative surveys now tell us about 2 to 3 percent are. But sexual preference has long been among the subjects upon which people have tended to lie. I think I can use Big Data to give a better answer to this question than we have ever had.

First, more on that survey data. Surveys tell us there are far more gay men in tolerant states than intolerant states. For example, according to a Gallup survey, the proportion of the population that is gay is almost twice as high in Rhode Island, the state with the highest support for gay marriage, than Mississippi, the state with the lowest support for gay marriage.

There are two likely explanations for this. First, gay men born in intolerant states may move to tolerant states. Second, gay men in intolerant states may not divulge that they are gay; they are even more likely to lie.

Some insight into explanation number one—gay mobility— can be gleaned from another Big Data source: Facebook, which allows users to list what gender they are interested in. About 2.5 percent of male Facebook users who list a gender of interest say they are interested in men; that corresponds roughly with what the surveys indicate. And Facebook too shows big differences in the gay population in states with high versus low tolerance: Facebook has the gay population more than twice as high in Rhode Island as in Mississippi.

Facebook also can provide information on how people move around. I was able to code the hometown of a sample of openly gay Facebook users. This allowed me to directly estimate how many gay men move out of intolerant states into more toler-ant parts of the country. The answer? There is clearly some mobility—from Oklahoma City to San Francisco, for example. But I estimate that men packing up their Judy Garland CDs and heading to someplace more open-minded can explain less than half of the difference in the openly gay population in tolerant versus intolerant states.*

In addition, Facebook allows us to focus in on high school students. This is a special group, because high school boys rarely get to choose where they live. If mobility explained the state-by-state differences in the openly gay population, these differences should not appear among high school users. So what does the high school data say? There are far fewer openly gay high school boys in intolerant states. Only two in one thousand male high school students in Mississippi are openly gay. So it ain't just mobility.

If a similar number of gay men are born in every state and mobility cannot fully explain why some states have so many more openly gay men, the closet must be playing a big role. Which brings us back to Google, with which so many people have proved willing to share so much.

Might there be a way to use porn searches to test how many

---

*   Some may find it offensive that I associate a male preference for Judy Garland with a preference for having sex with men, even in jest. And I certainly don't mean to imply that all—or even most—gay men have a fascination with divas. But search data demonstrates that there is something to the stereotype. I estimate that a man who searches for information about Judy Garland is three times more likely to search for gay porn than straight porn. Some stereotypes, Big Data tells us, are true.

gay men there *really* are in different states? Indeed, there is. Countrywide, I estimate—using data from Google searches and Google AdWords—that about 5 percent of male porn searches are for gay-male porn. (These would include searches for such terms as "Rocket Tube," a popular gay pornographic site, as well as "gay porn.")

And how does this vary in different parts of the country? Overall, there are more gay porn searches in tolerant states compared to intolerant states. This makes sense, given that some gay men move out of intolerant places into tolerant places. But the differences are not nearly as large as the differences suggested by either surveys or Facebook. In Mississippi, I estimate that 4.8 percent of male porn searches are for gay porn, far higher than the numbers suggested by either surveys or Facebook and reasonably close to the 5.2 percent of pornography searches that are for gay porn in Rhode Island.

So how many American men are gay? This measure of pornography searches by men—roughly 5 percent are same-sex—seems a reasonable estimate of the true size of the gay population in the United States. And there is another, less straightforward way to get at this number. It requires some data science. We could utilize the relationship between tolerance and the openly gay population. Bear with me a bit here.

My preliminary research indicates that in a given state every 20 percentage points of support for gay marriage means about one and a half times as many men from that state will identify openly as gay on Facebook. Based on this, we can estimate how many men born in a hypothetically fully tolerant place—where, say, 100 percent of people supported gay marriage—would be openly gay. My estimate is about 5 percent would be, which fits the data from porn searches nicely. The closest we might have to growing up in a fully tolerant environment is high school boys in California's Bay Area. About 4 percent of them are openly gay on Facebook. That seems in line with my calculation.

I should note that I have not yet been able to come up with an estimate of same-sex attraction for women. The pornography numbers are less useful here, since far fewer women watch pornography, making the sample less representative. And of those who do, even women who are primarily attracted to men in real life seem to enjoy viewing lesbian porn. Fully 20 percent of videos watched by women on PornHub are lesbian.

Five percent of American men being gay is an estimate, of course. Some men are bisexual; some—especially when young—are not sure what they are. Obviously, you can't count this as precisely as you might the number of people who vote or attend a movie.

But one consequence of my estimate is clear: an awful lot of men in the United States, particularly in intolerant states, are still in the closet. They don't reveal their sexual preferences on Facebook. They don't admit it on surveys. And in many cases, they may even be married to women.

It turns out that wives suspect their husbands of being gay rather frequently. They demonstrate that suspicion in the surprisingly common search: "Is my husband gay?" "Gay" is 10 percent more likely to complete searches that begin "Is my husband . . ." than the second-place word, "cheating." It is eight times more common than "an alcoholic" and ten times more common than "depressed."

Most tellingly perhaps, searches questioning a husband's

sexuality are far more prevalent in the least tolerant regions. The states with the highest percentage of women asking this question are South Carolina and Louisiana. In fact, in twenty-one of the twenty-five states where this question is most frequently asked, support for gay marriage is lower than the national average.

Google and porn sites aren't the only useful data resources when it comes to men's sexuality. There is more evidence available in Big Data on what it means to live in the closet. I analyzed ads on Craigslist for males looking for "casual encounters." The percentage of these ads that are seeking casual encounters with men tends to be larger in less tolerant states. Among the states with the highest percentages are Kentucky, Louisiana, and Alabama.

And for even more of a glimpse into the closet, let's return to Google search data and get a little more granular. One of the most common searches made immediately before or after "gay porn" is "gay test." (These tests presume to tell men whether or not they are homosexual.) And searches for "gay test" are about twice as prevalent in the least tolerant states.

What does it mean to go back and forth between searching for "gay porn" and searching for "gay test"? Presumably, it suggests a fairly confused if not tortured mind. It's reasonable to suspect that some of these men are hoping to confirm that their interest in gay porn does not actually mean they're gay.

The Google search data does not allow us to see a particular user's search history over time. However, in 2006, AOL released a sample of their users' searches to academic researchers. Here are some of one anonymous user's searches over a six-day period.

Friday 03:49:55	free gay picks [*sic*]
Friday 03:59:37	locker room gay picks
Friday 04:00:14	gay picks
Friday 04:00:35	gay sex picks
Friday 05:08:23	a long gay quiz
Friday 05:10:00	a good gay test
Friday 05:25:07	gay tests for a confused man
Friday 05:26:38	gay tests
Friday 05:27:22	am i gay tests
Friday 05:29:18	gay picks
Friday 05:30:01	naked men picks
Friday 05:32:27	free nude men picks
Friday 05:38:19	hot gay sex picks
Friday 05:41:34	hot man butt sex
Wednesday 13:37:37	am i gay tests
Wednesday 13:41:20	gay tests
Wednesday 13:47:49	hot man butt sex
Wednesday 13:50:31	free gay sex vidio [*sic*]

This certainly reads like a man who is not comfortable with his sexuality. And the Google data tells us there are still many men like him. Most of them, in fact, live in states that are less tolerant of same-sex relationships.

For an even closer look at the people behind these numbers, I asked a psychiatrist in Mississippi, who specializes in helping closeted gay men, if any of his patients might want to talk to me. One man reached out. He told me he was a retired professor, in his sixties, and married to the same woman for more than forty years.

About ten years ago, overwhelmed with stress, he saw the

psychiatrist and finally acknowledged his sexuality. He has always known he was attracted to men, he says, but thought that this was universal and something that all men just hid. Shortly after beginning therapy, he had his first, and only, gay sexual encounter, with a student of his who was in his late twenties, an experience he describes as "wonderful."

He and his wife do not have sex. He says that he would feel guilty ever ending his marriage or openly dating a man. He regrets virtually every one of his major life decisions.

The retired professor and his wife will go another night without romantic love, without sex. Despite enormous progress, the persistence of intolerance will cause millions of other Americans to do the same.

You may not be shocked to learn that 5 percent of men are gay and that many remain in the closet. There have been times when most people would have been shocked. And there are still places where many people would be shocked as well.

"In Iran we don't have homosexuals like in your country," Mahmoud Ahmadinejad, then president of Iran, insisted in 2007. "In Iran we do not have this phenomenon." Likewise, Anatoly Pakhomov, mayor of Sochi, Russia, shortly before his city hosted the 2014 Winter Olympics, said of gay people, "We do not have them in our city." Yet internet behavior reveals significant interest in gay porn in Sochi and Iran.

This raises an obvious question: are there any common sexual interests in the United States today that are still considered shocking? It depends what you consider common and how easily shocked you are.

Most of the top searches on PornHub are not surprising—
they include terms like "teen," "threesome," and "blowjob" for
men, phrases like "passionate love making," "nipple sucking,"
and "man eating pussy" for women.

Leaving the mainstream, PornHub data does tell us about
some fetishes that you might not have ever guessed existed.
There are women who search for "anal apples" and "humping stuffed animals." There are men who search for "snot fetish" and "nude crucifixion." But these searches are rare—only
about ten every month even on this huge porn site.

Another related point that becomes quite clear when reviewing PornHub data: there's someone out there for everyone. Women, not surprisingly, often search for "tall" guys,
"dark" guys, and "handsome" guys. But they also sometimes
search for "short" guys, "pale" guys, and "ugly" guys. There
are women who search for "disabled" guys, "chubby guy with
small dick," and "fat ugly old man." Men frequently search
for "thin" women, women with "big tits," and women with
"blonde" hair. But they also sometimes search for "fat" women,
women with "tiny tits," and women with "green hair." There
are men who search for "bald" women, "midget" women, and
women with "no nipples." This data can be cheering for those
who are not tall, dark, and handsome or thin, big-breasted, and
blonde.*

---

* I think this data also has implications for one's optimal dating strategy. Clearly, one should put oneself out there, get rejected a lot, and
not take rejection personally. This process will allow you, eventually,
to find the mate who is most attracted to someone like you. Again, no
matter what you look like, these people exist. Trust me.

What about other searches that are both common and surprising? Among the 150 most common searches by men, the most surprising for me are the incestuous ones I discussed in the chapter on Freud. Other little-discussed objects of men's desire are "shemales" (77th most common search) and "granny" (110th most common search). Overall, about 1.4 percent of men's PornHub searches are for women with penises. About 0.6 percent (0.4 percent for men under the age of thirty-four) are for the elderly. Only 1 in 24,000 PornHub searches by men are explicitly for preteens; that may have something to do with the fact that PornHub, for obvious reasons, bans all forms of child pornography and possessing it is illegal.

Among the top PornHub searches by women is a genre of pornography that, I warn you, will disturb many readers: sex featuring violence against women. Fully 25 percent of female searches for straight porn emphasize the pain and/or humiliation of the woman—"painful anal crying," "public disgrace," and "extreme brutal gangbang," for example. Five percent look for nonconsensual sex—"rape" or "forced" sex—even though these videos are banned on PornHub. And search rates for all these terms are at least twice as common among women as among men. If there is a genre of porn in which violence is perpetrated against a woman, my analysis of the data shows that it almost always appeals disproportionately to women.

Of course, when trying to come to terms with this, it is really important to remember that there is a difference between fantasy and real life. Yes, of the minority of women who visit PornHub, there is a subset who search—unsuccessfully—for rape imagery. To state the obvious, this does not mean women want to be raped in real life and it certainly doesn't make rape any less horrific a crime. What the porn data does tell us is that sometimes people have fantasies they wish they didn't have and which they may never mention to others.

Closets are not just repositories of fantasies. When it comes to sex, people keep many secrets—about how much they are having, for example.

In the introduction, I noted that Americans report using far more condoms than are sold every year. You might therefore think this means they are just saying they use condoms more often during sex than they actually do. The evidence suggests they also exaggerate how frequently they are having sex to begin with. About 11 percent of women between the ages of fifteen and forty-four say they are sexually active, not currently pregnant, and not using contraception. Even with relatively conservative assumptions about how many times they are having sex, scientists would expect 10 percent of them to become pregnant every month. But this would already be more than the total number of pregnancies in the United States (which is 1 in 113 women of childbearing age). In our sex-obsessed culture it can be hard to admit that you are just not having that much.

But if you're looking for understanding or advice, you have, once again, an incentive to tell Google. On Google, there are sixteen times more complaints about a spouse not wanting sex than about a married partner not being willing to talk. There are five and a half times more complaints about an unmarried partner not wanting sex than an unmarried partner refusing to text back.

And Google searches suggest a surprising culprit for many of these sexless relationships. There are twice as many complaints that a boyfriend won't have sex than that a girlfriend won't have sex. By far, the number one search complaint about a boyfriend is "My boyfriend won't have sex with me." (Google searches are not broken down by gender, but, since the previous analysis said that 95 percent of men are straight, we can guess that not too many "boyfriend" searches are coming from men.)

How should we interpret this? Does this really imply that boyfriends withhold sex more than girlfriends? Not necessarily. As mentioned earlier, Google searches can be biased in favor of stuff people are uptight talking about. Men may feel more comfortable telling their friends about their girlfriend's lack of sexual interest than women are telling their friends about their boyfriend's. Still, even if the Google data does not imply that boyfriends are really twice as likely to avoid sex as girlfriends, it does suggest that boyfriends avoiding sex is more common than people let on.

Google data also suggests a reason people may be avoiding sex so frequently: enormous anxiety, with much of it misplaced. Start with men's anxieties. It isn't news that men worry about how well-endowed they are, but the degree of this worry is rather profound.

Men Google more questions about their sexual organ than any other body part: more than about their lungs, liver, feet, ears, nose, throat, and brain combined. Men conduct more searches for how to make their penises bigger than how to tune a guitar, make an omelet, or change a tire. Men's top Googled concern about steroids isn't whether they may damage their health but whether taking them might diminish the size of their penis. Men's top Googled question related to how their body or mind would change as they aged was whether their penis would get smaller.

Side note: One of the more common questions for Google regarding men's genitalia is "How big is my penis?" That men turn to Google, rather than a ruler, with this question is, in my opinion, a quintessential expression of our digital era.*

Do women care about penis size? Rarely, according to Google searches. For every search women make about a partner's phallus, men make roughly 170 searches about their own. True, on the rare occasions women do express concerns about a partner's penis, it is frequently about its size, but not necessarily that it's small. More than 40 percent of complaints about a partner's penis size say that it's too big. "Pain" is the most Googled word used in searches with the phrase "___ during sex." ("Bleeding," "peeing," "crying," and "farting" round out the top five.) Yet only 1 percent of men's searches looking to change their penis size are seeking information on how to make it smaller.

Men's second-most-common sex question is how to make their sexual encounters longer. Once again, the insecurities of men do not appear to match the concerns of women. There are roughly the same number of searches asking how to make a boyfriend climax more quickly as climax more slowly. In fact, the most common concern women have related to a boyfriend's

---

* I wanted to call this book *How Big Is My Penis? What Google Searches Teach Us About Human Nature*, but my editor warned me that would be a tough sell, that people might be too embarrassed to buy a book with that title in an airport bookstore. Do you agree?

orgasm isn't about when it happened but why it isn't happening at all.

We don't often talk about body image issues when it comes to men. And while it's true that overall interest in personal appearance skews female, it's not as lopsided as stereotypes would suggest. According to my analysis of Google AdWords, which measures the websites people visit, interest in beauty and fitness is 42 percent male, weight loss is 33 percent male, and cosmetic surgery is 39 percent male. Among all searches with "how to" related to breasts, about 20 percent ask how to get rid of man breasts.

But, even if the number of men who lack confidence in their bodies is higher than most people would think, women still outpace them when it comes to insecurity about how they look. So what can this digital truth serum reveal about women's self-doubt? Every year in the United States, there are more than seven million searches looking into breast implants. Official statistics tell us that about 300,000 women go through with the procedure annually.

Women also show a great deal of insecurity about their behinds, although many women have recently flip-flopped on what it is they don't like about them.

In 2004, in some parts of the United States, the most common search regarding changing one's butt was how to make it smaller. The desire to make one's bottom bigger was overwhelmingly concentrated in areas with large black populations. Beginning in 2010, however, the desire for bigger butts grew in the rest of the United States. This interest, if not the posterior distribution itself, has tripled in four years. In 2014, there were more searches asking how to make your butt bigger than smaller in every state. These days, for every five searches looking into breast implants in the United States, there is one looking into butt implants. (Thank you, Kim Kardashian!)

Does women's growing preference for a larger bottom match men's preferences? Interestingly, yes. "Big butt porn" searches, which also used to be concentrated in black communities, have recently shot up in popularity throughout the United States.

What else do men want in a woman's body? As mentioned earlier, and as most will find blindingly obvious, men show a preference for large breasts. About 12 percent of nongeneric pornographic searches are looking for big breasts. This is nearly twenty times higher than the search volume for small-breast porn.

That said, it is not clear that this means men want women to get breast implants. About 3 percent of big-breast porn searches explicitly say they want to see natural breasts.

Google searches about one's wife and breast implants are evenly split between asking how to persuade her to get implants and perplexity as to why she wants them.

Or consider the most common search about a girlfriend's breasts: "I love my girlfriend's boobs." It is not clear what men are hoping to find from Google when making this search.

Women, like men, have questions about their genitals. In fact, they have nearly as many questions about their vaginas as men have about their penises. Women's worries about their vaginas are often health related. But at least 30 percent of their questions take up other concerns. Women want to know how to shave it, tighten it, and make it taste better. A strikingly common concern, as touched upon earlier, is how to improve its odor.

Women are most frequently concerned that their vaginas smell like fish, followed by vinegar, onions, ammonia, garlic, cheese, body odor, urine, bread, bleach, feces, sweat, metal, feet, garbage, and rotten meat.

In general, men do not make many Google searches involving a partner's genitalia. Men make roughly the same number of searches about a girlfriend's vagina as women do about a boyfriend's penis.

When men do search about a partner's vagina, it is usually to complain about what women worry about most: the odor. Mostly, men are trying to figure out how to tell a woman about a bad odor without hurting her feelings. Sometimes, however, men's questions about odor reveal their own insecurities. Men occasionally ask for ways to use the smell to detect cheating— if it smells like condoms, for example, or another man's semen.

What should we make of all this secret insecurity? There is clearly some good news here. Google gives us legitimate reasons to worry less than we do. Many of our deepest fears about how our sexual partners perceive us are unjustified. Alone, at their computers, with no incentive to lie, partners reveal themselves to be fairly nonsuperficial and forgiving. In fact, we are all so busy judging our own bodies that there is little energy left over to judge other people's.

There is also probably a connection between two of the big concerns revealed in the sexual searches on Google: lack of sex and an insecurity about one's sexual attractiveness and performance. Maybe these are related. Maybe if we worried less about sex, we'd have more of it.

What else can Google searches tell us about sex? We can do a battle of the sexes, to see who is most generous. Take all searches looking for ways to get better at performing oral sex on the opposite gender. Do men look for more tips or women? Who is more sexually generous, men or women? Women, duh. Adding up all the possibilities, I estimate the ratio is 2:1 in favor of women looking for advice on how to better perform oral sex on their partner.

And when men do look for tips on how to give oral sex, they are frequently not looking for ways of pleasing another person. Men make as many searches looking for ways to perform oral sex on themselves as they do how to give a woman an orgasm. (This is among my favorite facts in Google search data.)

THE TRUTH ABOUT HATE AND PREJUDICE

Sex and romance are hardly the only topics cloaked in shame and, therefore, not the only topics about which people keep secrets. Many people are, for good reason, inclined to keep their prejudices to themselves. I suppose you could call it progress that many people today feel they will be judged if they admit they judge other people based on their ethnicity, sexual orientation, or religion. But many Americans still do. (This is another section, I warn readers, that includes disturbing material.)

You can see this on Google, where users sometimes ask questions such as "Why are black people rude?" or "Why are Jews evil?" Below, in order, are the top five negative words used in searches about various groups.

	1.	2.	3.	4.	5.
AFRICAN AMERICANS	rude	racist	stupid	ugly	lazy
JEWS	evil	racist	ugly	cheap	greedy
MUSLIMS	evil	terrorists	bad	violent	dangerous
MEXICANS	racist	stupid	ugly	lazy	dumb
ASIANS	ugly	racist	annoying	stupid	cheap
GAYS	evil	wrong	stupid	annoying	selfish
CHRISTIANS	stupid	crazy	dumb	delusional	wrong

A few patterns among these stereotypes stand out. For example, African Americans are the only group that faces a "rude" stereotype. Nearly every group is a victim of a "stupid" stereotype; the only two that are not: Jews and Muslims. The "evil" stereotype is applied to Jews, Muslims, and gays but not black people, Mexicans, Asians, and Christians.

Muslims are the only group stereotyped as terrorists. When a Muslim American plays into this stereotype, the response can be instantaneous and vicious. Google search data can give us a minute-by-minute peek into such eruptions of hate-fueled rage.

Consider what happened shortly after the mass shooting in San Bernardino, California, on December 2, 2015. That morning, Rizwan Farook and Tashfeen Malik entered a meeting of Farook's coworkers armed with semiautomatic pistols and semiautomatic rifles and murdered fourteen people. That evening, literally minutes after the media first reported one of the shooters' Muslim-sounding name, a disturbing number of Californians had decided what they wanted to do with Muslims: kill them.

The top Google search in California with the word "Muslims" in it at the time was "kill Muslims." And overall, Americans searched for the phrase "kill Muslims" with about the same frequency that they searched for "martini recipe," "migraine symptoms," and "Cowboys roster." In the days following the San Bernardino attack, for every American concerned with "Islamophobia," another was searching for "kill Muslims." While hate searches were approximately 20 percent of all searches about Muslims before the attack, more than half of all search volume about Muslims became hateful in the hours that followed it.

And this minute-by-minute search data can tell us how difficult it can be to calm this rage. Four days after the shooting, then-president Obama gave a prime-time address to the country. He wanted to reassure Americans that the government could both stop terrorism and, perhaps more important, quiet this dangerous Islamophobia.

Obama appealed to our better angels, speaking of the importance of inclusion and tolerance. The rhetoric was powerful and moving. The *Los Angeles Times* praised Obama for "[warning] against allowing fear to cloud our judgment." The *New York Times* called the speech both "tough" and "calming." The website Think Progress praised it as "a necessary tool of good governance, geared towards saving the lives of Muslim Americans." Obama's speech, in other words, was judged a major success. But was it?

Google search data suggests otherwise. Together with Evan Soltas, then at Princeton, I examined the data. In his speech, the president said, "It is the responsibility of all Americans— of every faith—to reject discrimination." But searches calling

Muslims "terrorists," "bad," "violent," and "evil" doubled during and shortly after the speech. President Obama also said, "It is our responsibility to reject religious tests on who we admit into this country." But negative searches about Syrian refugees, a mostly Muslim group then desperately looking for a safe haven, rose 60 percent, while searches asking how to help Syrian refugees dropped 35 percent. Obama asked Americans to "not forget that freedom is more powerful than fear." Yet searches for "kill Muslims" tripled during his speech. In fact, just about every negative search we could think to test regarding Muslims shot up during and after Obama's speech, and just about every positive search we could think to test declined.

In other words, Obama seemed to say all the right things. All the traditional media congratulated Obama on his healing words. But new data from the internet, offering digital truth serum, suggested that the speech actually backfired in its main goal. Instead of calming the angry mob, as everybody thought he was doing, the internet data tells us that Obama actually inflamed it. Things that we think are working can have the exact opposite effect from the one we expect. Sometimes we need internet data to correct our instinct to pat ourselves on the back.

So what should Obama have said to quell this particular form of hatred currently so virulent in America? We'll circle back to that later. Right now we're going to take a look at an age-old vein of prejudice in the United States, the form of hate that in fact stands out above the rest, the one that has been the most destructive and the topic of the research that began this book. In my work with Google search data, the single most telling fact I have found regarding hate on the internet is the popularity of the word "nigger."

Either singular or in its plural form, the word "nigger" is included in seven million American searches every year. (Again, the word used in rap songs is almost always "nigga," not "nigger," so there's no significant impact from hip-hop lyrics to account for.) Searches for "nigger jokes" are seventeen times more common than searches for "kike jokes," "gook jokes," "spic jokes," "chink jokes," and "fag jokes" combined.

When are searches for "nigger(s)"—or "nigger jokes"—most common? Whenever African-Americans are in the news. Among the periods when such searches were highest was the immediate aftermath of Hurricane Katrina, when television and newspapers showed images of desperate black people in New Orleans struggling for their survival. They also shot up during Obama's first election. And searches for "nigger jokes" rise on average about 30 percent on Martin Luther King Jr. Day.

The frightening ubiquity of this racial slur throws into doubt some current understandings of racism.

Any theory of racism has to explain a big puzzle in America. On the one hand, the overwhelming majority of black Americans think they suffer from prejudice—and they have ample evidence of discrimination in police stops, job interviews, and jury decisions. On the other hand, very few white Americans will admit to being racist.

The dominant explanation among political scientists recently has been that this is due, in large part, to widespread *implicit* prejudice. White Americans may mean well, this theory goes, but they have a subconscious bias, which influences their treatment of black Americans. Academics invented an ingenious way to test for such a bias. It is called the implicit-association test.

The tests have consistently shown that it takes most people milliseconds longer to associate black faces with positive words, such as "good," than with negative words, such as "awful." For white faces, the pattern is reversed. The extra time it takes is evidence of someone's implicit prejudice—a prejudice the person may not even be aware of.

There is, though, an alternative explanation for the discrimination that African-Americans feel and whites deny: hidden *explicit* racism. Suppose there is a reasonably widespread conscious racism of which people are very much aware but to which they won't confess—certainly not in a survey. That's what the search data seems to be saying. There is nothing implicit about searching for "nigger jokes." And it's hard to imagine that Americans are Googling the word "nigger" with the same frequency as "migraine" and "economist" without *explicit* racism having a major impact on African-Americans. Prior to the Google data, we didn't have a convincing measure of this virulent animus. Now we do. We are, therefore, in a position to see what it explains.

It explains, as discussed earlier, why Obama's vote totals in 2008 and 2012 were depressed in many regions. It also correlates with the black-white wage gap, as a team of economists recently reported. The areas that I had found make the most racist searches, in other words, underpay black people. And then there is the phenomenon of Donald Trump's candidacy. As noted in the introduction, when Nate Silver, the polling guru, looked for the geographic variable that correlated most strongly with support in the 2016 Republican primary for Trump, he found it in the map of racism I had developed. That variable was searches for "nigger(s)."

Scholars have recently put together a state-by-state measure of implicit prejudice against black people, which has enabled me to compare the effects of *explicit* racism, as measured by Google searches, and *implicit* bias. For example, I tested how much each worked against Obama in both of his presidential elections. Using regression analysis, I found that, to predict where Obama underperformed, an area's racist Google searches explained a lot. An area's performance on implicit-association tests added little.

To be provocative and to encourage more research in this area, let me put forth the following conjecture, ready to be tested by scholars across a range of fields. The primary explanation for discrimination against African Americans today is not the fact that the people who agree to participate in lab experiments make subconscious associations between negative words and black people; it is the fact that millions of white Americans continue to do things like search for "nigger jokes."

The discrimination black people regularly experience in the United States appears to be fueled more widely by explicit, if hidden, hostility. But, for other groups, subconscious prejudice may have a more fundamental impact. For example, I was able to use Google searches to find evidence of implicit prejudice against another segment of the population: young girls.

And who, might you ask, would be harboring bias against girls?

Their parents.

It's hardly surprising that parents of young children are often excited by the thought that their kids might be gifted. In fact, of all Google searches starting "Is my 2-year-old," the most common next word is "gifted." But this question is not asked equally about young boys and young girls. Parents are two and a half times more likely to ask "Is my son gifted?" than "Is my daughter gifted?" Parents show a similar bias when using other phrases related to intelligence that they may shy away from saying aloud, like, "Is my son a genius?"

Are parents picking up on legitimate differences between young girls and boys? Perhaps young boys are more likely than young girls to use big words or otherwise show objective signs of giftedness? Nope. If anything, it's the opposite. At young ages, girls have consistently been shown to have larger vocabularies and use more complex sentences. In American schools, girls are 9 percent more likely than boys to be in gifted programs. Despite all this, parents looking around the dinner table appear to see more gifted boys than girls.* In fact, on every search term related to intelligence I tested, including those indicating its absence, parents were more likely to be inquiring about their sons rather than their daughters. There are also more searches for "is my son behind" or "stupid" than comparable searches for daughters. But searches with negative words like "behind" and "stupid" are less specifically skewed toward sons than searches with positive words, such as "gifted" or "genius."

What then are parents' overriding concerns regarding their daughters? Primarily, anything related to appearance. Consider questions about a child's weight. Parents Google "Is my daughter

---

* To further test the hypothesis that parents treat kids of different genders differently, I am working on obtaining data from parenting websites. This would include a much larger number of parents than those who make these particular, specific searches.

overweight?" roughly twice as frequently as they Google "Is my son overweight?" Parents are about twice as likely to ask how to get their daughters to lose weight as they are to ask how to get their sons to do the same. Just as with giftedness, this gender bias is not grounded in reality. About 28 percent of girls are over-weight, while 35 percent of boys are. Even though scales measure more overweight boys than girls, parents see—or worry about—overweight girls much more frequently than overweight boys.

Parents are also one and a half times more likely to ask whether their daughter is beautiful than whether their son is handsome. And they are nearly three times more likely to ask whether their daughter is ugly than whether their son is ugly. (How Google is expected to know whether a child is beautiful or ugly is hard to say.)

In general, parents seem more likely to use positive words in questions about sons. They are more apt to ask whether a son is "happy" and less apt to ask whether a son is "depressed."

Liberal readers may imagine that these biases are more common in conservative parts of the country, but I didn't find any evidence of that. In fact, I did not find a significant relation-ship between any of these biases and the political or cultural makeup of a state. Nor is there evidence that these biases have decreased since 2004, the year for which Google search data is first available. It would seem this bias against girls is more widespread and deeply ingrained than we'd care to believe.

Sexism is not the only place our stereotypes about prejudice may be off.

Vikingmaiden88 is twenty-six years old. She enjoys reading history and writing poetry. Her signature quote is from Shakespeare. I gleaned all this from her profile and posts on Stormfront.org, America's most popular online hate site. I also learned that Vikingmaiden88 has enjoyed the content on the site of the newspaper I work for, the *New York Times*. She wrote an enthusiastic post about a particular *Times* feature.

I recently analyzed tens of thousands of such Stormfront profiles, in which registered members can enter their location, birth date, interests, and other information.

Stormfront was founded in 1995 by Don Black, a former Ku Klux Klan leader. Its most popular "social groups" are "Union of National Socialists" and "Fans and Supporters of Adolf Hitler." Over the past year, according to Quantcast, roughly 200,000 to 400,000 Americans visited the site every month. A recent Southern Poverty Law Center report linked nearly one hundred murders in the past five years to registered Stormfront members.

Stormfront members are not whom I would have guessed.

They tend to be young, at least according to self-reported birth dates. The most common age at which people join the site is nineteen. And four times more nineteen-year-olds sign up than forty-year-olds. Internet and social network users lean young, but not nearly that young.

Profiles do not have a field for gender. But I looked at all the posts and complete profiles of a random sample of American users, and it turns out that you can work out the gender of most of the membership: I estimate that about 30 percent of Stormfront members are female.

The states with the most members per capita are Montana, Alaska, and Idaho. These states tend to be overwhelmingly white. Does this mean that growing up with little diversity fosters hate?

Probably not. Rather, since those states have a higher proportion of non-Jewish white people, they have more potential members for a group that attacks Jews and nonwhites. The percentage of Stormfront's target audience that joins is actually higher in areas with more minorities. This is particularly true when you look at Stormfront's members who are eighteen and younger and therefore do not themselves choose where they live.

Among this age group, California, a state with one of the largest minority populations, has a membership rate 25 percent higher than the national average.

One of the most popular social groups on the site is "In Support of Anti-Semitism." The percentage of members who join this group is positively correlated with a state's Jewish population. New York, the state with the highest Jewish population, has above-average per capita membership in this group.

In 2001, Dna88 joined Stormfront, describing himself as a "good looking, racially aware" thirty-year-old Internet developer living in "Jew York City." In the next four months, he wrote more than two hundred posts, like "Jewish Crimes Against Humanity" and "Jewish Blood Money," and directed people to a website, jewwatch.com, which claims to be a "scholarly library" on "Zionist criminality."

Stormfront members complain about minorities' speaking different languages and committing crimes. But what I found most interesting were the complaints about competition in the dating market.

A man calling himself William Lyon Mackenzie King, after a former prime minister of Canada who once suggested that

"Canada should remain a white man's country," wrote in 2003 that he struggled to "contain" his "rage" after seeing a white woman "carrying around her half black ugly mongrel niglet." In her profile, Whitepride26, a forty-one-year-old student in Los Angeles, says, "I dislike blacks, Latinos, and sometimes Asians, especially when men find them more attractive" than "a white female."

Certain political developments play a role. The day that saw the biggest single increase in membership in Stormfront's history, by far, was November 5, 2008, the day after Barack Obama was elected president. There was, however, no increased interest in Stormfront during Donald Trump's candidacy and only a small rise immediately after he won. Trump rode a wave of white nationalism. There is no evidence here that he created a wave of white nationalism.

Obama's election led to a surge in the white nationalist movement. Trump's election seems to be a response to that.

One thing that does not seem to matter: economics. There was no relationship between monthly membership registration and a state's unemployment rate. States disproportionately affected by the Great Recession saw no comparative increase in Google searches for Stormfront.

But perhaps what was most interesting—and surprising— were some of the topics of conversation Stormfront members have. They are similar to those my friends and I talk about. Maybe it was my own naïveté, but I would have imagined white nationalists inhabiting a different universe from that of my friends and me. Instead they have long threads praising *Game of Thrones* and discussing the comparative merits of on-line dating sites, like PlentyOfFish and OkCupid.

And the key fact that shows that Stormfront users are inhabiting similar universes as people like me and my friends: the popularity of the *New York Times* among Stormfront users. It isn't just VikingMaiden88 hanging around the *Times* site. The site is popular among many of its members. In fact, when you compare Stormfront users to people who visit the Yahoo News site, it turns out that the Stormfront crowd is twice as likely to visit nytimes.com.

Members of a hate site perusing the oh-so-liberal nytimes .com? How could this possibly be? If a substantial number of Stormfront members get their news from nytimes.com, it means our conventional wisdom about white nationalists is wrong. It also means our conventional wisdom about how the internet works is wrong.

THE TRUTH ABOUT THE INTERNET

The internet, most everybody agrees, is driving Americans apart, causing most people to hole up in sites geared toward people like them. Here's how Cass Sunstein of Harvard Law School described the situation: "Our communications market is rapidly moving [toward a situation where] people restrict themselves to their own points of view—liberals watching and reading mostly or only liberals; moderates, moderates; conservatives, conservatives; Neo-Nazis, Neo-Nazis."

This view makes sense. After all, the internet gives us a virtually unlimited number of options from which we can consume the news. I can read whatever I want. You can read whatever you want. VikingMaiden88 can read whatever she wants. And people, if left to their own devices, tend to seek out viewpoints that confirm what they believe. Thus, surely, the internet must be creating extreme political segregation.

There is one problem with this standard view. The data tells us that it is simply not true.

The evidence against this piece of conventional wisdom comes from a 2011 study by Matt Gentzkow and Jesse Shapiro, two economists whose work we discussed earlier.

Gentzkow and Shapiro collected data on the browsing behavior of a large sample of Americans. Their dataset also included the ideology—self-reported—of their subjects: whether people considered themselves more liberal or conservative. They used this data to measure the political segregation on the internet.

How? They performed an interesting thought experiment.

Suppose you randomly sampled two Americans who happen to both be visiting the same news website. What is the probability one of them will be liberal and the other conservative? How frequently, in other words, do liberals and conservatives "meet" on news sites?

To think about this further, suppose liberals and conservatives on the internet never got their online news from the same place. In other words, liberals exclusively visited liberal websites, conservatives exclusively conservative ones. If this were the case, the chances that two Americans on a given news site have opposing political views would be 0 percent. The internet would be perfectly *segregated*. Liberals and conservatives would never mix.

Suppose, in contrast, that liberals and conservatives did not differ at all in how they got their news. In other words, a liberal and a conservative were equally likely to visit any particular news site. If this were the case, the chances that two Americans on a given news website have opposing political views would be roughly 50 percent. The internet would be perfectly *desegregated*. Liberals and conservatives would perfectly mix.

So what does the data tell us? In the United States, according to Gentzkow and Shapiro, the chances that two people visiting the same news site have different political views is about 45 percent. In other words, the internet is far closer to perfect desegregation than perfect segregation. Liberals and conservatives are "meeting" each other on the web all the time.

What really puts the lack of segregation on the internet in perspective is comparing it to segregation in other parts of our lives. Gentzkow and Shapiro could repeat their analysis for various offline interactions. What are the chances that two family members have different political views? Two neighbors? Two colleagues? Two friends?

Using data from the General Social Survey, Gentzkow and Shapiro found that all these numbers were lower than the chances that two people on the same news website have different politics.

PROBABILITY THAT SOMEONE YOU MEET HAS OPPOSING POLITICAL VIEWS

On a News Website	45.2%
Coworker	41.6%
Offline Neighbor	40.3
Family Member	37%
Friend	34.7%

In other words, you are more likely to come across someone with opposing views online than you are offline.

Why isn't the internet more segregated? There are two factors that limit political segregation on the internet.

First, somewhat surprisingly, the internet news industry is dominated by a few massive sites. We usually think of the internet as appealing to the fringes. Indeed, there are sites for everybody, no matter your viewpoints. There are landing spots for pro-gun and anti-gun crusaders, cigar rights and dollar coin activists, anarchists and white nationalists. But these sites together account for a small fraction of the internet's news traffic. In fact, in 2009, four sites—Yahoo News, AOL News, msnbc.com, and cnn.com—collected more than half of news views. Yahoo News remains the most popular news site among Americans, with close to 90 million unique monthly visitors—or some 600 times Stormfront's audience. Mass media sites like Yahoo News appeal to a broad, politically diverse audience.

The second reason the internet isn't all that segregated is that many people with strong political opinions visit sites of the opposite viewpoint, if only to get angry and argue. Political junkies do not limit themselves only to sites geared toward them. Someone who visits thinkprogress.org and moveon.org—two extremely liberal sites—is more likely than the average internet user to visit foxnews.com, a right-leaning site. Someone who visits rushlimbaugh.com or glennbeck.com—two extremely conservative sites—is more likely than the average internet user to visit nytimes.com, a more liberal site.

Gentzkow and Shapiro's study was based on data from 2004–09, relatively early in the history of the internet. Might the internet have grown more compartmentalized since then?

Have social media and, in particular, Facebook altered their conclusion? Clearly, if our friends tend to share our political views, the rise of social media should mean a rise of echo chambers. Right?

Again, the story is not so simple. While it is true that people's friends on Facebook are more likely than not to share their political views, a team of data scientists—Eytan Bakshy, Solomon Messing, and Lada Adamic—have found that a surprising amount of the information people get on Facebook comes from people with opposing views.

How can this be? Don't our friends tend to share our political views? Indeed, they do. But there is one crucial reason that Facebook may lead to a more diverse political discussion than offline socializing. People, on average, have substantially more friends on Facebook than they do offline. And these weak ties facilitated by Facebook are more likely to be people with opposite political views.

In other words, Facebook exposes us to weak social connections—the high school acquaintance, the crazy third cousin, the friend of the friend of the friend you sort of, kind of, maybe know. These are people you might never go bowling with or to a barbecue with. You might not invite them over to a dinner party. But you do Facebook friend them. And you do see their links to articles with views you might have never otherwise considered.

In sum, the internet actually brings people of different political views together. The average liberal may spend her morning with her liberal husband and liberal kids; her afternoon with her liberal coworkers; her commute surrounded by liberal bumper stickers; her evening with her liberal yoga classmates.

When she comes home and peruses a few conservative comments on cnn.com or gets a Facebook link from her Republican high school acquaintance, this may be her highest conservative exposure of the day.

I probably never encounter white nationalists in my favorite coffee shop in Brooklyn. But VikingMaiden88 and I both frequent the *New York Times* site.

THE TRUTH ABOUT CHILD ABUSE AND ABORTION

The internet can give us insights into not just disturbing attitudes but also disturbing behaviors. Indeed, Google data may be effective at alerting us to crises that are missed by all the usual sources. People, after all, turn to Google when they are in trouble.

Consider child abuse during the Great Recession.

When this major economic downturn started in late 2007, many experts were naturally worried about the effect it might have on children. After all, many parents would be stressed and depressed, and these are major risk factors for maltreatment. Child abuse might skyrocket.

Then the official data came in, and it seemed that the worry was unfounded. Child protective service agencies reported that they were getting fewer cases of abuse. Further, these drops were largest in states that were hardest hit by the recession. "The doom-and-gloom predictions haven't come true," Richard Gelles, a child welfare expert at the University of Pennsylvania, told the Associated Press in 2011. Yes, as counterintuitive as it may have seemed, child abuse seemed to have plummeted during the recession.

But did child abuse really drop with so many adults out of work and extremely distressed? I had trouble believing this. So I turned to Google data.

It turns out, some kids make some tragic, and heart-wrenching, searches on Google—such as "my mom beat me" or "my dad hit me." And these searches present a different—and agonizing—picture of what happened during this time. The number of searches like this shot up during the Great Recession, closely tracking the unemployment rate.

Here's what I think happened: it was the reporting of child abuse cases that declined, not the child abuse itself. After all, it is estimated that only a small percentage of child abuse cases are reported to authorities anyway. And during a recession, many of the people who tend to report child abuse cases (teachers and police officers, for example) and handle cases (child protective service workers) are more likely to be overworked or out of work.

There were many stories during the economic downturn of people trying to report potential cases facing long wait times and giving up.

Indeed, there is more evidence, this time not from Google, that child abuse actually rose during the recession. When a child dies due to abuse or neglect it has to be reported. Such deaths, although rare, did rise in states that were hardest hit by the recession.

And there is some evidence from Google that more people were suspecting abuse in hard-hit areas. Controlling for pre-recession rates and national trends, states that had comparatively suffered the most had increased search rates for child abuse and neglect. For every percentage point increase in the unemployment rate, there was an associated 3 percent increase in the search rate for "child abuse" or "child neglect." Presumably, most of these people never successfully reported the abuse, as these states had the biggest drops in the reporting.

Searches by suffering kids increase. The rate of child deaths spike. Searches by people suspecting abuse go up in hard-hit states. But reporting of cases goes down. A recession seems to cause more kids to tell Google that their parents are hitting or beating them and more people to suspect that they see abuse. But the overworked agencies are able to handle fewer cases.

I think it's safe to say that the Great Recession did make child abuse worse, although the traditional measures did not show it.

Anytime I suspect people may be suffering off the books now, I turn to Google data. One of the potential benefits of this new data, and knowing how to interpret it, is the possibility of helping vulnerable people who might otherwise go overlooked by authorities.

So when the Supreme Court was recently looking into the effects of laws making it more difficult to get an abortion, I turned to the query data. I suspected women affected by this legislation might look into off-the-books ways to terminate a pregnancy. They did. And these searches were highest in states that had passed laws restricting abortions.

The search data here is both useful and troubling.

In 2015, in the United States, there were more than 700,000 Google searches looking into self-induced abortions. By comparison, there were some 3.4 million searches for abortion clinics that year. This suggests that a significant percentage of women considering an abortion have contemplated doing it themselves.

Women searched, about 160,000 times, for ways of getting abortion pills through unofficial channels—"buy abortion pills online" and "free abortion pills." They asked Google about abortion by herbs like parsley or by vitamin C. There were some 4,000 searches looking for directions on coat hanger abortions, including about 1,300 for the exact phrase "how to do a coat hanger abortion." There were also a few hundred looking into abortion through bleaching one's uterus and punching one's stomach.

What drives interest in self-induced abortion? The geography and timing of the Google searches point to a likely culprit: when it's hard to get an official abortion, women look into off-the-books approaches.

Search rates for self-induced abortion were fairly steady from 2004 through 2007. They began to rise in late 2008, coinciding with the financial crisis and the recession that followed. They took a big leap in 2011, jumping 40 percent. The Guttmacher Institute, a reproductive rights organization, singles out 2011 as the beginning of the country's recent crackdown on abortion; ninety-two state provisions that restrict access to abortion were enacted. Looking by comparison at Canada, which has not seen a crackdown on reproductive rights, there was no comparable increase in searches for self-induced abortions during this time.

The state with the highest rate of Google searches for self-induced abortions is Mississippi, a state with roughly three million people and, now, just one abortion clinic. Eight of the ten states with the highest search rates for self-induced abortions are considered by the Guttmacher Institute to be hostile or very hostile to abortion. None of the ten states with the lowest search rates for self-induced abortion are in either category.

Of course, we cannot know from Google searches how many women successfully give themselves abortions, but evidence suggests that a significant number may. One way to illuminate this is to compare abortion and birth data.

In 2011, the last year with complete state-level abortion data, women living in states with few abortion clinics had many fewer legal abortions.

Compare the ten states with the most abortion clinics per capita (a list that includes New York and California) to the ten states with the fewest abortion clinics per capita (a list that includes Mississippi and Oklahoma). Women living in states with the fewest abortion clinics had 54 percent fewer legal abortions—a difference of eleven abortions for every thousand women between the ages of fifteen and forty-four. Women living in states with the fewest abortion clinics also had more live births. However, the difference was not enough to make up for the lower number of abortions. There were six more live births for every thousand women of childbearing age.

In other words, there appear to have been some missing pregnancies in parts of the country where it was hardest to get an abortion. The official sources don't tell us what happened to those five missing births for each thousand women in states where it is hard to get an abortion.

Google provides some pretty good clues.

We can't blindly trust government data. The government may tell us that child abuse or abortion has fallen and politicians may celebrate this achievement. But the results we think we're seeing may be an artifact of flaws in the methods of data collection. The truth may be different—and, sometimes, far darker.

THE TRUTH ABOUT YOUR FACEBOOK FRIENDS

This book is about Big Data, in general. But this chapter has mostly emphasized Google searches, which I have argued reveal a hidden world very different from the one we think we see. So are other Big Data sources digital truth serum, as well? The fact is, many Big Data sources, such as Facebook, are often the opposite of digital truth serum.

On social media, as in surveys, you have no incentive to tell the truth. On social media, much more so than in surveys, you have a large incentive to make yourself look good. Your online presence is not anonymous, after all. You are courting an audience and telling your friends, family members, colleagues, acquaintances, and strangers who you are.

To see how biased data pulled from social media can be, consider the relative popularity of the *Atlantic*, a respected, highbrow monthly magazine, versus the *National Enquirer*, a gossipy, often-sensational magazine. Both publications have similar average circulations, selling a few hundred thousand copies. (The *National Enquirer* is a weekly, so it actually sells more total copies.) There are also a comparable number of Google searches for each magazine.

However, on Facebook, roughly 1.5 million people either

like the *Atlantic* or discuss articles from the *Atlantic* on their profiles. Only about 50,000 like the *Enquirer* or discuss its contents.

ATLANTIC VS. NATIONAL ENQUIRER POPULARITY COMPARED BY DIFFERENT SOURCES

Circulation	Roughly 1 *Atlantic* for every 1 *National Enquirer*
Google Searches	1 *Atlantic* for every 1 *National Enquirer*
Facebook Likes	27 *Atlantic* for every 1 *National Enquirer*

For assessing magazine popularity, circulation data is the ground truth. Google data comes close to matching it. And Facebook data is overwhelmingly biased against the trashy tabloid, making it the worst data for determining what people really like.

And as with reading preferences, so with life. On Facebook, we show our cultivated selves, not our true selves. I use Facebook data in this book, in fact in this chapter, but always with this caveat in mind.

To gain a better understanding of what social media misses, let's return to pornography for a moment. First, we need to address the common belief that the internet is dominated by smut. This isn't true. The majority of content on the internet is nonpornographic. For instance, of the top ten most visited websites, not one is pornographic. So the popularity of porn, while enormous, should not be overstated.

Yet, that said, taking a close look at how we like and share pornography makes it clear that Facebook, Instagram, and

Twitter only provide a limited window into what's truly popular on the internet. There are large subsets of the web that operate with massive popularity but little social presence.

The most popular video of all time, as of this writing, is Psy's "Gangnam Style," a goofy pop music video that satirizes trendy Koreans. It's been viewed about 2.3 billion times on YouTube alone since its debut in 2012. And its popularity is clear no matter what site you are on. It's been shared across different social media platforms tens of millions of times.

The most popular pornographic video of all time may be "Great Body, Great Sex, Great Blowjob." It's been viewed more than 80 million times. In other words, for every thirty views of "Gangnam Style," there has been about at least one view of "Great Body, Great Sex, Great Blowjob." If social media gave us an accurate view of the videos people watched, "Great Body, Great Sex, Great Blowjob" should be posted millions of times. But this video has been shared on social media only a few dozen times and always by porn stars, not by average users. People clearly do not feel the need to advertise their interest in this video to their friends.

Facebook is digital brag-to-my-friends-about-how-good-my-life-is serum. In Facebook world, the average adult seems to be happily married, vacationing in the Caribbean, and perusing the *Atlantic*. In the real world, a lot of people are angry, on supermarket checkout lines, peeking at the *National Enquirer*, ignoring the phone calls from their spouse, whom they haven't slept with in years. In Facebook world, family life seems perfect. In the real world, family life is messy. It can occasionally be so messy that a small number of people even regret having children. In Facebook world, it seems every young adult is at a cool party Saturday night. In the real world, most are home alone, binge-watching shows on Netflix. In Facebook world, a girlfriend posts twenty-six happy pictures from her getaway with her boyfriend. In the real world, immediately after posting this, she Googles "my boyfriend won't have sex with me." And, perhaps at the same time, the boyfriend watches "Great Body, Great Sex, Great Blowjob."

DIGITAL TRUTH	DIGITAL LIES
• Searches	• Social media posts
• Views	• Social media likes
• Clicks	• Dating profiles
• Swipes	

THE TRUTH ABOUT YOUR CUSTOMERS

In the early morning of September 5, 2006, Facebook introduced a major update to its home page. The early versions of Facebook had only allowed users to click on profiles of their friends to learn what they were doing. The website, considered a big success, had at the time 9.4 million users.

But after months of hard work, engineers had created something they called "News Feed," which would provide users with updates on the activities of all their friends.

Users immediately reported that they hated News Feed. Ben Parr, a Northwestern undergraduate, created "Students Against Facebook news feed." He said that "news feed is just too creepy, too stalker-esque, and a feature that has to go." Within a few days, the group had 700,000 members echoing

Parr's sentiment. One University of Michigan junior told the *Michigan Daily*, "I'm really creeped out by the new Facebook. It makes me feel like a stalker."

David Kirkpatrick tells this story in his authorized account of the website's history, *The Facebook Effect: The Inside Story of the Company That Is Connecting the World*. He dubs the introduction of News Feed "the biggest crisis Facebook has ever faced." But Kirkpatrick reports that when he interviewed Mark Zuckerberg, cofounder and head of the rapidly growing company, the CEO was unfazed.

The reason? Zuckerberg had access to digital truth serum: numbers on people's clicks and visits to Facebook. As Kirkpatrick writes:

> Zuckerberg in fact knew that people liked the News Feed, no matter what they were saying in the groups. He had the data to prove it. People were spending more time on Facebook, on average, than before News Feed launched. And they were doing more there—dramatically more. In August, users viewed 12 billion pages on the service. But by October, with News Feed under way, they viewed 22 billion.

And that was not all the evidence at Zuckerberg's disposal. Even the viral popularity of the anti–News Feed group was evidence of the power of News Feed. The group was able to grow so rapidly precisely because so many people had heard that their friends had joined—and they learned this through their News Feed.

In other words, while people were joining in a big public

uproar over how unhappy they were about seeing all the details of their friends' lives on Facebook, they were coming back to Facebook to see all the details of their friends' lives. News Feed stayed. Facebook now has more than one billion daily active users.

In his book *Zero to One*, Peter Thiel, an early investor in Facebook, says that great businesses are built on secrets, either secrets about nature or secrets about people. Jeff Seder, as discussed in Chapter 3, found the natural secret that left ventricle size predicted horse performance. Google found the natural secret of how powerful the information in links can be.

Thiel defines "secrets about people" as "things that people don't know about themselves or things they hide because they don't want others to know." These kinds of businesses, in other words, are built on people's lies.

You could argue that all of Facebook is founded on an unpleasant secret about people that Zuckerberg learned while at Harvard. Zuckerberg, early in his sophomore year, created a website for his fellow students called Facemash. Modeled on a site called "Am I Hot or Not?," Facemash would present pictures of two Harvard students and then have other students judge who was better looking.

The sophomore's site was greeted with outrage. The *Harvard Crimson*, in an editorial, accused young Zuckerberg of "catering to the worst side" of people. Hispanic and African-American groups accused him of sexism and racism. Yet, before Harvard administrators shut down Zuckerberg's internet access—just a few hours after the site was founded—450 people had viewed the site and voted 22,000 times on different images. Zuckerberg had learned an important secret: people can claim they're furious, they can decry something as distasteful, and yet they'll still click.

And he learned one more thing: for all their professions of seriousness, responsibility, and respect for others' privacy, people, even Harvard students, had a great interest in evaluating people's looks. The views and votes told him that. And later—since Facemash proved too controversial—he took this knowledge of just how interested people could be in superficial facts about others they sort of knew and harnessed it into the most successful company of his generation.

Netflix learned a similar lesson early on in its life cycle: don't trust what people tell you; trust what they do.

Originally, the company allowed users to create a queue of movies they wanted to watch in the future but didn't have time for at the moment. This way, when they had more time, Netflix could remind them of those movies.

However, Netflix noticed something odd in the data. Users were filling their queues with plenty of movies. But days later, when they were reminded of the movies on the queue, they rarely clicked.

What was the problem? Ask users what movies they plan to watch in a few days, and they will fill the queue with aspirational, highbrow films, such as black-and-white World War II documentaries or serious foreign films. A few days later, however, they will want to watch the same movies they usually want to watch: lowbrow comedies or romance films. People were consistently lying to themselves.

Faced with this disparity, Netflix stopped asking people to tell them what they wanted to see in the future and started building a model based on millions of clicks and views from similar customers. The company began greeting its users with suggested lists of films based not on what they claimed to like but on what the data said they were likely to view. The result: customers visited Netflix more frequently and watched more movies.

"The algorithms know you better than you know yourself," says Xavier Amatriain, a former data scientist at Netflix.

THE OUTSIZE VALUE OF IGNORING WHAT PEOPLE TELL YOU

WHAT PEOPLE SAY	REALITY	IPSO FACTO . . .
They don't want to stalk their friends.	There is little in this world they want more than to keep up with and judge their friends.	Mark Zuckerberg, cofounder of Facebook, is worth $55.2 billion.
They don't want to buy products that are produced in sweatshops.	They will buy nice, "reasonably priced" products.	Phil Knight, cofounder of Nike, is worth $25.4 billion.
They want to listen to news in the morning.	They want to hear about midgets having sex with porn stars in the morning.	Howard Stern is worth $500 million.
They have no interest in reading about bondage, dominance, and sadomasochism.	They want to read about BDSM between a young college graduate and a business magnate.	*50 Shades of Gray* has sold 125 million copies.
They want politicians to outline their policy positions.	They want politicians to spare them the details but seem tough and self-assured.	Donald Trump

CAN WE HANDLE THE TRUTH?

You may find parts of this chapter depressing. Digital truth serum has revealed an abiding interest in judging people based on their looks; the continued existence of millions of closeted gay men; a meaningful percentage of women fantasizing about rape; widespread animus against African-Americans; a hidden child abuse and self-induced abortion crisis; and an outbreak of violent Islamophobic rage that only got worse when the president appealed for tolerance. Not exactly cheery stuff. Often, after I give a talk on my research, people come up to me and say, "Seth, it's all very interesting. But it's *so* depressing."

I can't pretend there isn't a darkness in some of this data. If people consistently tell us what they think we want to hear, we will generally be told things that are more comforting than the truth. Digital truth serum, on average, will show us that the world is worse than we have thought.

Do we need to know this? Learning about Google searches, porn data, and who clicks on what might not make you think, "This is great. We can understand who we really are." You might instead think, "This is horrible. We can understand who we really are."

But the truth helps—and not just for Mark Zuckerberg or others looking to attract clicks or customers. There are at least three ways that this knowledge can improve our lives.

First, there can be comfort in knowing that you are not alone in your insecurities and embarrassing behavior. It can be nice to know others are insecure about their bodies. It is probably nice for many people—particularly those who aren't having much sex—to know the whole world isn't fornicating like rabbits. And it may be valuable for a high school boy in Mississippi with a crush on the quarterback to know that, despite the low numbers of openly gay men around him, plenty of others feel the same kinds of attraction.

There's another area—one I haven't yet discussed—where Google searches can help show you are not alone. When you were young, a teacher may have told you that, if you have a question, you should raise your hand and ask it because if you're confused, others are, too. If you were anything like me, you ignored your teacher's advice and sat there silently, afraid to open your mouth. Your questions were too dumb, you thought; everyone else's were more profound. The anonymous, aggregate Google data can tell us once and for all how right our teachers were. Plenty of basic, sub-profound questions lurk in other minds, too.

Consider the top questions Americans had during Obama's 2014 State of the Union speech. (See the color photo at end of the book.)

YOU'RE NOT THE ONLY ONE WONDERING: TOP GOOGLED QUESTIONS DURING THE STATE OF THE UNION

How old is Obama?

Who is sitting next to Biden?

Why is Boehner wearing a green tie?

Why is Boehner orange?

Now, you might read these questions and think they speak poorly of our democracy. To be more concerned about the color of someone's tie or his skin tone instead of the content of the president's speech doesn't reflect well on us. To not know who

John Boehner, then the Speaker of the House of Representatives, is also doesn't say much for our political engagement.

I prefer instead to think of such questions as demonstrating the wisdom of our teachers. These are the types of questions people usually don't raise, because they sound too silly. But lots of people have them—and Google them.

In fact, I think Big Data can give a twenty-first-century update to a famous self-help quote: "Never compare your insides to everyone else's outsides."

A Big Data update may be: "Never compare your Google searches to everyone else's social media posts."

Compare, for example, the way that people describe their husbands on public social media and in anonymous searches.

TOP WAYS PEOPLE DESCRIBE THEIR HUSBANDS

SOCIAL MEDIA POSTS	SEARCHES
the best	gay
my best friend	a jerk
amazing	amazing
the greatest	annoying
so cute	mean

Since we see other people's social media posts but not their searches, we tend to exaggerate how many women consistently think their husbands are "the best," "the greatest," and "so cute." * We tend to minimize how many women think their

---

* I analyzed Twitter data. I thank Emma Pierson for help downloading this. I did not include descriptors of what one's husband is doing right now, which are prevalent on social media but wouldn't really make

husbands are "a jerk," "annoying," and "mean." By analyzing anonymous and aggregate data, we may all understand that we're not the only ones who find marriage, and life, difficult. We may learn to stop comparing our searches to everyone else's social media posts.

The second benefit of digital truth serum is that it alerts us to people who are suffering. The Human Rights Campaign has asked me to work with them in helping educate men in certain states about the possibility of coming out of the closet. They are looking to use the anonymous and aggregate Google search data to help them decide where best to target their resources. Similarly, child protective service agencies have contacted me to learn in what parts of the country there may be far more child abuse than they are recording.

One surprising topic I was also contacted about: vaginal odors. When I first wrote about this in the *New York Times*, of all places, I did so in an ironic tone. The section made me, and others, chuckle.

However, when I later explored some of the message boards that come up when someone makes these searches they included numerous posts from young girls convinced that their lives were ruined due to anxiety about vaginal odor. It's no joke. Sex ed experts have contacted me, asking how they can best incorporate some of the internet data to reduce the paranoia among young girls.

---

sense on search. Even these descriptions tilt toward the favorable. The top ways to describe what a husband is doing right now on social media are "working" and "cooking."

While I feel a bit out of my depth on all these matters, they are serious, and I believe data science can help.

The final—and, I think, most powerful—value in this digital truth serum is indeed its ability to lead us from problems to solutions. With more understanding, we might find ways to reduce the world's supply of nasty attitudes.

Let's return to Obama's speech about Islamophobia. Recall that every time Obama argued that people should respect Muslims more, the very people he was trying to reach became more enraged.

Google searches, however, reveal that there was one line that did trigger the type of response then-president Obama might have wanted. He said, "Muslim Americans are our friends and our neighbors, our co-workers, our sports heroes and, yes, they are our men and women in uniform, who are willing to die in defense of our country."

After this line, for the first time in more than a year, the top Googled noun after "Muslim" was not "terrorists," "extremists," or "refugees." It was "athletes," followed by "soldiers." And, in fact, "athletes" kept the top spot for a full day afterward.

When we lecture angry people, the search data implies that their fury can grow. But subtly provoking people's curiosity, giving new information, and offering new images of the group that is stoking their rage may turn their thoughts in different, more positive directions.

Two months after that original speech, Obama gave another televised speech on Islamophobia, this time at a mosque. Perhaps someone in the president's office had read Soltas's and my *Times* column, which discussed what had worked and what didn't. For the content of this speech was noticeably different.

Obama spent little time insisting on the value of tolerance. Instead, he focused overwhelmingly on provoking people's curiosity and changing their perceptions of Muslim Americans. Many of the slaves from Africa were Muslim, Obama told us; Thomas Jefferson and John Adams had their own copies of the Koran; the first mosque on U.S. soil was in North Dakota; a Muslim American designed skyscrapers in Chicago. Obama again spoke of Muslim athletes and armed service members but also talked of Muslim police officers and firefighters, teachers and doctors.

And my analysis of the Google searches suggests this speech was more successful than the previous one. Many of the hateful, rageful searches against Muslims dropped in the hours after the president's address.

There are other potential ways to use search data to learn what causes, or reduces, hate. For example, we might look at how racist searches change after a black quarterback is drafted in a city or how sexist searches change after a woman is elected to office. We might see how racism responds to community policing or how sexism responds to new sexual harassment laws.

Learning of our subconscious prejudices can also be useful. For example, we might all make an extra effort to delight in little girls' minds and show less concern with their appearance. Google search data and other wellsprings of truth on the internet give us an unprecedented look into the darkest corners of the human psyche. This is at times, I admit, difficult to face. But it can also be empowering. We can use the data to fight the darkness. Collecting rich data on the world's problems is the first step toward fixing them.

5

ZOOMING IN

My brother, Noah, is four years younger than I. Most people, upon first meeting us, find us eerily similar. We both talk too loudly, are balding in the same way, and have great difficulty keeping our apartments tidy.

But there are differences: I count pennies. Noah buys the best. I love Leonard Cohen and Bob Dylan. For Noah, it's Cake and Beck.

Perhaps the most notable difference between us is our attitude toward baseball. I am obsessed with baseball and, in particular, my love of the New York Mets has always been a core part of my identity. Noah finds baseball impossibly boring, and his hatred of the sport has long been a core part of his identity.*

---

* Full disclosure: When I was fact-checking this book, Noah denied that his hatred of America's pastime is a key part of his personality. He does admit to hating baseball, but he believes his kindness, love of

Seth Stephens-Davidowitz
Baseball-o-Phile

Noah Stephens-Davidowitz
Baseball-o-Phobe

How can two guys with such similar genes, raised by the same parents, in the same town, have such opposite feelings about baseball? What determines the adults we become? More fundamentally, what's *wrong* with Noah? There's a growing field within developmental psychology that mines massive adult databases and correlates them with key childhood events. It can help us tackle this and related questions. We might call this increasing use of Big Data to answer psychological questions Big Psych.

To see how this works, let's consider a study I conducted on how childhood experiences influence which baseball team you support—or whether you support any team at all. For this study, I used Facebook data on "likes" of baseball teams. (In the

---

children, and intelligence are the core elements of his personality—and that his attitudes about baseball would not even make the top ten. However, I concluded that it's sometimes hard to see one's own identity objectively and, as an outside observer, I am able to see that hating baseball is indeed fundamental to who Noah is, whether he's able to recognize it or not. So I left it in.

previous chapter I noted that Facebook data can be deeply misleading on sensitive topics. With this study, I am assuming that nobody, not even a Phillies fan, is embarrassed to acknowledge a rooting interest in a particular team on Facebook.)

To begin with, I downloaded the number of males of every age who "like" each of New York's two baseball teams. Here are the percent that are Mets fans, by year of birth.

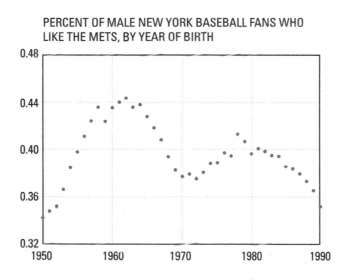

PERCENT OF MALE NEW YORK BASEBALL FANS WHO
LIKE THE METS, BY YEAR OF BIRTH

The higher the point, the more Mets fans. The popularity of the team rises and falls then rises and falls again, with the Mets being very popular among those born in 1962 and 1978. I'm guessing baseball fans might have an idea as to what's going on here. The Mets have won just two World Series: in 1969 and 1986. These men were roughly seven to eight years old when the Mets won. Thus a huge predictor of Mets fandom, for boys at least, is whether the Mets won a World Series when they were around the age seven or eight.

In fact, we can extend this analysis. I downloaded information on Facebook showing how many fans of every age "like" every one of a comprehensive selection of Major League Baseball teams.

I found that there are also an unusually high number of male Baltimore Orioles fans born in 1962 and male Pittsburgh Pirates fans born in 1963. Those men were eight-year-old boys when these teams were champions. Indeed, calculating the age of peak fandom for all the teams I studied, then figuring out how old these fans would have been, gave me this chart:

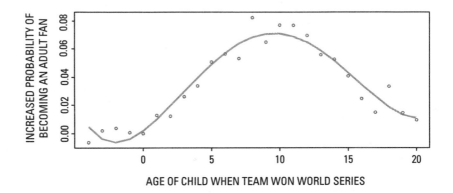

AGE OF CHILD WHEN TEAM WON WORLD SERIES

Once again we see that the most important year in a man's life, for the purposes of cementing his favorite baseball team as an adult, is when he is more or less eight years old. Overall, five to fifteen is the key period to win over a boy. Winning when a man is nineteen or twenty is about one-eighth as important in determining who he will root for as winning when he is eight. By then, he will already either love a team for life or he won't.

You might be asking, what about women baseball fans? The patterns are much less sharp, but the peak age appears to be twenty-two years old.

This is my favorite study. It relates to two of my most beloved topics: baseball and the sources of my adult discontent. I was firmly hooked in 1986 and have been suffering along—rooting for the Mets—ever since. Noah had the good sense to be born four years later and was spared this pain.

Now, baseball is not the most important topic in the world, or so my Ph.D. advisors repeatedly told me. But this methodology might help us tackle similar questions, including how people develop their political preferences, sexual proclivities, musical taste, and financial habits. (I would be particularly interested on the origins of my brother's wacky ideas on the latter two subjects.) My prediction is that we will find that many of our adult behaviors and interests, even those that we consider fundamental to who we are, can be explained by the arbitrary facts of when we were born and what was going on in certain key years while we were young.

Indeed, some work has already been done on the origin of political preferences. Yair Ghitza, chief scientist at Catalist, a data analysis company, and Andrew Gelman, a political scientist and statistician at Columbia University, tried to test the conventional idea that most people start out liberal and become increasingly conservative as they age. This is the view expressed in a famous quote often attributed to Winston Churchill: "Any man who is under 30, and is not a liberal, has no heart; and any man who is over 30, and is not a conservative, has no brains."

Ghitza and Gelman pored through sixty years of survey data, taking advantage of more than 300,000 observations on voting preferences. They found, contrary to Churchill's claim, that teenagers sometimes tilt liberal and sometimes tilt conservative. As do the middle-aged and the elderly.

These researchers discovered that political views actually

form in a way not dissimilar to the way our sports team preferences do. There is a crucial period that imprints on people for life. Between the key ages of fourteen and twenty-four, numerous Americans will form their views based on the popularity of the current president. A popular Republican or unpopular Democrat will influence many young adults to become Republicans. An unpopular Republican or popular Democrat puts this impressionable group in the Democratic column.

And these views, in these key years, will, on average, last a lifetime.

To see how this works, compare Americans born in 1941 and those born a decade later.

Those in the first group came of age during the presidency of Dwight D. Eisenhower, a popular Republican. In the early 1960s, despite being under thirty, this generation strongly tilted toward the Republican Party. And members of this generation have consistently tilted Republican as they have aged.

Americans born ten years later—baby boomers—came of age during the presidencies of John F. Kennedy, an extremely popular Democrat; Lyndon B. Johnson, an initially popular Democrat; and Richard M. Nixon, a Republican who eventually resigned in disgrace. Members of this generation have tilted liberal their entire lives.

With all this data, the researchers were able to determine the single most important year for developing political views: age eighteen.

And they found that these imprint effects are substantial. Their model estimates that the Eisenhower experience resulted in about a 10 percentage point lifetime boost for Republicans among Americans born in 1941. The Kennedy, Johnson, and Nixon experience gave Democrats a 7 percentage point advantage among Americans born in 1952.

I've made it clear that I am skeptical of survey data, but I am impressed with the large number of responses examined here. In fact, this study could not have been done with one small survey. The researchers needed the hundreds of thousands of observations, aggregated from many surveys, to see how preferences change as people age.

Data size was also crucial for my baseball study. I needed to zoom in not only on fans of each team but on people of every age. Millions of observations are required to do this and Facebook and other digital sources routinely offer such numbers.

This is where the bigness of Big Data really comes into play. You need a lot of pixels in a photo in order to be able to zoom in with clarity on one small portion of it. Similarly, you need a lot of observations in a dataset in order to be able to zoom in with clarity on one small subset of that data—for example, how popular the Mets are among men born in 1978. A small survey of a couple of thousand people won't have a large enough sample of such men.

This is the third power of Big Data: Big Data allows us to meaningfully zoom in on small segments of a dataset to gain new insights on who we are. And we can zoom in on other dimensions besides age. If we have enough data, we can see how people in particular towns and cities behave. And we can see how people carry on hour-by-hour or even minute-by-minute.

In this chapter, human behavior gets its close-up.

WHAT'S REALLY GOING ON IN OUR COUNTIES, CITIES, AND TOWNS?

In hindsight it's surprising. But when Raj Chetty, then a professor at Harvard, and a small research team first got a hold of a rather large dataset—all Americans' tax records since 1996—they were not certain anything would come of it. The IRS had handed over the data because they thought the researchers might be able to use it to help clarify the effects of tax policy.

The initial attempts Chetty and his team made to use this Big Data led, in fact, to numerous dead ends. Their investigations of the consequences of state and federal tax policies reached mostly the same conclusions everybody else had just by using surveys. Perhaps Chetty's answers, using the hundreds of millions of IRS data points, were a bit more precise. But getting the same answers as everybody else, with a little more precision, is not a major social science accomplishment. It is not the type of work that top journals are eager to publish.

Plus, organizing and analyzing all the IRS data was time-consuming. Chetty and his team—drowning in data—were taking more time than everybody else to find the same answers as everybody else.

It was beginning to look like the Big Data skeptics were right. You didn't need data for hundreds of millions of Americans to understand tax policy; a survey of ten thousand people was plenty. Chetty and his team were understandably discouraged.

And then, finally, the researchers realized their mistake. "Big Data is not just about doing the same thing you would have done with surveys except with more data," Chetty explains. They were asking little data questions of the massive collection of data they had been handed. "Big Data really should allow you to use completely different designs than what you would have with a survey," Chetty adds. "You can, for example, zoom in on geographies."

In other words, with data on hundreds of millions of people, Chetty and his team could spot patterns among cities, towns, and neighborhoods, large and small.

As a graduate student at Harvard, I was in a seminar room when Chetty presented his initial results using the tax records of every American. Social scientists refer in their work to observations—how many data points they have. If a social scientist is working with a survey of eight hundred people, he would say, "We have eight hundred observations." If he is working with a laboratory experiment with seventy people, he would say, "We have seventy observations."

"We have one-point-two billion observations," Chetty said, straight-faced. The audience giggled nervously.

Chetty and his coauthors began, in that seminar room and then in a series of papers, to give us important new insights into how America works.

Consider this question: is America a land of opportunity? Do you have a shot, if your parents are not rich, to become rich yourself?

The traditional way to answer this question is to look at a representative sample of Americans and compare this to similar data from other countries.

Here is the data for a variety of countries on equality of opportunity. The question asked: what is the chance that a person with parents in the bottom 20 percent of the income distribution reaches the top 20 percent of the income distribution?

CHANCES A PERSON WITH POOR PARENTS WILL BECOME RICH (SELECTED COUNTRIES)

United States	7.5
United Kingdom	9.0
Denmark	11.7
Canada	13.5

As you can see, America does *not* score well.

But this simple analysis misses the real story. Chetty's team zoomed in on geography. They found the odds differ a huge amount depending on where in the United States you were born.

CHANCES A PERSON WITH POOR PARENTS WILL BECOME RICH (SELECTED PARTS OF THE UNITED STATES)

San Jose, CA	12.9
Washington, DC	10.5
United States Average	*7.5*
Chicago, IL	6.5
Charlotte, NC	4.4

In some parts of the United States, the chance of a poor kid succeeding is as high as in any developed country in the world. In other parts of the United States, the chance of a poor kid succeeding is lower than in any developed country in the world.

These patterns would never be seen in a small survey, which might only include a few people in Charlotte and San Jose, and which therefore would prevent you from zooming in like this.

In fact, Chetty's team could zoom in even further. Because they had so much data—data on every single American—they could even zoom in on the small groups of people who moved from city to city to see how that might have affected their prospects: those who moved from New York City to Los Angeles, Milwaukee to Atlanta, San Jose to Charlotte. This allowed them to test for causation, not just correlation (a distinction I'll discuss in the next chapter). And, yes, moving to the right city in one's formative years made a significant difference.

So is America a "land of opportunity"?

The answer is neither yes nor no. The answer is: some parts are, and some parts aren't.

As the authors write, "The U.S. is better described as a collection of societies, some of which are 'lands of opportunity' with high rates of mobility across generations, and others in which few children escape poverty."

So what is it about parts of the United States where there is high income mobility? What makes some places better at equaling the playing field, of allowing a poor kid to have a pretty good life? Areas that spend more on education provide a better chance to poor kids. Places with more religious people and lower crime do better. Places with more black people do worse. Interestingly, this has an effect on not just the black kids but on the white kids living there as well. Places with lots of single mothers do worse. This effect too holds not just for kids of single mothers but for kids of married parents living in places with lots of single mothers. Some of these results suggest that a poor kid's peers matter. If his friends have a difficult background and little opportunity, he may struggle more to escape poverty.

The data tells us that some parts of America are better at giving kids a chance to escape poverty. So what places are best at giving people a chance to escape the grim reaper?

We like to think of death as the great equalizer. Nobody, after all, can avoid it. Not the pauper nor the king, the homeless man nor Mark Zuckerberg. Everybody dies.

But if the wealthy can't avoid death, data tells us that they can now delay it. American women in the top 1 percent of income live, on average, ten years longer than American women in the bottom 1 percent of income. For men, the gap is fifteen years.

How do these patterns vary in different parts of the United States? Does your life expectancy vary based on where you live? Is this variation different for rich and poor people? Again, by zooming in on geography, Raj Chetty's team found the answers.

Interestingly, for the wealthiest Americans, life expectancy is hardly affected by where they live. If you have excesses of money, you can expect to make it roughly eighty-nine years as a woman and about eighty-seven years as a man. Rich people everywhere tend to develop healthier habits—on average, they exercise more, eat better, smoke less, and are less likely to suffer from obesity. Rich people can afford the treadmill, the organic avocados, the yoga classes. And they can buy these things in any corner of the United States.

For the poor, the story is different. For the poorest Americans, life expectancy varies tremendously depending on where they live. In fact, living in the right place can add five years to a poor person's life expectancy.

So why do some places seem to allow the impoverished to live so much longer? What attributes do cities where poor people live the longest share?

Here are four attributes of a city—three of them do not correlate with poor people's life expectancy, and one of them does. See if you can guess which one matters.

WHAT MAKES POOR PEOPLE IN A CITY LIVE MUCH LONGER?

The city has a high level of religiosity.

The city has low levels of pollution.

The city has a higher percentage of residents covered by health
insurance.

A lot of rich people live in the city.

The first three—religion, environment, and health insurance—do not correlate with longer life spans for the poor. The variable that does matter, according to Chetty and the others who worked on this study? How many rich people live in a city. More rich people in a city means the poor there live longer. Poor people in New York City, for example, live a lot longer than poor people in Detroit.

Why is the presence of rich people such a powerful predictor of poor people's life expectancy? One hypothesis—and this is speculative—was put forth by David Cutler, one of the authors of the study and one of my advisors. Contagious behavior may be driving some of this.

There is a large amount of research showing that habits are contagious. So poor people living near rich people may pick up a lot of their habits. Some of these habits—say, pretentious vocabulary—aren't likely to affect one's health. Others—working out—will definitely have a positive impact. Indeed, poor people living near rich people exercise more, smoke less, and are less likely to suffer from obesity.

My personal favorite study by Raj Chetty's team, which had access to that massive collection of IRS data, was their inquiry into why some people cheat on their taxes while others do not. Explaining this study is a bit more complicated.

The key is knowing that there is an easy way for self-employed people with one child to maximize the money they receive from the government. If you report that you had taxable income of exactly $9,000 in a given year, the government will write you a check for $1,377—that amount represents the Earned Income Tax Credit, a grant to supplement the earnings of the working poor, minus your payroll taxes. Report any more than that, and your payroll taxes will go up. Report any less than that, and the Earned Income Tax Credit drops. A taxable income of $9,000 is the sweet spot.

And, wouldn't you know it, $9,000 is the most common taxable income reported by self-employed people with one child.

Did these Americans adjust their work schedules to make sure they earned the perfect income? Nope. When these workers were randomly audited—a very rare occurrence—it was almost always found that they made nowhere near $9,000—they earned either substantially less or substantially more.

In other words, they cheated on their taxes by pretending they made the amount that would give them the fattest check from the government.

So how typical was this type of tax fraud and who among the self-employed with one child was most likely to commit it? It turns out, Chetty and colleagues reported, that there were huge differences across the United States in how common this type of cheating was. In Miami, among people in this category, an astonishing 30 percent reported they made $9,000. In Philadelphia, just 2 percent did.

What predicts who is going to cheat? What is it about places that have the greater number of cheaters and those that have lower numbers? We can correlate rates of cheating with other city-level demographics and it turns out that there are two strong predictors: a high concentration of people in the area qualifying for the Earned Income Tax Credit and a high concentration of tax professionals in the neighborhood.

What do these factors indicate? Chetty and the authors had an explanation. The key motivator for cheating on your taxes in this manner was information.

Most self-employed one-kid taxpayers simply did not know that the magic number for getting a big fat check from the government was $9,000. But living near others who might—either their neighbors or tax assisters—dramatically increased the odds that they would learn about it.

In fact, Chetty's team found even more evidence that knowledge drove this kind of cheating. When Americans moved from an area where this variety of tax fraud was low to an area where it was high, they learned and adopted the trick. Through time, cheating spread from region to region throughout the United States. Like a virus, cheating on taxes is contagious.

Now stop for a moment and think about how revealing this study is. It demonstrated that, when it comes to figuring out who will cheat on their taxes, the key isn't determining who is honest and who is dishonest. It is determining who knows how to cheat and who doesn't.

So when someone tells you they would never cheat on their taxes, there's a pretty good chance that they are—you guessed it—lying. Chetty's research suggests that many would if they knew how.

If you want to cheat on your taxes (and I am *not* recommending this), you should live near tax professionals or live near tax cheaters who can show you the way. If you want to have kids who are world-famous, where should you live? This ability to zoom in on data and get really granular can help answer this question, too.

I was curious where the most successful Americans come from, so one day I decided to download Wikipedia. (You can do that sort of thing nowadays.)

With a little coding, I had a dataset of more than 150,000 Americans deemed by Wikipedia's editors to be notable enough to warrant an entry. The dataset included county of birth, date of birth, occupation, and gender. I merged it with county-level birth data gathered by the National Center for Health Statistics. For every county in the United States, I calculated the odds of making it into Wikipedia if you were born there.

Is being profiled in Wikipedia a meaningful marker of notable achievement? There are certainly limitations. Wikipedia's editors skew young and male, which may bias the sample. And some types of notability are not particularly worthy. Ted Bundy, for example, rates a Wikipedia entry because he killed dozens of young women. That said, I was able to remove criminals without affecting the results much.

I limited the study to baby boomers (those born between 1946 and 1964) because they have had nearly a full lifetime to become notable. Roughly one in 2,058 American-born baby boomers were deemed notable enough to warrant a Wikipedia entry. About 30 percent made it through achievements in art or entertainment, 29 percent through sports, 9 percent via politics, and 3 percent in academia or science.

The first striking fact I noticed in the data was the enormous geographic variation in the likelihood of becoming a big success, at least on Wikipedia's terms. Your chances of achieving notability were highly dependent on where you were born.

Roughly one in 1,209 baby boomers born in California reached Wikipedia. Only one in 4,496 baby boomers born in West Virginia did. Zoom in by county and the results become more telling. Roughly one in 748 baby boomers born in Suffolk County, Massachusetts, where Boston is located, made it to Wikipedia. In some other counties, the success rate was twenty times lower.

Why do some parts of the country appear to be so much

better at churning out America's movers and shakers? I closely examined the top counties. It turns out that nearly all of them fit into one of two categories.

First, and this surprised me, many of these counties contained a sizable college town. Just about every time I saw the name of a county that I had not heard of near the top of the list, like Washtenaw, Michigan, I found out that it was dominated by a classic college town, in this case Ann Arbor. The counties graced by Madison, Wisconsin; Athens, Georgia; Columbia, Missouri; Berkeley, California; Chapel Hill, North Carolina; Gainesville, Florida; Lexington, Kentucky; and Ithaca, New York, are all in the top 3 percent.

Why is this? Some of it is may well be due to the gene pool: sons and daughters of professors and graduate students tend to be smart (a trait that, in the game of big success, can be mighty useful). And, indeed, having more college graduates in an area is a strong predictor of the success of the people born there.

But there is most likely something more going on: early exposure to innovation. One of the fields where college towns are most successful in producing top dogs is music. A kid in a college town will be exposed to unique concerts, unusual radio stations, and even independent record stores. And this isn't limited to the arts. College towns also incubate more than their expected share of notable businesspeople. Maybe early exposure to cutting-edge art and ideas helps them, too.

The success of college towns does not just cross regions. It crosses race. African-Americans were noticeably underrepresented on Wikipedia in nonathletic fields, especially business and science. This undoubtedly has a lot to do with discrimination. But one small county, where the 1950 population was

84 percent black, produced notable baby boomers at a rate near those of the highest counties.

Of fewer than 13,000 boomers born in Macon County, Alabama, fifteen made it to Wikipedia—or one in 852. Every single one of them is black. Fourteen of them were from the town of Tuskegee, home of Tuskegee University, a historically black college founded by Booker T. Washington. The list included judges, writers, and scientists. In fact, a black child born in Tuskegee had the same probability of becoming a notable in a field outside of sports as a white child born in some of the highest-scoring, majority-white college towns.

The second attribute most likely to make a county's natives successful was the presence in that county of a big city. Being born in San Francisco County, Los Angeles County, or New York City all offered among the highest probabilities of making it to Wikipedia. (I grouped New York City's five counties together because many Wikipedia entries did not specify a borough of birth.)

Urban areas tend to be well supplied with models of success. To see the value of being near successful practitioners of a craft when young, compare New York City, Boston, and Los Angeles. Among the three, New York City produces notable journalists at the highest rate; Boston produces notable scientists at the highest rate; and Los Angeles produces notable actors at the highest rate. Remember, we are talking about people who were born there, not people who moved there. And this holds true even after subtracting people with notable parents in that field.

Suburban counties, unless they contained major college towns, performed far worse than their urban counterparts.

My parents, like many boomers, moved away from crowded sidewalks to tree-shaded streets—in this case from Manhattan to Bergen County, New Jersey—to raise their three children. This was potentially a mistake, at least from the perspective of having notable children. A child born in New York City is 80 percent more likely to make it into Wikipedia than a kid born in Bergen County. These are just correlations, but they do suggest that growing up near big ideas is better than growing up with a big backyard.

The stark effects identified here might be even stronger if I had better data on places lived throughout childhood, since many people grow up in different counties than the one where they were born.

The success of college towns and big cities is striking when you just look at the data. But I also delved more deeply to undertake a more sophisticated empirical analysis.

Doing so showed that there was another variable that was a strong predictor of a person's securing an entry in Wikipedia: the proportion of immigrants in your county of birth. The greater the percentage of foreign-born residents in an area, the higher the proportion of children born there who go on to notable success. (Take that, Donald Trump!) If two places have similar urban and college populations, the one with more immigrants will produce more prominent Americans. What explains this?

A lot of it seems to be directly attributable to the children of immigrants. I did an exhaustive search of the biographies of the hundred most famous white baby boomers, according to the Massachusetts Institute of Technology's Pantheon project, which is also working with Wikipedia data. Most of these were entertainers. At least thirteen had foreign-born mothers, including Oliver Stone, Sandra Bullock, and Julianne Moore. This rate is more than three times higher than the national average during this period. (Many had fathers who were immigrants, including Steve Jobs and John Belushi, but this data was more difficult to compare to national averages, since information on fathers is not always included on birth certificates.)

What about variables that don't impact success? One that I found more than a little surprising was how much money a state spends on education. In states with similar percentages of its residents living in urban areas, education spending did not correlate with rates of producing notable writers, artists, or business leaders.

It is interesting to compare my Wikipedia study to one of Chetty's team's studies discussed earlier. Recall that Chetty's team was trying to figure out what areas are good at allowing people to reach the upper middle class. My study was trying to figure out what areas are good at allowing people to reach fame. The results are strikingly different.

Spending a lot on education helps kids reach the upper middle class. It does little to help them become a notable writer, artist, or business leader. Many of these huge successes hated school. Some dropped out.

New York City, Chetty's team found, is not a particularly good place to raise a child if you want to ensure he reaches the upper middle class. It is a great place, my study found, if you want to give him a chance at fame.

When you look at the factors that drive success, the large variation between counties begins to make sense. Many counties combine all the main ingredients for success. Return, again, to Boston. With numerous universities, it is stewing in innovative ideas. It is an urban area with many extremely accomplished people offering youngsters examples of how to make it. And it draws plenty of immigrants, whose children are driven to apply these lessons.

What if an area has none of these qualities? Is it destined to produce fewer superstars? Not necessarily. There is another path: extreme specialization. Roseau County, Minnesota, a small rural county with few foreigners and no major universities, is a good example. Roughly 1 in 740 people born here made it into Wikipedia. Their secret? All nine were professional hockey players, no doubt helped by the county's world-class youth and high school hockey programs.

So is the point here—assuming you're not so interested in raising a hockey star—to move to Boston or Tuskegee if you want to give your future children the utmost advantage? It can't hurt. But there are larger lessons here. Usually, economists and sociologists focus on how to avoid bad outcomes, such as poverty and crime. Yet the goal of a great society is not only to leave fewer people behind; it is to help as many people as possible to really stand out. Perhaps this effort to zoom in on the places where hundreds of thousands of the most famous Americans were born can give us some initial strategies: encouraging immigration, subsidizing universities, and supporting the arts, among them.

Usually, I study the United States. So when I think of zooming in by geography, I think of zooming in on our cities and towns—of looking at places like Macon County, Alabama, and Roseau County, Minnesota. But another huge—and still growing—advantage of data from the internet is that it is easy to collect data from around the world. We can then see how countries differ. And data scientists get an opportunity to tip-toe into anthropology.

One somewhat random topic I recently explored: how does pregnancy play out in different countries around the world? I examined Google searches by pregnant women. The first thing I found was a striking similarity in the physical symptoms about which women complain.

I tested how often various symptoms were searched in combination with the word "pregnant." For example, how often is "pregnant" searched in conjunction with "nausea," "back pain," or "constipation"? Canada's symptoms were very close to those in the United States. Symptoms in countries like Britain, Australia, and India were all roughly similar, too.

Pregnant women around the world apparently also crave the same things. In the United States, the top Google search in this category is "craving ice during pregnancy." The next four are salt, sweets, fruit, and spicy food. In Australia, those cravings don't differ all that much: the list features salt, sweets, chocolate, ice, and fruit. What about India? A similar story: spicy food, sweets, chocolate, salt, and ice cream. In fact, the top five are very similar in all of the countries I looked at.

Preliminary evidence suggests that no part of the world has stumbled upon a diet or environment that drastically changes the physical experience of pregnancy.

But the thoughts that surround pregnancy most definitely do differ.

Start with questions about what pregnant women can

safely do. The top questions in the United States: can pregnant women "eat shrimp," "drink wine," "drink coffee," or "take Tylenol"?

When it comes to such concerns, other countries don't have much in common with the United States or one another. Whether pregnant women can "drink wine" is not among the top ten questions in Canada, Australia, or Britain. Australia's concerns are mostly related to eating dairy products while pregnant, particularly cream cheese. In Nigeria, where 30 percent of the population uses the internet, the top question is whether pregnant women can drink cold water.

Are these worries legitimate? It depends. There is strong evidence that pregnant women are at an increased risk of listeria from unpasteurized cheese. Links have been established between drinking too much alcohol and negative outcomes for the child. In some parts of the world, it is believed that drinking cold water can give your baby pneumonia; I don't know of any medical support for this.

The huge differences in questions posed around the world are most likely caused by the overwhelming flood of information coming from disparate sources in each country: legitimate scientific studies, so-so scientific studies, old wives' tales, and neighborhood chatter. It is difficult for women to know what to focus on—or what to Google.

We can see another clear difference when we look at the top searches for "how to ___ during pregnancy?" In the United States, Australia, and Canada, the top search is "how to prevent stretch marks during pregnancy." But in Ghana, India, and Nigeria, preventing stretch marks is not even in the top five. These countries tend to be more concerned with how to have sex or how to sleep.

TOP FIVE SEARCHES (IN ORDER) FOR "HOW TO ___ DURING PREGNANCY"

UNITED STATES	INDIA	AUSTRALIA	BRITAIN	NIGERIA	SOUTH AFRICA
prevent stretch marks	sleep	prevent stretch marks	lose weight	have sex	have sex
lose weight	do sex	lose weight	prevent stretch marks	lose weight	lose weight
have sex	have sex	avoid stretch marks	avoid stretch marks	make love	prevent stretch marks
avoid stretch marks	sex	sleep	sleep	stay healthy	sleep
stay fit	take care	have sex	have sex	stop vomiting	stop vomiting

TOP FIVE SEARCHES BEGINNING WITH "CAN PREGNANT WOMEN ___?"

UNITED STATES	eat shrimp	drink wine	drink coffee	take Tylenol	eat sushi
BRITAIN	eat prawns	eat smoked salmon	eat cheesecake	eat mozzarella	eat mayonnaise
AUSTRALIA	eat cream cheese	eat prawns	eat bacon	eat sour cream	eat feta cheese

(continued on next page)

NIGERIA	drink cold water	drink wine	drink coffee	have sex	take moringa (edible plant)
SINGAPORE	drink green tea	eat ice cream	eat durian	drink coffee	eat pineapple
SPAIN	eat pâté	eat jamón	take paracetamol (pain relief)	eat tuna	sunbathe
GERMANY	fly	eat salami	go in sauna	eat honey	eat mozzarella
BRAZIL	dye their hair	take Dipirona (pain relief)	take paracetamol	ride a bike	fly

There is undoubtedly more to learn from zooming in on aspects of health and culture in different corners of the world. But my preliminary analysis suggests that Big Data will tell us that humans are even less powerful than we realized when it comes to transcending our biology. Yet we come up with remarkably different interpretations of what it all means.

HOW WE FILL OUR MINUTES AND HOURS

"The adventures of a young man whose principal interests are rape, ultra-violence, and Beethoven."

That was how Stanley Kubrick's controversial *A Clockwork Orange* was advertised. In the movie, the fictional young protagonist, Alex DeLarge, committed shocking acts of vio-

lence with chilling detachment. In one of the film's most noto-
rious scenes, he raped a woman while belting out "Singin' in
the Rain."

Almost immediately, there were reports of copycat in-
cidents. Indeed, a group of men raped a seventeen-year-old
girl while singing the same song. The movie was shut down
in many European countries, and some of the more shocking
scenes were removed for a version shown in America.

There are, in fact, many examples of real life imitating art,
with men seemingly hypnotized by what they had just seen
on-screen. A showing of the gang movie *Colors* was followed
by a violent shooting. A showing of the gang movie *New Jack
City* was followed by riots.

Perhaps most disturbing, four days after the release of
The Money Train, men used lighter fluid to ignite a subway
toll booth, almost perfectly mimicking a scene in the film.
The only difference between the fictional and real-world ar-
son: In the movie, the operator escaped. In real life, he burned
to death.

There is also some evidence from psychological experiments that subjects exposed to a violent film will report more
anger and hostility, even if they don't precisely imitate one of
the scenes.

In other words, anecdotes and experiments suggest violent
movies can incite violent behavior. But how big an effect do
they really have? Are we talking about one or two murders
every decade or hundreds of murders every year? Anecdotes
and experiments can't answer this.

To see if Big Data could, two economists, Gordon Dahl

and Stefano DellaVigna, merged together three Big Datasets for the years 1995 to 2004: FBI hourly crime data, box-office numbers, and a measure of the violence in every movie from kids-in-mind.com.

The information they were using was complete—every movie and every crime committed in every hour in cities throughout the United States. This would prove important.

Key to their study was the fact that on some weekends, the most popular movie was a violent one—*Hannibal* or *Dawn of the Dead,* for example—while on other weekends, the most popular movie was nonviolent, such as *Runaway Bride* or *Toy Story.*

The economists could see exactly how many murders, rapes, and assaults were committed on weekends when a prominent violent movie was released and compare that to the number of murders, rapes, and assaults there were on weekends when a prominent peaceful movie was released.

So what did they find? When a violent movie was shown, did crime rise, as some experiments suggest? Or did it stay the same?

On weekends with a popular violent movie, the economists found, crime dropped.

You read that right. On weekends with a popular violent movie, when millions of Americans were exposed to images of men killing other men, crime dropped—significantly.

When you get a result this strange and unexpected, your first thought is that you've done something wrong. Each author carefully went over the coding. No mistakes. Your second thought is that there is some other variable that will explain these results. They checked if time of year affected the results.

It didn't. They collected data on weather, thinking perhaps somehow this was driving the relationship. It wasn't.

"We checked all our assumptions, everything we were doing," Dahl told me. "We couldn't find anything wrong."

Despite the anecdotes, despite the lab evidence, and as bizarre as it seemed, showing a violent movie somehow caused a big drop in crime. How could this possibly be?

The key to figuring it out for Dahl and DellaVigna was utilizing their Big Data to zoom in closer. Survey data traditionally provided information that was annual or at best perhaps monthly. If we are really lucky, we might get data for a weekend. By comparison, as we've increasingly been using comprehensive datasets, rather than small-sample surveys, we have been able to home in by the hour and even the minute. This has allowed us to learn a lot more about human behavior.

Sometimes fluctuations over time are amusing, if not earth-shattering. EPCOR, a utility company in Edmonton, Canada, reported minute-by-minute water consumption data during the 2010 Olympic gold medal hockey match between the United States and Canada, which an estimated 80 percent of Canadians watched. The data tells us that shortly after each period ended, water consumption shot up. Toilets across Edmonton were clearly flushing.

Google searches can also be broken down by the minute, revealing some interesting patterns in the process. For example, searches for "unblocked games" soar at 8 A.M. on weekdays and stay high through 3 P.M., no doubt in response to schools' attempts to block access to mobile games on school property without banning students' cell phones.

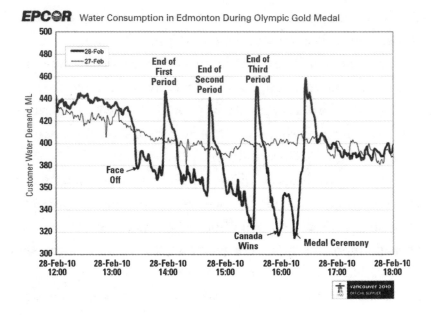

Search rates for "weather," "prayer," and "news" peak before 5:30 A.M., evidence that most people wake up far earlier than I do. Search rates for "suicide" peak at 12:36 A.M. and are at the lowest levels around 9 A.M., evidence that most people are far less miserable in the morning than I am.

The data shows that the hours between 2 and 4 A.M. are prime time for big questions: What is the meaning of consciousness? Does free will exist? Is there life on other planets? The popularity of these questions late at night may be a result, in part, of cannabis use. Search rates for "how to roll a joint" peak between 1 and 2 A.M.

And in their large dataset, Dahl and DellaVigna could look at how crime changed by the hour on those movies weekends. They found that the drop in crime when popular violent movies were shown—relative to other weekends—began in the early evening.

Crime was lower, in other words, before the violent scenes even started, when theatergoers may have just been walking in.

Can you guess why? Think, first, about who is likely to choose to attend a violent movie. It's young men—particularly young, aggressive men.

Think, next, about where crimes tend to be committed. Rarely in a movie theater. There have been exceptions, most notably a 2012 premeditated shooting in a Colorado theater. But, by and large, men go to theaters unarmed and sit, silently.

Offer young, aggressive men the chance to see *Hannibal*, and they will go to the movies. Offer young, aggressive men *Runaway Bride* as their option, and they will take a pass and instead go out, perhaps to a bar, club, or a pool hall, where the incidence of violent crime is higher.

Violent movies keep potentially violent people off the streets.

Puzzle solved. Right? Not quite yet. There was one more strange thing in the data. The effects started right when the movies started showing; however, they did not stop after the movie ended and the theater closed. On evenings where violent movies were showing, crime was lower well into the night, from midnight to 6 A.M.

Even if crime was lower while the young men were in the movie theater, shouldn't it rise after they left and were no longer preoccupied? They had just watched a violent movie, which experiments say makes people more angry and aggressive.

Can you think of any explanations for why crime still dropped after the movie ended? After much thought, the authors, who were crime experts, had another "Aha" moment.

They knew that alcohol is a major contributor to crime. The authors had sat in enough movie theaters to know that virtually no theaters in the United States serve liquor. Indeed, the authors found that alcohol-related crimes plummeted in late-night hours after violent movies.

Of course, Dahl and DellaVigna's results were limited. They could not, for instance, test the months-out, lasting effects—to see how long the drop in crime might last. And it's still possible that consistent exposure to violent movies ultimately leads to more violence. However, their study does put the immediate impact of violent movies, which has been the main theme in these experiments, into perspective. Perhaps a violent movie does influence some people and make them unusually angry and aggressive. However, do you know what undeniably influences people in a violent direction? Hanging out with other potentially violent men and drinking.*

---

* This story shows how things that seem bad may be good if they prevent something worse. Ed McCaffrey, a Stanford-educated former wide receiver, uses this argument to justify letting all four of his sons play football: "These guys have energy. And, so, if they're not playing football, they're skateboarding, they're climbing trees, they're playing tag in the backyard, they're doing paintball. I mean, they're not going to sit there and do nothing. And, so, the way I look at it is, hey, at least there's rules within the sport of football. . . . My kids have been to the emergency room for falling off decks, getting in bike crashes, skateboarding, falling out of trees. I mean, you name it . . . Yea, it's a violent collision sport. But, also, my guys just have the personality, where, at least they're not squirrel-jumping off mountains and doing crazy stuff like that. So, it's organized aggression, I guess." McCaffrey's argument, made in an interview on *The Herd with Colin Cowherd*, is one I had never heard before. After reading the Dahl/DellaVigna paper, I take the argument seriously. An

This makes sense now. But it didn't make sense before Dahl and DellaVigna began analyzing piles of data.

One more important point that becomes clear when we zoom in: the world is complicated. Actions we take today can have distant effects, most of them unintended. Ideas spread—sometimes slowly; other times exponentially, like viruses. People respond in unpredictable ways to incentives.

These connections and relationships, these surges and swells, cannot be traced with tiny surveys or traditional data methods. The world, quite simply, is too complex and too rich for little data.

OUR DOPPELGANGERS

In June 2009, David "Big Papi" Ortiz looked like he was done. During the previous half decade, Boston had fallen in love with their Dominican-born slugger with the friendly smile and gapped teeth.

He had made five consecutive All-Star games, won an MVP Award, and helped end Boston's eighty-six-year championship drought. But in the 2008 season, at the age of thirty-two, his numbers fell off. His batting average had dropped 68 points, his on-base percentage 76 points, his slugging percentage 114 points. And at the start of the 2009 season, Ortiz's numbers were dropping further.

Here's how Bill Simmons, a sportswriter and passion-

---

advantage of huge real-world datasets, rather than laboratory data, is that they can pick up these kinds of effects.

ate Boston Red Sox fan, described what was happening in the early months of the 2009 season: "It's clear that David Ortiz no longer excels at baseball. . . . Beefy sluggers are like porn stars, wrestlers, NBA centers and trophy wives: When it goes, it goes." Great sports fans trust their eyes, and Simmons's eyes told him Ortiz was finished. In fact, Simmons predicted he would be benched or released shortly.

Was Ortiz really finished? If you're the Boston general manager, in 2009, do you cut him? More generally, how can we predict how a baseball player will perform in the future? Even more generally, how can we use Big Data to predict what people will do in the future?

A theory that will get you far in data science is this: look at what sabermetricians (those who have used data to study baseball) have done and expect it to spread out to other areas of data science. Baseball was among the first fields with comprehensive datasets on just about everything, and an army of smart people willing to devote their lives to making sense of that data. Now, just about every field is there or getting there. Baseball comes first; every other field follows. Sabermetrics eats the world.

The simplest way to predict a baseball player's future is to assume he will continue performing as he currently is. If a player has struggled for the past 1.5 years, you might guess that he will struggle for the next 1.5 years.

By this methodology, Boston should have cut David Ortiz.

However, there might be more relevant information. In the 1980s, Bill James, who most consider the founder of sabermetrics, emphasized the importance of age. Baseball players, James found, peaked early—at around the age of twenty-seven.

Teams tended to ignore just how much players decline as they age. They overpaid for aging players.

By this more advanced methodology, Boston should definitely have cut David Ortiz.

But this age adjustment might miss something. Not all players follow the same path through life. Some players might peak at twenty-three, others at thirty-two. Short players may age differently from tall players, fat players from skinny players. Baseball statisticians found that there were types of players, each following a different aging path. This story was even worse for Ortiz: "beefy sluggers" indeed do, on average, peak early and collapse shortly past thirty.

If Boston considered his recent past, his age, and his size, they should, without a doubt, have cut David Ortiz.

Then, in 2003, statistician Nate Silver introduced a new model, which he called PECOTA, to predict player performance. It proved to be the best—and, also, the coolest. Silver searched for players' doppelgangers. Here's how it works. Build a database of every Major League Baseball player ever, more than 18,000 men. And include everything you know about those players: their height, age, and position; their home runs, batting average, walks, and strikeouts for each year of their careers. Now, find the twenty ballplayers who look most similar to Ortiz right up until that point in his career—those who played like he did when he was 24, 25, 26, 27, 28, 29, 30, 31, 32, and 33. In other words, find his doppelgangers. Then see how Ortiz's doppelgangers' careers progressed.

A doppelganger search is another example of zooming in. It zooms in on the small subset of people most similar to a given person. And, as with all zooming in, it gets better the more data you have. It turns out, Ortiz's doppelgangers gave a very different prediction for Ortiz's future. Ortiz's doppelgangers included Jorge Posada and Jim Thome. These players started their careers a bit slow; had amazing bursts in their late twenties, with world-class power; and then struggled in their early thirties.

Silver then predicted how Ortiz would do based on how these doppelgangers ended up doing. And here's what he found: they regained their power. For trophy wives, Simmons may be right: when it goes, it goes. But for Ortiz's doppelgangers, when it went, it came back.

The doppelganger search, the best methodology ever used to predict baseball player performance, said Boston should be patient with Ortiz. And Boston indeed was patient with their aging slugger. In 2010, Ortiz's average rose to .270. He hit 32 home runs and made the All-Star team. This began a string of four consecutive All-Star games for Ortiz. In 2013, batting in his traditional third spot in the lineup, at the age of thirty-seven, Ortiz batted .688 as Boston defeated St. Louis, 4 games to 2, in the World Series. Ortiz was voted World Series MVP.*

As soon as I finished reading Nate Silver's approach to predicting the trajectory of ballplayers, I immediately began thinking about whether I might have a doppelganger, too.

---

* You can probably tell by this part of the book I tend to be cynical about good stories. I wanted one feel-good story in here, so I am leaving my cynicism to a footnote. I suspect PECOTA just found out that Ortiz was a steroid user who stopped using steroids and would start using them again. From the standpoint of prediction, it is actually pretty cool if PECOTA was able to detect that—but it makes it a less moving story.

Doppelganger searches are promising in many fields, not just athletics. Could I find the person who shares the most interests with me? Maybe if I found the person most similar to me, we could hang out. Maybe he would know some restaurants we would like. Maybe he could introduce me to things I had no idea I might have an affinity for.

A doppelganger search zooms in on individuals and even on the traits of individuals. And, as with all zooming in, it gets sharper the more data you have. Suppose I searched for my doppelganger in a dataset of ten or so people. I might find someone who shared my interest in books. Suppose I searched for my doppelganger in a dataset of a thousand or so people. I might find someone who had a thing for popular physics books. But suppose I searched for my doppelganger in a dataset of hundreds of millions of people. Then I might be able to find someone who was really, truly similar to me.

One day, I went doppelganger hunting on social media. Using the entire corpus of Twitter profiles, I looked for the people on the planet who have the most common interests with me.

You can certainly tell a lot about my interests from whom I follow on my Twitter account. Overall, I follow some 250 people, showing my passions for sports, politics, comedy, science, and morose Jewish folksingers.

So is there anybody out there in the universe who follows all 250 of these accounts, my Twitter twin? Of course not. Doppelgangers aren't identical to us, only similar. Nor is there anybody who follows 200 of the accounts I follow. Or even 150.

However, I did eventually find an account that followed an

amazing 100 of the accounts I follow: Country Music Radio Today. Huh? It turns out, Country Music Radio Today was a bot (it no longer exists) that followed 750,000 Twitter profiles in the hope that they would follow back.

I have an ex-girlfriend who I suspect would get a kick out of this result. She once told me I was more like a robot than a human being.

All joking aside, my initial finding that my doppelganger was a bot that followed 750,000 random accounts does make an important point about doppelganger searches. For a doppelganger search to be truly accurate, you don't want to find someone who merely likes the same things you like. You also want to find someone who dislikes the things you dislike.

My interests are apparent not just from the accounts I follow but from those I choose not to follow. I am interested in sports, politics, comedy, and science but not food, fashion, or theater. My follows show that I like Bernie Sanders but not Elizabeth Warren, Sarah Silverman but not Amy Schumer, the *New Yorker* but not the *Atlantic*, my friends Noah Popp, Emily Sands, and Josh Gottlieb but not my friend Sam Asher. (Sorry, Sam. But your Twitter feed is a snooze.)

Of all 200 million people on Twitter, who has the most similar profile to me? It turns out my doppelganger is *Vox* writer Dylan Matthews. This was kind of a letdown, for the purposes of improving my media consumption, as I already follow Matthews on Twitter and Facebook and compulsively read his *Vox* posts. So learning he was my doppelganger hasn't really changed my life. But it's still pretty cool to know the person most similar to you in the world, especially if it's someone you admire. And when I finish this book and stop being a hermit, maybe Matthews and I can hang out and discuss the writings of James Surowiecki.

The Ortiz doppelganger search was neat for baseball fans. And my doppelganger search was entertaining, at least to me. But what else can these searches reveal? For one thing, doppelganger searches have been used by many of the biggest internet companies to dramatically improve their offerings and user experience. Amazon uses something like a doppelganger search to suggest what books you might like. They see what people similar to you select and base their recommendations on that.

Pandora does the same in picking what songs you might want to listen to. And this is how Netflix figures out the movies you might like. The impact has been so profound that when Amazon engineer Greg Linden originally introduced doppelganger searches to predict readers' book preferences, the improvement in recommendations was so good that Amazon founder Jeff Bezos got to his knees and shouted, "I'm not worthy!" to Linden.

But what is really interesting about doppelganger searches, considering their power, is not how they're commonly being used now. It is how frequently they are not used. There are major areas of life that could be vastly improved by the kind of personalization these searches allow. Take our health, for instance.

Isaac Kohane, a computer scientist and medical researcher at Harvard, is trying to bring this principle to medicine. He wants to organize and collect all of our health information so that instead of using a one-size-fits-all approach, doctors can find patients just like you. Then they can employ more personalized, more focused diagnoses and treatments.

Kohane considers this a natural extension for the medical field and not even a particularly radical one. "What is a diagnosis?" Kohane asks. "A diagnosis really is a statement that you share properties with previously studied populations. When I diagnose you with a heart attack, God forbid, I say you have a pathophysiology that I learned from other people means you have had a heart attack."

A diagnosis is, in essence, a primitive kind of doppelganger search. The problem is that the datasets doctors use to make their diagnoses are small. These days a diagnosis is based on a doctor's experience with the population of patients he or she has treated and perhaps supplemented by academic papers from small populations that other researchers have encountered. As we've seen, though, for a doppelganger search to really get good, it would have to include many more cases.

Here is a field where some Big Data could really help. So what's taking so long? Why isn't it already widely used? The problem lies with data collection. Most medical reports still exist on paper, buried in files, and for those that are computerized, they're often locked up in incompatible formats. We often have better data, Kohane notes, on baseball than on health. But simple measures would go a long way. Kohane talks repeatedly of "low-hanging fruit." He believes, for instance, that merely creating a complete dataset of children's height and weight charts and any diseases they might have would be revolutionary for pediatrics. Each child's growth path then could be compared to every other child's growth path. A computer could find children who were on a similar trajectory and automatically flag any troubling patterns. It might detect a child's height leveling off prematurely, which in certain scenarios would likely point to one of two possible causes: hypothyroidism or a brain tumor.

Early diagnosis in both cases would be a huge boon. "These are rare birds," according to Kohane, "one-in-ten-thousand kind of events. Children, by and large, are healthy. I think we could diagnose them earlier, at least a year earlier. One hundred percent, we could."

James Heywood is an entrepreneur who has a different approach to deal with difficulties linking medical data. He created a website, PatientsLikeMe.com, where individuals can report their own information—their conditions, treatments, and side effects. He's already had a lot of success charting the varying courses diseases can take and how they compare to our common understanding of them.

His goal is to recruit enough people, covering enough conditions, so that people can find their health doppelganger. Heywood hopes that you can find people of your age and gender, with your history, reporting symptoms similar to yours—and see what has worked for them. That would be a very different kind of medicine, indeed.

DATA STORIES

In many ways the act of zooming in is more valuable to me than the particular findings of a particular study, because it offers a new way of seeing and talking about life.

When people learn that I am a data scientist and a writer, they sometimes will share some fact or survey with me. I often find this data boring—static and lifeless. It has no story to tell.

Likewise, friends have tried to get me to join them in reading novels and biographies. But these hold little interest for me as well. I always find myself asking, "Would that happen in other situations? What's the more general principle?" Their stories feel small and unrepresentative.

What I have tried to present in this book is something that, for me, is like nothing else. It is based on data and numbers; it is illustrative and far-reaching. And yet the data is so rich that you can visualize the people underneath it. When we zoom in on every minute of Edmonton's water consumption, I *see* the people getting up from their couch at the end of the period. When we zoom in on people moving from Philadelphia to Miami and starting to cheat on their taxes, I *see* these people talking to their neighbors in their apartment complex and learning about the tax trick. When we zoom in on baseball fans of every age, I *see* my own childhood and my brother's childhood and millions of adult men still crying over a team that won them over when they were eight years old.

At the risk of once again sounding grandiose, I think the economists and data scientists featured in this book are creating not only a new tool but a new genre. What I have tried to present in this chapter, and much of this book, is data so big and so rich, allowing us to zoom in so close that, without limiting ourselves to any particular, unrepresentative human being, we can still tell complex and evocative stories.

6

ALL THE WORLD'S A LAB

February 27, 2000, started as an ordinary day on Google's Mountain View campus. The sun was shining, the bikers were pedaling, the masseuses were massaging, the employees were hydrating with cucumber water. And then, on this ordinary day, a few Google engineers had an idea that unlocked the secret that today drives much of the internet. The engineers found the best way to get you clicking, coming back, and staying on their sites.

Before describing what they did, we need to talk about correlation versus causality, a huge issue in data analysis—and one that we have not yet adequately addressed.

The media bombard us with correlation-based studies seemingly every day. For example, we have been told that those of us who drink a moderate amount of alcohol tend to be in better health. That is a correlation.

Does this mean drinking a moderate amount will improve

one's health—a causation? Perhaps not. It could be that good health causes people to drink a moderate amount. Social scientists call this reverse causation. Or it could be that there is an independent factor that causes both moderate drinking and good health. Perhaps spending a lot of time with friends leads to both moderate alcohol consumption and good health. Social scientists call this omitted-variable bias.

How, then, can we more accurately establish causality? The gold standard is a randomized, controlled experiment. Here's how it works. You randomly divide people into two groups. One, the treatment group, is asked to do or take something. The other, the control group, is not. You then see how each group responds. The difference in the outcomes between the two groups is your causal effect.

For example, to test whether moderate drinking causes good health, you might randomly pick some people to drink one glass of wine per day for a year, randomly choose others to drink no alcohol for a year, and then compare the reported health of both groups. Since people were randomly assigned to the two groups, there is no reason to expect one group would have better initial health or have socialized more. You can trust that the effects of the wine are causal. Randomized, controlled experiments are the most trusted evidence in any field. If a pill can pass a randomized, controlled experiment, it can be dispensed to the general populace. If it cannot pass this test, it won't make it onto pharmacy shelves.

Randomized experiments have increasingly been used in the social sciences as well. Esther Duflo, a French economist at MIT, has led the campaign for greater use of experiments in developmental economics, a field that tries to figure out the best ways to help the poorest people in the world. Consider Duflo's study, with colleagues, of how to improve education in rural India, where more than half of middle school students cannot read a simple sentence. One potential reason students struggle so much is that teachers don't show up consistently. On a given day in some schools in rural India, more than 40 percent of teachers are absent.

Duflo's test? She and her colleagues randomly divided schools into two groups. In one (the treatment group), in addition to their base pay, teachers were paid a small amount—50 rupees, or about $1.15—for every day they showed up to work. In the other, no extra payment for attendance was given. The results were remarkable. When teachers were paid, teacher absenteeism dropped in half. Student test performance also improved substantially, with the biggest effects on young girls. By the end of the experiment, girls in schools where teachers were paid to come to class were 7 percentage points more likely to be able to write.

According to a *New Yorker* article, when Bill Gates learned of Duflo's work, he was so impressed he told her, "We *need* to fund you."

THE ABCS OF A/B TESTING

So randomized experiments are the gold standard for proving causality, and their use has spread through the social sciences. Which brings us back to Google's offices on February 27, 2000. What did Google do on that day that revolutionized the internet?

On that day, a few engineers decided to perform an experiment on Google's site. They randomly divided users into two groups. The treatment group was shown twenty links on the search results pages. The control group was shown the usual ten. The engineers then compared the satisfaction of the two groups based on how frequently they returned to Google.

This is a revolution? It doesn't seem so revolutionary. I already noted that randomized experiments have been used by pharmaceutical companies and social scientists. How can copying them be such a big deal?

The key point—and this was quickly realized by the Google engineers—is that experiments in the digital world have a huge advantage relative to experiments in the offline world. As convincing as offline randomized experiments can be, they are also resource-intensive. For Duflo's study, schools had to be contacted, funding had to be arranged, some teachers had to be paid, and all students had to be tested. Offline experiments can cost thousands or hundreds of thousands of dollars and take months or years to conduct.

In the digital world, randomized experiments can be cheap and fast. You don't need to recruit and pay participants. Instead, you can write a line of code to randomly assign them to a group. You don't need users to fill out surveys. Instead, you can measure mouse movements and clicks. You don't need to hand-code and analyze the responses. You can build a program to automatically do that for you. You don't have to contact anybody. You don't even have to tell users they are part of an experiment.

This is the fourth power of Big Data: it makes randomized experiments, which can find truly causal effects, much, much easier to conduct—anytime, more or less anywhere, as long as you're online. In the era of Big Data all the world's a lab.

This insight quickly spread through Google and then the rest of Silicon Valley, where randomized controlled experiments have been renamed "A/B testing." In 2011, Google engineers ran seven thousand A/B tests. And this number is only rising.

If Google wants to know how to get more people to click on ads on their sites, they may try two shades of blue in ads—one shade for Group A, another for Group B. Google can then compare click rates. Of course, the ease of such testing can lead to overuse. Some employees felt that because testing was so effortless, Google was overexperimenting. In 2009, one frustrated designer quit after Google went through forty-one marginally different shades of blue in A/B testing. But this designer's stand in favor of art over obsessive market research has done little to stop the spread of the methodology.

Facebook now runs a thousand A/B tests per day, which means that a small number of engineers at Facebook start more randomized, controlled experiments in a given day than the entire pharmaceutical industry starts in a year.

A/B testing has spread beyond the biggest tech firms. A former Google employee, Dan Siroker, brought this methodology to Barack Obama's first presidential campaign, which A/B-tested home page designs, email pitches, and donation forms. Then Siroker started a new company, Optimizely, which allows organizations to perform rapid A/B testing. In 2012,

Optimizely was used by Obama as well as his opponent, Mitt Romney, to maximize sign-ups, volunteers, and donations. It's also used by companies as diverse as Netflix, TaskRabbit, and *New York* magazine.

To see how valuable testing can be, consider how Obama used it to get more people engaged with his campaign. Obama's home page initially included a picture of the candidate and a button below the picture that invited people to "Sign Up."

Was this the best way to greet people? With the help of Siroker, Obama's team could test whether a different picture and button might get more people to actually sign up. Would more people click if the home page instead featured a picture of Obama with a more solemn face? Would more people click if the button instead said "Join Now"? Obama's team showed users different combinations of pictures and buttons and measured how many of them clicked the button. See if you can predict the winning picture and winning button.

Pictures Tested

Buttons Tested

The winner was the picture of Obama's family and the button "Learn More." And the victory was huge. By using that combination, Obama's campaign team estimated it got 40 per-

Winning Combination

cent more people to sign up, netting the campaign roughly $60 million in additional funding.

There is another great benefit to the fact that all this gold-standard testing can be done so cheap and easy: it further frees us from our reliance upon our intuition, which, as noted in Chapter 1, has its limitations. A fundamental reason for A/B testing's importance is that people are unpredictable. Our intuition often fails to predict how they will respond.

Was your intuition correct on Obama's optimal website?

Here are some more tests for your intuition. The *Boston Globe* A/B-tests headlines to figure out which ones get the most people to click on a story. Try to guess the winners from these pairs:

**ONE OF THESE HEADLINES WAS WAY BETTER
THAN THE OTHER IN GETTING CLICKS.**

	HEADLINE A	HEADLINE B
1.	Can the SnotBot drone save the whales?	Can this drone help save the whales?
2.	Of course "deflated balls" is a top search term in Massachusetts	This top Mass. Google search term is pretty embarrassing
3.	Hookup contest at heart of St. Paul rape trial	No charges in prep school sex scandal
4.	Woman makes bank off rare baseball card	Woman makes $179,000 off rare baseball card
5.	MBTA projects annual operating deficit will double by 2020	Get ready: the MBTA's deficit is about to double
6.	How Massachusetts helped win you the right to birth control access	How Boston University helped end "crimes against chastity"
7.	When the first subway opened in Boston	Cartoons from when the first subway opened in Boston
8.	Victim and family in prep-school rape trial blame toxic culture	Victim and family in prep-school rape trial releases statement
9.	Guy in "Free Brady" hat is only one able to foil Miley Cyrus prank	Pats fan gets an eyeful for recognizing an undercover Miley Cyrus

Finished your guesses? The answers are in bold below.

	HEADLINE A	HEADLINE B	WINNER?
1.	**Can the SnotBot drone save the whales?**	Can this drone help save the whales?	53% more clicks for A
2.	Of course "deflated balls" is a top search term in Massachusetts	**This top Mass. Google search term is pretty embarrassing**	986% more clicks for B

(continued on next page)

	HEADLINE A	HEADLINE B	WINNER?
3.	Hookup contest at heart of St. Paul rape trial	**No charges in prep school sex scandal**	108% more clicks for B
4.	**Woman makes bank off rare baseball card**	Woman makes $179,000 off rare baseball card	38% more clicks for A
5.	MBTA projects annual operating deficit will double by 2020	**Get ready: the MBTA's deficit is about to double**	62% more clicks for B
6.	How Massachusetts helped win you the right to birth control access	**How Boston University helped end "crimes against chastity"**	188% more clicks for B
7.	**When the first subway opened in Boston**	Cartoons from when the first subway opened in Boston	33% more clicks for A
8.	Victim and family in prep-school rape trial blame toxic culture	**Victim and family in prep-school rape trial releases statement**	76% more clicks for B
9.	Guy in "Free Brady" hat is only one able to foil Miley Cyrus prank	**Pats fan gets an eyeful for recognizing an undercover Miley Cyrus**	67% more clicks for B

I predict you got more than half right, perhaps by considering what you would click on. But you probably did not guess all of these correctly.

Why? What did you miss? What insights into human behavior did you lack? What lessons can you learn from your mistakes?

We usually ask questions such as these after making bad predictions.

But look how difficult it is to draw general conclusions from the *Globe* headlines. In the first headline test, changing a single word, "this" to "SnotBot," led to a big win. This might suggest more details win. But in the second headline, "deflated balls," the detailed term, loses. In the fourth headline, "makes bank" beats the number $179,000. This might suggest slang terms win. But the slang term "hookup contest" loses in the third headline.

The lesson of A/B testing, to a large degree, is to be wary of general lessons. Clark Benson is the CEO of ranker.com, a news and entertainment site that relies heavily on A/B testing to choose headlines and site design. "At the end of the day, you can't assume anything," Benson says. "Test literally everything."

Testing fills in gaps in our understanding of human nature. These gaps will always exist. If we knew, based on our life experience, what the answer would be, testing would not be of value. But we don't, so it is.

Another reason A/B testing is so important is that seemingly small changes can have big effects. As Benson puts it, "I'm constantly amazed with minor, minor factors having outsized value in testing."

In December 2012, Google changed its advertisements. They added a rightward-pointing arrow surrounded by a square.

Notice how bizarre this arrow is. It points rightward to absolutely nothing. In fact, when these arrows first appeared, many Google customers were critical. Why were they adding meaningless arrows to the ad, they wondered?

Well, Google is protective of its business secrets, so they don't say exactly how valuable the arrows were. But they did say that these arrows had won in A/B testing. The reason Google added them is that they got a lot more people to click. And this minor, seemingly meaningless change made Google and their ad partners oodles of money.

So how can you find these small tweaks that produce outsize profits? You have to test lots of things, even many that seem trivial. In fact, Google's users have noted numerous times that ads have been changed a tiny bit only to return to their previous form. They have unwittingly become members of treatment groups in A/B tests—but at the cost only of seeing these slight variations.

Centering Experiment (Didn't Work)

Best Selling iPad 2 Case
The ZAGGmate™ - Tough Aluminum Case
with build in Bluetooth Keyboard
www.zagg.com

Green Star Experiment (Didn't Work)

Foster's Hollywood Restaurant **Reviews**, Madrid, Spain ...
www.tripadvisor.co.uk > ... > Madrid > Madrid Restaurants ▾ TripAdvisor ▾
★ ★ ★ ☆ ☆ Rating: 3 - 118 reviews
Foster's Hollywood, Madrid: See 118 unbiased **reviews** of **Foster's Hollywood**, rated 3 of 5 on TripAdvisor and ranked #3647 of 6489 restaurants in Madrid

New Font Experiment (Didn't Work)

Live Stock Market News
Free Charts, News and Tips from UTVi Experts. Visit us Today!
UTVi.com/Stocks

The above variations never made it to the masses. They lost. But they were part of the process of picking winners. The road to a clickable arrow is paved with ugly stars, faulty positionings, and gimmicky fonts.

It may be fun to guess what makes people click. And if you are a Democrat, it might be nice to know that testing got Obama more money. But there is a dark side to A/B testing.

In his excellent book *Irresistible*, Adam Alter writes about the rise of behavioral addictions in contemporary society. Many people are finding aspects of the internet increasingly difficult to turn off.

My favorite dataset, Google searches, can give us some clues as to what people find most addictive. According to Google, most addictions remain the ones people have struggled with for many decades—drugs, sex, and alcohol, for example. But the internet is starting to make its presence felt on the list—with "porn" and "Facebook" now among the top ten reported addictions.

TOP ADDICTIONS REPORTED TO GOOGLE, 2016

Drugs	Alcohol	Gambling
Sex	Sugar	Facebook
Porn	Love	

A/B testing may be playing a role in making the internet so darn addictive.

Tristan Harris, a "design ethicist," was quoted in *Irresistible* explaining why people have such a hard time resisting certain sites on the internet: "There are a thousand people on the other side of the screen whose job it is to break down the self-regulation you have."

And these people are using A/B testing.

Through testing, Facebook may figure out that making a particular button a particular color gets people to come back to their site more often. So they change the button to that color. Then they may figure out that a particular font gets people to come back to their site more often. So they change the text to that font. Then they may figure out that emailing people at a certain time gets them coming back to their site more often. So they email people at that time.

Pretty soon, Facebook becomes a site optimized to maximize how much time people spend on Facebook. In other words, find enough winners of A/B tests and you have an addictive site. It is the type of feedback that cigarette companies never had.

A/B testing is increasingly a tool of the gaming industry. As Alter discusses, World of Warcraft A/B-tests various versions of its game. One mission might ask you to kill someone. Another might ask you to save something. Game designers can give different samples of players' different missions and then see which ones keep more people playing. They might find, for example, that the mission that asked you to save a person got people to return 30 percent more often. If they test many, many missions, they start finding more and more winners. These 30 percent wins add up, until they have a game that keeps many adult men holed up in their parents' basement.

If you are a little disturbed by this, I am with you. And we will talk a bit more about the ethical implications of this and other aspects of Big Data near the end of this book. But for better or worse, experimentation is now a crucial tool in the data scientists' tool kit. And there is another form of experimentation sitting in that tool kit. It has been used to ask a variety of questions, including whether TV ads really work.

NATURE'S CRUEL—BUT ENLIGHTENING—EXPERIMENTS

It's January 22, 2012, and the New England Patriots are playing the Baltimore Ravens in the AFC Championship game.

There's a minute left in the game. The Ravens are down, but they've got the ball. The next sixty seconds will determine which team will play in the Super Bowl. The next sixty seconds will help seal players' legacies. And the last minute of this game will do something that, for an economist, is far more profound: the last sixty seconds will help finally tell us, once and for all, Do advertisements work?

The notion that ads improve sales is obviously crucial to our economy. But it is maddeningly hard to prove. In fact, this is a textbook example of exactly how difficult it is to distinguish between correlation and causation.

There's no doubt that products that advertise the most also have the highest sales. Twentieth Century Fox spent $150 million marketing the movie *Avatar*, which became the highest-grossing film of all time. But how much of the $2.7 billion in *Avatar* ticket sales was due to the heavy marketing? Part of the reason 20th Century Fox spent so much money on promotion was presumably that they knew they had a desirable product.

Firms believe they know how effective their ads are. Economists are skeptical they really do. University of Chicago economics professor Steven Levitt, while collaborating with an electronics company, was underwhelmed when the firm tried to convince him they knew how much their ads worked. How, Levitt wondered, could they be so confident?

The company explained that, every year, in the days preceding Father's Day, they ramp up their TV ad spending. Sure enough, every year, before Father's Day, they have the highest sales. Uh, maybe that's just because a lot of kids buy electronics for their dads, particularly for Father's Day gifts, regardless of advertising.

"They got the causality completely backwards," says Levitt in a lecture. At least they might have. We don't know. "It's a really hard problem," Levitt adds.

As important as this problem is to solve, firms are reluctant to conduct rigorous experiments. Levitt tried to convince the electronics company to perform a randomized, controlled experiment to precisely learn how effective their TV ads were. Since A/B testing isn't possible on television yet, this would require seeing what happens without advertising in some areas.

Here's how the firm responded: "Are you crazy? We can't not advertise in twenty markets. The CEO would kill us." That ended Levitt's collaboration with the company.

Which brings us back to this Patriots-Ravens game. How can the results of a football game help us determine the causal effects of advertising? Well, it can't tell us the effects of a particular ad campaign from a particular company. But it can give evidence on the average effects of advertisements from many large campaigns.

It turns out, there is a hidden advertising experiment in games like this. Here's how it works. By the time these championship games are played, companies have purchased, and produced, their Super Bowl advertisements. When businesses decide which ads to run, they don't know which teams will play in the game.

But the results of the playoffs will have a huge impact on who actually watches the Super Bowl. The two teams that ultimately qualify will bring with them an enormous amount of viewers. If New England, which plays near Boston, wins, far more people in Boston will watch the Super Bowl than folks in Baltimore. And vice versa.

To the firms, it is the equivalent of a coin flip to determine whether tens of thousands of extra people in Baltimore or Boston will be exposed to their advertisement, a flip that will happen after their spots are purchased and produced.

Now, back to the field, where Jim Nantz on CBS is announcing the final results of this experiment.

> Here comes Billy Cundiff, to tie this game, and, in all likelihood, send it to overtime. The last two years, sixteen of sixteen on field goals. Thirty-two yards to tie it. And the kick. Look out! Look out! It's no good. . . . And the Patriots take the knee and will now take the journey to Indianapolis. They're heading to Super Bowl Forty-Six.

Two weeks later, Super Bowl XLVI would score a 60.3 audience share in Boston and a 50.2 share in Baltimore. Sixty

thousand more people in Boston would watch the 2012 advertisements.

The next year, the same two teams would meet for the AFC
Championship. This time, Baltimore would win. The extra ad
exposures for the 2013 Super Bowl advertisements would be
seen in Baltimore.

	2012 SUPER BOWL RATINGS (BOSTON PLAYS)	2013 SUPER BOWL RATINGS (BALTIMORE PLAYS)
Boston	56.7	48.0
Baltimore	47.9	59.6

Hal Varian, chief economist at Google; Michael D. Smith,
economist at Carnegie Mellon; and I used these two games and
all the other Super Bowls from 2004 to 2013 to test whether—
and, if so, how much—Super Bowl ads work. Specifically we
looked at whether when a company advertises a movie in the
Super Bowl, they see a big jump in ticket sales in the cities that
had higher viewership for the game.

They indeed do. People in cities of teams that qualify for
the Super Bowl attend movies that were advertised during the
Super Bowl at a significantly higher rate than do those in cities of teams that just missed qualifying. More people in those
cities saw the ad. More people in those cities decided to go to
the film.

One alternative explanation might be that having a team
in the Super Bowl makes you more likely to go see movies.
However, we tested a group of movies that had similar budgets
and were released at similar times but that did not advertise in

the Super Bowl. There was no increased attendance in the cities of the Super Bowl teams.

Okay, as you might have guessed, advertisements work. This isn't too surprising.

But it's not just that they work. The ads were incredibly effective. In fact, when we first saw the results, we double- and triple- and quadruple-checked them to make sure they were right—because the returns were so large. The average movie in our sample paid about $3 million for a Super Bowl ad slot. They got $8.3 million in increased ticket sales, a 2.8-to-1 return on their investment.

This result was confirmed by two other economists, Wesley R. Hartmann and Daniel Klapper, who independently and earlier came up with a similar idea. These economists studied beer and soft drink ads run during the Super Bowl, while also utilizing the increased ad exposures in the cities of teams that qualify. They found a 2.5-to-1 return on investment. As expensive as these Super Bowl ads are, our results and theirs suggest they are so effective in upping demand that companies are actually dramatically underpaying for them.

And what does all of this mean for our friends back at the electronics company Levitt had worked with? It's possible that Super Bowl ads are more cost-effective than other forms of advertising. But at the very least our study does suggest that all that Father's Day advertising is probably a good idea.

One virtue of the Super Bowl experiment is that it wasn't necessary to intentionally assign anyone to treatment or control groups. It happened based on the lucky bounces in a football game. It happened, in other words, naturally. Why is that an advantage? Because nonnatural, randomly controlled experiments, while super-powerful and easier to do in the digital age, still are not always possible.

Sometimes we can't get our act together in time. Sometimes, as with that electronics company that didn't want to run an experiment on its ad campaign, we are too invested in the answer to test it.

Sometimes experiments are impossible. Suppose you are interested in how a country responds to losing a leader. Does it go to war? Does its economy stop functioning? Does nothing much change? Obviously, we can't just kill a significant number of presidents and prime ministers and see what happens. That would be not only impossible but immoral. Universities have built up, over many decades, institutional review boards (IRBs) that determine if a proposed experiment is ethical.

So if we want to know causal effects in a certain scenario and it is unethical or otherwise unfeasible to do an experiment, what can we do? We can utilize what economists—defining nature broadly enough to include football games—call natural experiments.

For better or worse (okay, clearly worse), there is a huge random component to life. Nobody knows for sure what or who is in charge of the universe. But one thing is clear: whoever is running the show—the laws of quantum mechanics, God, a pimply kid in his underwear simulating the universe on his computer—they, She, or he is *not* going through IRB approval.

Nature experiments on us all the time. Two people get

shot. One bullet stops just short of a vital organ. The other doesn't. These bad breaks are what make life unfair. But, if it is any consolation, the bad breaks do make life a little easier for economists to study. Economists use the arbitrariness of life to test for causal effects.

Of forty-three American presidents, sixteen have been victims of serious assassination attempts, and four have been killed. The reasons that some lived were essentially random.

Compare John F. Kennedy and Ronald Reagan. Both men had bullets headed directly for their most vulnerable body parts. JFK's bullet exploded his brain, killing him shortly afterward. Reagan's bullet stopped centimeters short of his heart, allowing doctors to save his life. Reagan lived, while JFK died, with no rhyme or reason—just luck.

These attempts on leaders' lives and the arbitrariness with which they live or die is something that happens throughout the world. Compare Akhmad Kadyrov, of Chechyna, and Adolf Hitler, of Germany. Both men have been inches away from a fully functioning bomb. Kadyrov died. Hitler had changed his schedule, wound up leaving the booby-trapped room a few minutes early to catch a train, and thus survived.

And we can use nature's cold randomness—killing Kennedy but not Reagan—to see what happens, on average, when a country's leader is assassinated. Two economists, Benjamin F. Jones and Benjamin A. Olken, did just that. The control group here is any country in the years immediately after a near-miss assassination—for example, the United States in the mid-1980s. The treatment group is any country in the years immediately after a completed assassination—for example, the United States in the mid-1960s.

What, then, is the effect of having your leader murdered? Jones and Olken found that successful assassinations dramatically alter world history, taking countries on radically different paths. A new leader causes previously peaceful countries to go to war and previously warring countries to achieve peace. A new leader causes economically booming countries to start busting and economically busting countries to start booming.

In fact, the results of this assassination-based natural experiment overthrew a few decades of conventional wisdom on how countries function. Many economists previously leaned toward the view that leaders largely were impotent figureheads pushed around by external forces. Not so, according to Jones and Olken's analysis of nature's experiment.

Many would not consider this examination of assassination attempts on world leaders an example of Big Data. The number of assassinated or almost assassinated leaders in the study was certainly small—as was the number of wars that did or did not result. The economic datasets necessary to characterize the trajectory of an economy were large but for the most part predate digitalization.

Nonetheless, such natural experiments—though now used almost exclusively by economists—are powerful and will take on increasing importance in an era with more, better, and larger datasets. This is a tool that data scientists will not long forgo.

And yes, as should be clear by now, economists are playing a major role in the development of data science. At least I'd like to think so, since that was my training.

Where else can we find natural experiments—in other words, situations where the random course of events places people in treatment and control groups?

The clearest example is a lottery, which is why economists love them—not playing them, which we find irrational, but studying them. If a Ping-Pong ball with a three on it rises to the top, Mr. Jones will be rich. If it's a ball with a six instead, Mr. Johnson will be.

To test the causal effects of monetary windfalls, economists compare those who win lotteries to those who buy tickets but lose. These studies have generally found that winning the lottery does not make you happy in the short run but does in the long run.*

Economists can also utilize the randomness of lotteries to see how one's life changes when a neighbor gets rich. The data shows that your neighbor winning the lottery can have an impact on your own life. If your neighbor wins the lottery, for example, you are more likely to buy an expensive car, such as a BMW. Why? Almost certainly, economists maintain, the cause is jealousy after your richer neighbor purchased his own expensive car. Chalk it up to human nature. If Mr. Johnson sees Mr. Jones driving a brand-new BMW, Mr. Johnson wants one, too.

Unfortunately, Mr. Johnson often can't afford this BMW, which is why economists found that neighbors of lottery winners are significantly more likely to go bankrupt. Keeping up with the Joneses, in this instance, is impossible.

---

* A famous 1978 paper that claimed that winning the lottery does not make you happy has largely been debunked.

But natural experiments don't have to be explicitly random, like lotteries. Once you start looking for randomness, you see it everywhere—and can use it to understand how our world works.

Doctors are part of a natural experiment. Every once in a while, the government, for essentially arbitrary reasons, changes the formula it uses to reimburse physicians for Medicare patients. Doctors in some counties see their fees for certain procedures rise. Doctors in other counties see their fees drop.

Two economists—Jeffrey Clemens and Joshua Gottlieb, a former classmate of mine—tested the effects of this arbitrary change. Do doctors always give patients the same care, the care they deem most necessary? Or are they driven by financial incentives?

The data clearly shows that doctors can be motivated by monetary incentives. In counties with higher reimbursements, some doctors order substantially more of the better-reimbursed procedures—more cataract surgeries, colonoscopies, and MRIs, for example.

And then, the big question: do their patients fare better after getting all this extra care? Clemens and Gottlieb reported only "small health impacts." The authors found no statistically significant impact on mortality. Give stronger financial incentives to doctors to order certain procedures, this natural experiment suggests, and some will order more procedures that don't make much difference for patients' health and don't seem to prolong their lives.

Natural experiments can help answer life-or-death questions. They can also help with questions that, to some young people, feel like life-or-death.

Stuyvesant High School (known as "Stuy") is housed in a ten-floor, $150 million tan, brick building overlooking the Hudson River, a few blocks from the World Trade Center, in lower Manhattan. Stuy is, in a word, impressive. It offers fifty-five Advanced Placement (AP) classes, seven languages, and electives in Jewish history, science fiction, and Asian-American literature. Roughly one-quarter of its graduates are accepted to an Ivy League or similarly prestigious college. Stuyvesant trained Harvard physics professor Lisa Randall, Obama strategist David Axelrod, Academy Award–winning actor Tim Robbins, and novelist Gary Shteyngart. Its commencement speakers have included Bill Clinton, Kofi Annan, and Conan O'Brien.

The only thing more remarkable than Stuyvesant's offerings and graduates is its cost: zero dollars. It is a public high school and probably the country's best. Indeed, a recent study used 27 million reviews by 300,000 students and parents to rank every public high school in the United States. Stuy ranked number one. It is no wonder, then, that ambitious, middle-class New York parents and their equally ambitious progeny can become obsessed with Stuy's brand.

For Ahmed Yilmaz,* the son of an insurance agent and teacher in Queens, Stuy was *"the* high school."

"Working-class and immigrant families see Stuy as a way out," Yilmaz explains. "If your kid goes to Stuy, he is going to go to a legit, top-twenty university. The family will be okay."

So how can you get into Stuyvesant High School? You

---

* I have changed his name and a few details.

have to live in one of the five boroughs of New York City and score above a certain number on the admission exam. That's it. No recommendations, no essay, no legacy admission, no affirmative action. One day, one test, one score. If your number is above a certain threshold, you're in.

Each November, approximately 27,000 New York youngsters sit for the admission exam. The competition is brutal. Fewer than 5 percent of those who take the test get into Stuy.

Yilmaz explains that his mother had "worked her ass off" and put what little money she had into his preparation for the test. After months spending every weekday afternoon and full weekends preparing, Yilmaz was confident he would get into Stuy. He still remembers the day he received the envelope with the results. He missed by two questions.

I asked him what it felt like. "What does it feel like," he responded, "to have your world fall apart when you're in middle school?"

His consolation prize was hardly shabby—Bronx Science, another exclusive and highly ranked public school. But it was not Stuy. And Yilmaz felt Bronx Science was more a specialty school meant for technical people. Four years later, he was rejected from Princeton. He attended Tufts and has shuffled through a few careers. Today he is a reasonably successful employee at a tech company, although he says his job is "mind-numbing" and not as well compensated as he'd like.

More than a decade later, Yilmaz admits that he sometimes wonders how life would have played out had he gone to Stuy. "Everything would be different," he says. "Literally, everyone I know would be different." He wonders if Stuyvesant High School would have led him to higher SAT scores, a university like Princeton or Harvard (both of which he considers significantly better than Tufts), and perhaps more lucrative or fulfilling employment.

It can be anything from entertaining to self-torture for human beings to play out hypotheticals. What would my life be like if I made the move on that girl or that boy? If I took that job? If I went to that school? But these what-ifs seem unanswerable. Life is not a video game. You can't replay it under different scenarios until you get the results you want.

Milan Kundera, the Czech-born writer, has a pithy quote about this in his novel *The Unbearable Lightness of Being*: "Human life occurs only once, and the reason we cannot determine which of our decisions are good and which bad is that in a given situation we can make only one decision; we are not granted a second, third or fourth life in which to compare various decisions."

Yilmaz will never experience a life in which he somehow managed to score two points higher on that test.

But perhaps there's a way we can gain some insight on how different his life may or may not have been by doing a study of large numbers of Stuyvesant High School students.

The blunt, naïve methodology would be to compare all the students who went to Stuyvesant and all those who did not. We could analyze how they performed on AP tests and SATs—and what colleges they were accepted into. If we did this, we would find that students who went to Stuyvesant score much higher on standardized tests and get accepted to substantially better universities. But as we've seen already in this chapter, this kind of evidence, by itself, is not convincing. Maybe the reason Stuyvesant students perform so much better is that Stuy attracts much better students in the first place. Correlation here does not prove causation.

To test the *causal* effects of Stuyvesant High School, we need to compare two groups that are almost identical: one that got the Stuy treatment and one that did not. We need a natural experiment. But where can we find it?

The answer: students, like Yilmaz, who scored very, very close to the cutoff necessary to attend Stuyvesant.* Students who just missed the cutoff are the control group; students who just made the cut are the treatment group.

There is little reason to suspect students on either side of the cutoff differ much in talent or drive. What, after all, causes a person to score just a point or two higher on a test than another? Maybe the lower-scoring one slept ten minutes too little or ate a less nutritious breakfast. Maybe the higher-scoring one had remembered a particularly difficult word on the test from a conversation she had with her grandmother three years earlier.

In fact, this category of natural experiments—utilizing sharp numerical cutoffs—is so powerful that it has its own name among economists: regression discontinuity. Anytime there is a precise number that divides people into two different groups—a discontinuity—economists can compare—or regress—the outcomes of people very, very close to the cutoff.

---

* In looking for people like Yilmaz who scored near the cutoff, I was blown away by the number of people—in their twenties through their fifties—who remember this test-taking experience from their early teens and speak about missing a cutoff in dramatic terms. This includes former congressman and New York City mayoral candidate Anthony Weiner, who says he missed Stuy by a single point. "They didn't want me," he told me, in a phone interview.

Two economists, M. Keith Chen and Jesse Shapiro, took advantage of a sharp cutoff used by federal prisons to test the effects of rough prison conditions on future crime. Federal inmates in the United States are given a score, based on the nature of their crime and their criminal history. The score determines the conditions of their prison stay. Those with a high enough score will go to a high-security correctional facility, which means less contact with other people, less freedom of movement, and likely more violence from guards or other inmates.

Again, it would not be fair to compare the entire universe of prisoners who went to high-security prisons to the entire universe of prisoners who went to low-security prisons. High-security prisons will include more murderers and rapists, low-security prisons more drug offenders and petty thieves.

But those right above or right below the sharp numerical threshold had virtually identical criminal histories and backgrounds. This one measly point, however, meant a very different prison experience.

The result? The economists found that prisoners assigned to harsher conditions were more likely to commit additional crimes once they left. The tough prison conditions, rather than deterring them from crime, hardened them and made them more violent once they returned to the outside world.

So what did such a "regression discontinuity" show for Stuyvesant High School? A team of economists from MIT and Duke—Atila Abdulkadiroğlu, Joshua Angrist, and Parag Pathak—performed the study. They compared the outcomes of New York pupils on both sides of the cutoff. In other words, these economists looked at hundreds of students who, like

Yilmaz, *missed* Stuyvesant by a question or two. They compared them to hundreds of students who had a better test day and *made* Stuy by a question or two. Their measures of success were AP scores, SAT scores, and the rankings of the colleges they eventually attended.

Their stunning results were made clear by the title they gave the paper: "Elite Illusion." The effects of Stuyvesant High School? Nil. Nada. Zero. Bupkus. Students on either side of the cutoff ended up with indistinguishable AP scores and indistinguishable SAT scores and attended indistinguishably prestigious universities.

The entire reason that Stuy students achieve more in life than non-Stuy students, the researchers concluded, is that better students attend Stuyvesant in the first place. Stuy does not *cause* you to perform better on AP tests, do better on your SATs, or end up at a better college.

"The intense competition for exam school seats," the economists wrote, "does not appear to be justified by improved learning for a broad set of students."

Why might it not matter which school you go to? Some more stories can help get at the answer. Consider two more students, Sarah Kaufmann and Jessica Eng, two young New Yorkers who both dreamed from an early age of going to Stuy. Kaufmann's score was just on the cutoff; she made it by one question. "I don't think anything could be that exciting again," Kaufmann recalls. Eng's score was just below the cutoff; she missed by one question. Kaufmann went to her dream school, Stuy. Eng did not.

So how did their lives end up? Both have since had successful, and rewarding, careers—as do most people who score in the top 5 percent of all New Yorkers on tests. Eng, ironically, enjoyed her high school experience more. Bronx Science, where she attended, was the only high school with a Holocaust museum. Eng discovered she loved curation and studied anthropology at Cornell.

Kaufmann felt a little lost in Stuy, where students were heavily focused on grades and she felt there was too much emphasis on testing, not on teaching. She called her experience "definitely a mixed bag." But it was a learning experience. She realized, for college, she would only apply to liberal arts schools, which had more emphasis on teaching. She got accepted to her dream school, Wesleyan University. There she found a passion for helping others, and she is now a public interest lawyer.

People adapt to their experience, and people who are going to be successful find advantages in any situation. The factors that make you successful are your talent and your drive. They are not who gives your commencement speech or other advantages that the biggest name-brand schools offer.

This is only one study, and it is probably weakened by the fact that most of the students who just missed the Stuyvesant cutoff ended up at another fine school. But there is growing evidence that, while going to a good school is important, there is little gained from going to the greatest possible school.

Take college. Does it matter if you go to one of the best universities in the world, such as Harvard, or a solid school such as Penn State?

Once again, there is a clear correlation between the ranking of one's school and how much money people make. Ten years into their careers, the average graduate of Harvard makes $123,000. The average graduate of Penn State makes $87,800.

But this correlation does not imply causation.

Two economists, Stacy Dale and Alan B. Krueger, thought of an ingenious way to test the causal role of elite universities on the future earning potential of their graduates. They had a large dataset that tracked a whole host of information on high school students, including where they applied to college, where they were accepted to college, where they attended college, their family background, and their income as adults.

To get a treatment and control group, Dale and Krueger compared students with similar backgrounds who were accepted by the same schools but chose different ones. Some students who got into Harvard attended Penn State—perhaps to be nearer to a girlfriend or boyfriend or because there was a professor they wanted to study under. These students, in other words, were just as talented, according to admissions committees, as those who went to Harvard. But they had different educational experiences.

So when two students, from similar backgrounds, both got into Harvard but one chose Penn State, what happened? The researchers' results were just as stunning as those on Stuyvesant High School. Those students ended up with more or less the same incomes in their careers. If future salary is the measure, similar students accepted to similarly prestigious schools who choose to attend different schools end up in about the same place.

Our newspapers are peppered with articles about hugely successful people who attended Ivy League schools: people like Microsoft founder Bill Gates and Facebook founders Mark Zuckerberg and Dustin Moskovitz, all of whom attended Harvard. (Granted, they all dropped out, raising additional questions about the value of an Ivy League education.)

There are also stories of people who were talented enough to get accepted to an Ivy League school, chose to attend a less prestigious school, and had extremely successful lives: people like Warren Buffett, who started at the Wharton School at the University of Pennsylvania, an Ivy League business school, but transferred to the University of Nebraska–Lincoln because it was cheaper, he hated Philadelphia, and he thought the Wharton classes were boring. The data suggests, earnings-wise at least, that choosing to attend a less prestigious school is a fine decision, for Buffett and others.

This book is called *Everybody Lies*. By this, I mostly mean that people lie—to friends, to surveys, and to themselves—to make themselves look better.

But the world also lies to us by presenting us with faulty, misleading data. The world shows us a huge number of successful Harvard graduates but fewer successful Penn State graduates, and we assume that there is a huge advantage to going to Harvard.

By cleverly making sense of nature's experiments, we can correctly make sense of the world's data—to find what's really useful and what is not.

Natural experiments relate to the previous chapter, as well. They often require zooming in—on the treatment and control groups: the cities in the Super Bowl experiment, the counties in the Medicare pricing experiment, the students close to the cutoff in the Stuyvesant experiment. And zooming in, as discussed in the previous chapter, often requires large, comprehensive datasets—of the type that are increasingly available as the world is digitized. Since we don't know when nature will choose to run her experiments, we can't set up a small survey to measure the results. We need a lot of existing data to learn from these interventions. We need Big Data.

There is one more important point to make about the experiments—either our own or those of nature—detailed in this chapter. Much of this book has focused on understanding the world—how much racism cost Obama, how many men are really gay, how insecure men and women are about their bodies. But these controlled or natural experiments have a more practical bent. They aim to improve our decision making, to help us learn interventions that work and those that do not.

Companies can learn how to get more customers. The government can learn how to use reimbursement to best motivate doctors. Students can learn what schools will prove most valuable. These experiments demonstrate the potential of Big Data to replace guesses, conventional wisdom, and shoddy correlations with what actually works—*causally*.

PART III

BIG DATA: HANDLE WITH CARE

7

BIG DATA, BIG SCHMATA? WHAT IT CANNOT DO

"Seth, Lawrence Summers would like to meet with you," the email said, somewhat cryptically. It was from one of my Ph.D. advisers, Lawrence Katz. Katz didn't tell me why Summers was interested in my work, though I later found out Katz had known all along.

I sat in the waiting room outside Summers's office. After some delay, the former Treasury secretary of the United States, former president of Harvard, and winner of some of the biggest awards in economics, summoned me inside.

Summers began the meeting by reading my paper on racism's effect on Obama, which his secretary had printed for him. Summers is a speed reader. As he reads, he occasionally sticks his tongue out and to the right, while his eyes rapidly shift left and right and down the page. Summers reading a social science paper reminds me of a great pianist performing a sonata. He is so focused he seems to lose track of all else. In fewer than five minutes, he had completed my thirty-page paper.

"You say that Google searches for 'nigger' suggest racism," Summers said. "That seems plausible. They predict where Obama gets less support than Kerry. That is interesting. Can we really think of Obama and Kerry as the same?"

"They were ranked as having similar ideologies by political scientists," I responded. "Also, there is no correlation between racism and changes in House voting. The result stays strong even when we add controls for demographics, church attendance, and gun ownership." This is how we economists talk. I had grown animated.

Summers paused and stared at me. He briefly turned to the TV in his office, which was tuned to CNBC, then stared at me again, then looked at the TV, then back at me. "Okay, I like this paper," Summers said. "What else are you working on?"

The next sixty minutes may have been the most intellectually exhilarating of my life. Summers and I talked about interest rates and inflation, policing and crime, business and charity. There is a reason so many people who meet Summers are enthralled. I have been fortunate to speak with some incredibly smart people in my life; Summers struck me as the smartest. He is obsessed with ideas, more than all else, which seems to be what often gets him in trouble. He had to resign his presidency at Harvard after suggesting the possibility that part of the reason for the shortage of women in the sciences might be that men have more variation in their IQs. If he finds an idea interesting, Summers tends to say it, even if it offends some ears.

It was now a half hour past the scheduled end time for our meeting. The conversation was intoxicating, but I still had no idea why I was there, nor when I was supposed to leave, nor how I would know when I was supposed to leave. I got the feeling, by this point, that Summers himself may have forgotten why he had set up this meeting.

And then he asked the million-dollar—or perhaps billion-dollar—question. "You think you can predict the stock market with this data?"

Aha. Here at last was the reason Summers had summoned me to his office.

Summers is hardly the first person to ask me this particular question. My father has generally been supportive of my unconventional research interests. But one time he did broach the subject. "Racism, child abuse, abortion," he said. "Can't you make any money off this expertise of yours?" Friends and other family members have raised the subject, as well. So have coworkers and strangers on the internet. Everyone seems to want to know whether I can use Google searches—or other Big Data—to pick stocks. Now it was the former Treasury secretary of the United States. This was more serious.

So *can* new Big Data sources successfully predict which ways stocks are headed? The short answer is no.

In the previous chapters we discussed the four powers of Big Data. This chapter is all about Big Data's limitations—both what we cannot do with it and, on occasion, what we ought not do with it. And one place to start is by telling the story of the failed attempt by Summers and myself to beat the markets.

In Chapter 3, we noted that new data is most likely to yield big returns when the existing research in a given field is weak. It is an unfortunate truth about the world that you will have a much easier time getting new insights about racism, child abuse, or abortion than you will getting a new, profitable insight into how a business is performing. That's because massive resources are already devoted to looking for even the slightest edge in measuring business performance. The competition in finance is fierce. That was already a strike against us.

Summers, who is not someone known for effusing about other people's intelligence, was certain the hedge funds were already way ahead of us. I was quite taken during our conversation by how much respect he had for them and how many of my suggestions he was convinced they'd beaten us to. I proudly shared with him an algorithm I had devised that allowed me to obtain more complete Google Trends data. He said it was clever. When I asked him if Renaissance, a quantitative hedge fund, would have figured out that algorithm, he chuckled and said, "Yeah, of course they would have figured that out."

The difficulty of keeping up with the hedge funds wasn't the only fundamental problem that Summers and I ran up against in using new, big datasets to beat the markets.

THE CURSE OF DIMENSIONALITY

Suppose your strategy for predicting the stock market is to find a lucky coin—but one that will be found through careful testing. Here's your methodology: You label one thousand coins—1 to 1,000. Every morning, for two years, you flip each coin, record whether it came up heads or tails, and then note whether the Standard & Poor's Index went up or down that day. You pore through all your data. And voilà! You've found something. It turns out that 70.3 percent of the time Coin 391 came up heads the S&P Index rose. The relationship is statistically significant, highly so. You have found your lucky coin!

Just flip Coin 391 every morning and buy stocks whenever it comes up heads. Your days of Target T-shirts and ramen noodle dinners are over. Coin 391 is your ticket to the good life!

Or not.

You have become another victim of one of the most diabolical aspects of "the curse of dimensionality." It can strike whenever you have lots of variables (or "dimensions")—in this case, one thousand coins—chasing not that many observations—in this case, 504 trading days over those two years. One of those dimensions—Coin 391, in this case—is likely to get lucky. Decrease the number of variables—flip only one hundred coins—and it will become much less likely that one of them will get lucky. Increase the number of observations—try to predict the behavior of the S&P Index for twenty years—and coins will struggle to keep up.

The curse of dimensionality is a major issue with Big Data, since newer datasets frequently give us exponentially more variables than traditional data sources—every search term, every category of tweet, etc. Many people who claim to predict the market utilizing some Big Data source have merely been entrapped by the curse. All they've really done is find the equivalent of Coin 391.

Take, for example, a team of computer scientists from Indiana University and Manchester University who claimed they could predict which way the markets would go based on what people were tweeting. They built an algorithm to code the world's day-to-day moods based on tweets. They used techniques similar to the sentiment analysis discussed in

Chapter 3. However, they coded not just one mood but many moods—happiness, anger, kindness, and more. They found that a preponderance of tweets suggesting calmness, such as "I feel calm," predicts that the Dow Jones Industrial Average is likely to rise six days later. A hedge fund was founded to exploit their findings.

What's the problem here?

The fundamental problem is that they tested too many things. And if you test enough things, just by random chance, one of them will be statistically significant. They tested many emotions. And they tested each emotion one day before, two days before, three days before, and up to seven days before the stock market behavior that they were trying to predict. And all these variables were used to try to explain just a few months of Dow Jones ups and downs.

Calmness six days earlier was not a legitimate predictor of the stock market. Calmness six days earlier was the Big Data equivalent of our hypothetical Coin 391. The tweet-based hedge fund was shut down one month after starting due to lackluster returns.

Hedge funds trying to time the markets with tweets are not the only ones battling the curse of dimensionality. So are the numerous scientists who have tried to find the genetic keys to who we are.

Thanks to the Human Genome Project, it is now possible to collect and analyze the complete DNA of people. The potential of this project seemed enormous.

Maybe we could find the gene that causes schizophrenia. Maybe we could discover the gene that causes Alzheimer's and Parkinson's and ALS. Maybe we could find the gene that causes—gulp—intelligence. Is there one gene that can add a whole bunch of IQ points? Is there one gene that makes a genius?

In 1998, Robert Plomin, a prominent behavioral geneticist, claimed to have found the answer. He received a dataset that included the DNA and IQs of hundreds of students. He compared the DNA of "geniuses"—those with IQs of 160 or higher—to the DNA of those with average IQs.

He found a striking difference in the DNA of these two groups. It was located in one small corner of chromosome 6, an obscure but powerful gene that was used in the metabolism of the brain. One version of this gene, named IGF2r, was twice as common in geniuses.

"First Gene to Be Linked with High Intelligence Is Reported Found," headlined the *New York Times*.

You may think of the many ethical questions Plomin's finding raised. Should parents be allowed to screen their kids for IGF2r? Should they be allowed to abort a baby with the low-IQ variant? Should we genetically modify people to give them a high IQ? Does IGF2r correlate with race? Do we want to know the answer to that question? Should research on the genetics of IQ continue?

Before bioethicists had to tackle any of these thorny questions, there was a more basic question for geneticists, including Plomin himself. Was the result accurate? Was it really true that IGF2r could predict IQ? Was it really true that geniuses were twice as likely to carry a certain variant of this gene?

Nope. A few years after his original study, Plomin got access to another sample of people that also included their DNA and IQ scores. This time, IGF2r did not correlate with IQ. Plomin—and this is a sign of a good scientist—retracted his claim.

This, in fact, has been a general pattern in the research into genetics and IQ. First, scientists report that they have found a genetic variant that predicts IQ. Then scientists get new data and discover their original assertion was wrong.

For example, in a recent paper, a team of scientists, led by Christopher Chabris, examined twelve prominent claims about genetic variants associated with IQ. They examined data from ten thousand people. They could not reproduce the correlation for any of the twelve.

What's the issue with all of these claims? The curse of dimensionality. The human genome, scientists now know, differs in millions of ways. There are, quite simply, too many genes to test.

If you test enough tweets to see if they correlate with the stock market, you will find one that correlates just by chance. If you test enough genetic variants to see if they correlate with IQ, you will find one that correlates just by chance.

How can you overcome the curse of dimensionality? You have to have some humility about your work and not fall in love with your results. You have to put these results through additional tests. For example, before you bet your life savings on Coin 391, you would want to see how it does over the next couple of years. Social scientists call this an "out-of-sample" test. And the more variables you try, the more humble you have to be. The more variables you try, the tougher the out-of-sample test has to be. It is also crucial to keep track of every test you attempt. Then you can know exactly how likely it is you are falling victim to the curse and how skeptical you should be of your results. Which brings us back to Larry Summers and me. Here's how we tried to beat the markets.

Summers's first idea was to use searches to predict future sales of key products, such as iPhones, that might shed light on the future performance of the stock of a company, such as Apple. There was indeed a correlation between searches for "iPhones" and iPhones sales. When people are Googling a lot for "iPhones," you can bet a lot of phones are being sold. However, this information was already incorporated into the Apple stock price. Clearly, when there were lots of Google searches for "iPhones," hedge funds had also figured out that it would be a big seller, regardless of whether they used the search data or some other source.

Summers's next idea was to predict future investment in developing countries. If a large number of investors were going to be pouring money into countries such as Brazil or Mexico in the near future, then stocks for companies in these countries would surely rise. Perhaps we could predict a rise in investment with key Google searches—such as "invest in Mexico" or "investment opportunities in Brazil." This proved a dead end. The problem? The searches were too rare. Instead of revealing meaningful patterns, this search data jumped all over the place.

We tried searches for individual stocks. Perhaps if people were searching for "GOOG," this meant they were about to buy Google. These searches seemed to predict that the stocks would be traded a lot. But they did not predict whether the stocks would rise or fall. One major limitation is that these searches did not tell us whether someone was interested in buying or selling the stock.

One day, I excitedly showed Summers a new idea I had: past searches for "buy gold" seemed to correlate with future increases in the price of gold. Summers told me I should test it going forward to see if it remained accurate. It stopped working, perhaps because some hedge fund had found the same relationship.

In the end, over a few months, we didn't find anything useful in our tests. Undoubtedly, if we had looked for a correlation with market performance in each of the billions of Google search terms, we would have found one that worked, however weakly. But it likely would have just been our own Coin 391.

THE OVEREMPHASIS ON WHAT IS MEASURABLE

In March 2012, Zoë Chance, a marketing professor at Yale, received a small white pedometer in her office mailbox in downtown New Haven, Connecticut. She aimed to study how this device, which measures the steps you take during the day and gives you points as a result, can inspire you to exercise more.

What happened next, as she recounted in a TEDx talk, was a Big Data nightmare. Chance became so obsessed and addicted to increasing her numbers that she began walking everywhere, from the kitchen to the living room, to the dining room, to the basement, in her office. She walked early in the morning, late at night, at nearly all hours of the day—twenty thousand steps in a given twenty-four hour period. She checked her pedometer hundreds of times per day, and much that remained of her human communication was with other pedometer users online, discussing strategies to improve scores. She remembers putting the pedometer on her three-year-old daughter when her daughter was walking, because she was so obsessed with getting the number higher.

Chance became so obsessed with maximizing this number that she lost all perspective. She forgot the reason someone would want to get the number higher—exercising, not having her daughter walk a few steps. Nor did she complete any academic research about the pedometer. She finally got rid of the device after falling late one night, exhausted, while trying to get in more steps. Though she is a data-driven researcher by profession, the experience affected her profoundly. "It makes me skeptical of whether having access to additional data is always a good thing," Chance says.

This is an extreme story. But it points to a potential problem with people using data to make decisions. Numbers can be seductive. We can grow fixated with them, and in so doing we can lose sight of more important considerations. Zoë Chance lost sight, more or less, of the rest of her life.

Even less obsessive infatuations with numbers can have drawbacks. Consider the twenty-first-century emphasis on testing in American schools—and judging teachers based on how their students score. While the desire for more objective measures of what happens in classrooms is legitimate, there are many things that go on there that can't readily be captured in numbers. Moreover, all of that testing pressured many teachers to teach to the tests—and worse. A small number, as was proven in a paper by Brian Jacob and Steven Levitt, cheated outright in administering those tests.

The problem is this: the things we can measure are often not exactly what we care about. We can measure how students do on multiple-choice questions. We can't easily measure critical thinking, curiosity, or personal development. Just trying to increase a single, easy-to-measure number—test scores or the number of steps taken in a day—doesn't always help achieve what we are really trying to accomplish.

In its efforts to improve its site, Facebook runs into this danger as well. The company has tons of data on how people use the site. It's easy to see whether a particular News Feed story was liked, clicked on, commented on, or shared. But, according to Alex Peysakhovich, a Facebook data scientist with whom I have written about these matters, not one of these is a perfect proxy for more important questions: What was the experience of using the site like? Did the story connect the user with her friends? Did it inform her about the world? Did it make her laugh?

Or consider baseball's data revolution in the 1990s. Many teams began using increasingly intricate statistics—rather than relying on old-fashioned human scouts—to make decisions. It was easy to measure offense and pitching but not fielding, so some organizations ended up underestimating the importance of defense. In fact, in his book *The Signal and the Noise*, Nate Silver estimates that the Oakland A's, a data-driven organization profiled in *Moneyball*, were giving up eight to ten wins per year in the mid-nineties because of their lousy defense.

The solution is not always more Big Data. A special sauce is often necessary to help Big Data work best: the judgment of humans and small surveys, what we might call small data. In an interview with Silver, Billy Beane, the A's then general manager and the main character in *Moneyball*, said that he actually had begun increasing his scouting budget.

To fill in the gaps in its giant data pool, Facebook too has to take an old-fashioned approach: asking people what they think. Every day as they load their News Feed, hundreds of Facebook users are presented with questions about the stories they see there. Facebook's automatically collected datasets (likes, clicks, comments) are supplemented, in other words, by smaller data ("Do you want to see this post in your News Feed?" "Why?"). Yes, even a spectacularly successful Big Data organization like Facebook sometimes makes use of the source of information much disparaged in this book: a small survey.

Indeed, because of this need for small data as a supplement to its mainstay—massive collections of clicks, likes, and posts—Facebook's data teams look different than you might guess. Facebook employs social psychologists, anthropologists, and sociologists precisely to find what the numbers miss.

Some educators, too, are becoming more alert to blind spots in Big Data. There is a growing national effort to supplement mass testing with small data. Student surveys have proliferated. So have parent surveys and teacher observations, where other experienced educators watch a teacher during a lesson.

"School districts realize they shouldn't be focusing solely on test scores," says Thomas Kane, a professor of education at Harvard. A three-year study by the Bill & Melinda Gates Foundation bears out the value in education of both big and small data. The authors analyzed whether test-score-based models, student surveys, or teacher observations were best at measuring which teachers most improved student learning. When they put the three measures together into a composite score, they got the best results. "Each measure adds something of value," the report concluded.

In fact, it was just as I was learning that many Big Data operations use small data to fill in the holes that I showed up in Ocala, Florida, to meet Jeff Seder. Remember, he was the Harvard-educated horse guru who used lessons learned from a huge dataset to predict the success of American Pharoah.

After sharing all the computer files and math with me, Seder admitted that he had another weapon: Patty Murray.

Murray, like Seder, has high intelligence and elite credentials—a degree from Bryn Mawr. She also left New York City for rural life. "I like horses more than humans," Murray admits. But Murray is a bit more traditional in her approaches to evaluating horses. She, like many horse agents, personally examines horses, seeing how they walk, checking for scars and bruises, and interrogating their owners.

Murray then collaborates with Seder as they pick the final horses they want to recommend. Murray sniffs out problems with the horses, problems that Seder's data, despite being the most innovative and important dataset ever collected on horses, still misses.

I am predicting a revolution based on the revelations of Big Data. But this does not mean we can just throw data at any question. And Big Data does not eliminate the need for all the other ways humans have developed over the millennia to understand the world. They complement each other.

8

MO DATA, MO PROBLEMS?
WHAT WE SHOULDN'T DO

Sometimes, the power of Big Data is so impressive it's scary. It raises ethical questions.

THE DANGER OF EMPOWERED CORPORATIONS

Recently, three economists—Oded Netzer and Alain Lemaire, both of Columbia, and Michal Herzenstein of the University of Delaware—looked for ways to predict the likelihood of whether a borrower would pay back a loan. The scholars utilized data from Prosper, a peer-to-peer lending site. Potential borrowers write a brief description of why they need a loan and why they are likely to make good on it, and potential lenders decide whether to provide them the money. Overall, about 13 percent of borrowers defaulted on their loan.

It turns out the language that potential borrowers use is a strong predictor of their probability of paying back. And it is an important indicator even if you control for other relevant information lenders were able to obtain about those potential borrowers, including credit ratings and income.

Listed below are ten phrases the researchers found that are commonly used when applying for a loan. Five of them positively correlate with paying back the loan. Five of them negatively correlate with paying back the loan. In other words, five tend to be used by people you can trust, five by people you cannot. See if you can guess which are which.

God	lower interest rate	after-tax
promise	will pay	hospital
debt-free	graduate	
minimum payment	thank you	

You might think—or at least hope—that a polite, openly religious person who gives his word would be among the most likely to pay back a loan. But in fact this is not the case. This type of person, the data shows, is less likely than average to make good on their debt.

Here are the phrases grouped by the likelihood of paying back.

TERMS USED IN LOAN APPLICATIONS BY PEOPLE MOST LIKELY TO PAY BACK

debt-free	after-tax	graduate
lower interest rate	minimum payment	

TERMS USED IN LOAN APPLICATIONS BY PEOPLE MOST LIKELY TO DEFAULT

God	will pay	hospital
promise	thank you	

Before we discuss the ethical implications of this study, let's think through, with the help of the study's authors, what it reveals about people. What should we make of the words in the different categories?

First, let's consider the language that suggests someone is more likely to make their loan payments. Phrases such as "lower interest rate" or "after-tax" indicate a certain level of financial sophistication on the borrower's part, so it's perhaps not surprising they correlate with someone more likely to pay their loan back. In addition, if he or she talks about positive achievements such as being a college "graduate" and being "debt-free," he or she is also likely to pay their loans.

Now let's consider language that suggests someone is unlikely to pay their loans. Generally, if someone tells you he will pay you back, he will not pay you back. The more assertive the promise, the more likely he will break it. If someone writes "I promise I will pay back, so help me God," he is among the least likely to pay you back. Appealing to your mercy— explaining that he needs the money because he has a relative in the "hospital"—also means he is unlikely to pay you back. In fact, mentioning any family member—a husband, wife, son, daughter, mother, or father—is a sign someone will not be paying back. Another word that indicates default is "explain," meaning if people are trying to explain why they are going to be able to pay back a loan, they likely won't.

The authors did not have a theory for why thanking people is evidence of likely default.

In sum, according to these researchers, giving a detailed plan of how he can make his payments and mentioning commitments he has kept in the past are evidence someone will pay back a loan. Making promises and appealing to your mercy is a clear sign someone will go into default. Regardless of the reasons—or what it tells us about human nature that making promises is a sure sign someone will, in actuality, not do something—the scholars found the test was an extremely valuable piece of information in predicting default. Someone who mentions God was 2.2 times more likely to default. This was among the single highest indicators that someone would not pay back.

But the authors also believe their study raises ethical questions. While this was just an academic study, some companies do report that they utilize online data in approving loans. Is this acceptable? Do we want to live in a world in which companies use the words we write to predict whether we will pay back a loan? It is, at a minimum, creepy—and, quite possibly, scary.

A consumer looking for a loan in the near future might have to worry about not merely her financial history but also her online activity. And she may be judged on factors that seem absurd—whether she uses the phrase "Thank you" or invokes "God," for example. Further, what about a woman who legitimately needs to help her sister in a hospital and will most certainly pay back her loan afterward? It seems awful to punish her because, on average, people claiming to need help for medical bills have often been proven to be lying. A world functioning this way starts to look awfully dystopian.

This is the ethical question: Do corporations have the right to judge our fitness for their services based on abstract but statistically predictive criteria not directly related to those services?

Leaving behind the world of finance, let's look at the larger implications on, for example, hiring practices. Employers are increasingly scouring social media when considering job candidates. That may not raise ethical questions if they're looking for evidence of bad-mouthing previous employers or revealing previous employers' secrets. There may even be some justification for refusing to hire someone whose Facebook or Instagram posts suggest excessive alcohol use. But what if they find a seemingly harmless indicator that correlates with something they care about?

Researchers at Cambridge University and Microsoft gave fifty-eight thousand U.S. Facebook users a variety of tests about their personality and intelligence. They found that Facebook likes are frequently correlated with IQ, extraversion, and conscientiousness. For example, people who like Mozart, thunderstorms, and curly fries on Facebook tend to have higher IQs. People who like Harley-Davidson motorcycles, the country music group Lady Antebellum, or the page "I Love Being a Mom" tend to have lower IQs. Some of these correlations may be due to the curse of dimensionality. If you test enough things, some will randomly correlate. But some interests may legitimately correlate with IQ.

Nonetheless, it would seem unfair if a smart person who happens to like Harleys couldn't get a job commensurate with his skills because he was, without realizing it, signaling low intelligence.

In fairness, this is not an entirely new problem. People have long been judged by factors not directly related to job performance—the firmness of their handshakes, the neatness of their dress. But a danger of the data revolution is that, as more of our life is quantified, these proxy judgments can get more esoteric yet more intrusive. Better prediction can lead to subtler and more nefarious discrimination.

Better data can also lead to another form of discrimination, what economists call price discrimination. Businesses are often trying to figure out what price they should charge for goods or services. Ideally they want to charge customers the maximum they are willing to pay. This way, they will extract the maximum possible profit.

Most businesses usually end up picking one price that everyone pays. But sometimes they are aware that the members of a certain group will, on average, pay more. This is why movie theaters charge more to middle-aged customers—at the height of their earning power—than to students or senior citizens and why airlines often charge more to last-minute purchasers. They price discriminate.

Big Data may allow businesses to get substantially better at learning what customers are willing to pay—and thus gouging certain groups of people. Optimal Decisions Group was a pioneer in using data science to predict how much consumers are willing to pay for insurance. How did they do it? They used a methodology that we have previously discussed in this book. They found prior customers most similar to those currently looking to buy insurance—and saw how high a premium they were willing to take on. In other words, they ran a doppelganger search. A doppelganger search is entertaining if it helps us predict whether a baseball player will return to his former greatness. A doppelganger search is great if it helps us cure someone's disease. But if a doppelganger search helps a corporation extract every last penny from you? That's not so cool. My spendthrift brother would have a right to complain if he got charged more online than tightwad me.

Gambling is one area in which the ability to zoom in on customers is potentially dangerous. Big casinos are using something like a doppelganger search to better understand their consumers. Their goal? To extract the maximum possible profit —to make sure more of your money goes into their coffers.

Here's how it works. Every gambler, casinos believe, has a "pain point." This is the amount of losses that will sufficiently frighten her so that she leaves your casino for an extended period of time. Suppose, for example, that Helen's "pain point" is $3,000. This means if she loses $3,000, you've lost a customer, perhaps for weeks or months. If Helen loses $2,999, she won't be happy. Who, after all, likes to lose money? But she won't be so demoralized that she won't come back tomorrow night.

Imagine for a moment that you are managing a casino. And imagine that Helen has shown up to play the slot machines. What is the optimal outcome? Clearly, you want Helen to get as close as possible to her "pain point" without crossing it. You want her to lose $2,999, enough that you make big profits but not so much that she won't come back to play again soon.

How can you do this? Well, there are ways to get Helen to stop playing once she has lost a certain amount. You can offer her free meals, for example. Make the offer enticing enough, and she will leave the slots for the food.

But there's one big challenge with this approach. How do you know Helen's "pain point"? The problem is, people have different "pain points." For Helen, it's $3,000. For John, it might be $2,000. For Ben, it might be $26,000. If you convince Helen to stop gambling when she lost $2,000, you left profits on the table. If you wait too long—after she has lost $3,000—you have lost her for a while. Further, Helen might not want to tell you her pain point. She may not even know what it is herself.

So what do you do? If you have made it this far in the book, you can probably guess the answer. You utilize data science. You learn everything you can about a number of your customers—their age, gender, zip code, and gambling behavior. And, from that gambling behavior—their winnings, losings, comings, and goings—you estimate their "pain point."

You gather all the information you know about Helen and find gamblers who are similar to her—her doppelgangers, more or less. Then you figure out how much pain they can withstand. It's probably the same amount as Helen. Indeed, this is what the casino Harrah's does, utilizing a Big Data warehouse firm, Terabyte, to assist them.

Scott Gnau, general manager of Terabyte, explains, in the excellent book *Super Crunchers*, what casino managers do when they see a regular customer nearing their pain point: "They come out and say, 'I see you're having a rough day. I know you like our steakhouse. Here, I'd like you to take your wife to dinner on us right now.'"

This might seem the height of generosity: a free steak dinner. But really it's self-serving. The casino is just trying to get customers to quit before they lose so much that they'll leave for an extended period of time. In other words, management is using sophisticated data analysis to try to extract as much money from customers, over the long term, as it can.

We have a right to fear that better and better use of online data will give casinos, insurance companies, lenders, and other corporate entities too much power over us.

On the other hand, Big Data has also been enabling consumers to score some blows against businesses that overcharge them or deliver shoddy products.

One important weapon is sites, such as Yelp, that publish reviews of restaurants and other services. A recent study by economist Michael Luca, of Harvard, has shown the extent to which businesses are at the mercy of Yelp reviews. Comparing those reviews to sales data in the state of Washington, he found that one fewer star on Yelp will make a restaurant's revenues drop 5 to 9 percent.

Consumers are also aided in their struggles with business by comparison shopping sites—like Kayak and Booking.com. As discussed in *Freakonomics*, when an internet site began reporting the prices different companies were charging for term life insurance, these prices fell dramatically. If an insurance company was overcharging, customers would know it and use someone else. The total savings to consumers? One billion dollars per year.

Data on the internet, in other words, can tell businesses which customers to avoid and which they can exploit. It can also tell customers the businesses they should avoid and who is trying to exploit them. Big Data to date has helped both sides in the struggle between consumers and corporations. We have to make sure it remains a fair fight.

THE DANGER OF EMPOWERED GOVERNMENTS

When her ex-boyfriend showed up at a birthday party, Adriana Donato knew he was upset. She knew that he was mad. She knew that he had struggled with depression. As he invited her for a drive, there was one thing Donato, a twenty-year-old zoology student, did not know. She did not know her ex-boyfriend, twenty-two-year-old James Stoneham, had spent the previous three weeks searching for information on how to murder somebody and about murder law, mixed in with the occasional search about Donato.

If she had known this, presumably she would not have gotten in the car. Presumably, she would not have been stabbed to death that evening.

In the movie *Minority Report*, psychics collaborate with police departments to stop crimes before they happen. Should Big Data be made available to police departments to stop crimes before they happen? Should Donato have at least been warned about her ex-boyfriend's foreboding searches? Should the police have interrogated Stoneham?

First, it must be acknowledged that there is growing evidence that Google searches related to criminal activity do correlate with criminal activity. Christine Ma-Kellams, Flora Or, Ji Hyun Baek, and Ichiro Kawachi have shown that Google searches related to suicide correlate strongly with state-level suicide rates. In addition, Evan Soltas and I have shown that weekly Islamophobic searches—such as "I hate Muslims" or "kill Muslims"—correlate with anti-Muslim hate crimes that week. If more people are making searches saying they want to do something, more people are going to do that thing.

So what should we do with this information? One simple, fairly uncontroversial idea: we can utilize the area-level data to allocate resources. If a city has a huge rise in suicide-related searches, we can up the suicide awareness in this city. The city government or nonprofits might run commercials explaining where people can get help, for example. Similarly, if a city has a huge rise in searches for "kill Muslims," police departments might be wise to change how they patrol the streets. They might dispatch more officers to protect the local mosque, for example.

But one step we should be very reluctant to take: going after individuals before any crime has been committed. This seems, to begin with, an invasion of privacy. There is a large ethical leap from the government having the search data of thousands or hundreds of thousands of people to the police department having the search data of an individual. There is a large ethical leap from protecting a local mosque to ransacking someone's house. There is a large ethical leap from advertising suicide prevention to locking someone up in a mental hospital against his will.

The reason to be extremely cautious using individual-level data, however, goes beyond even ethics. There is a data reason as well. It is a large leap for data science to go from trying to predict the actions of a city to trying to predict the actions of an individual.

Let's return to suicide for a moment. Every month, there are about 3.5 million Google searches in the United States related to suicide, with the majority of them suggesting suicidal ideation—searches such as "suicidal," "commit suicide," and "how to suicide." In other words, every month, there is more than one search related to suicide for every one hundred Americans. This brings to mind a quote from the philosopher Friedrich Nietzsche: "The thought of suicide is a great consolation: by means of it one gets through many a dark night." Google search data shows how true that is, how common the thought of suicide is. However, every month, there are fewer than four thousand suicides in the United States. Suicidal ideation is incredibly common. Suicide is not. So it wouldn't make a lot of sense for cops to be showing up at the door of everyone who has ever made some online noise about wanting to blow their brains out—if for no other reason than that the police wouldn't have time for anything else.

Or consider those incredibly vicious Islamophobic searches. In 2015, there were roughly 12,000 searches in the United States for "kill Muslims." There were 12 murders of Muslims reported as hate crimes. Clearly, the vast majority of people who make this terrifying search do not go through with the corresponding act.

There is some math that explains the difference between predicting the behavior of an individual and predicting the behavior in a city. Here's a simple thought experiment. Suppose there are one million people in a city and one mosque. Suppose, if someone does not search for "kill Muslims," there is only a 1-in-100,000,000 chance that he will attack a mosque. Suppose if someone does search for "kill Muslims," this chance rises sharply, to 1 in 10,000. Suppose Islamophobia has skyrocketed and searches for "kill Muslims" have risen from 100 to 1,000.

In this situation, math shows that the chances of a mosque being attacked has risen about fivefold, from about 2 percent to 10 percent. But the chances of an individual who searched for "kill Muslims" actually attacking a mosque remains only 1 in 10,000.

The proper response in this situation is not to jail all the people who searched for "kill Muslims." Nor is it to visit their houses. There is a tiny chance that any one of these people in particular will commit a crime. The proper response, however, would be to protect that mosque, which now has a 10 percent chance of being attacked.

Clearly, many horrific searches never lead to horrible actions.

That said, it is at least theoretically possible that there are some classes of searches that suggest a reasonably high probability of a horrible follow-through. It is at least theoretically possible, for example, that data scientists could in the future build a model that could have found that Stoneham's searches related to Donato were significant cause for concern.

In 2014, there were about 6,000 searches for the exact phrase "how to kill your girlfriend" and 400 murders of girlfriends. If all of these murderers had made this exact search beforehand, that would mean 1 in 15 people who searched "how to kill your girlfriend" went through with it. Of course, many, probably most, people who murdered their girlfriends did not make this exact search. This would mean the true probability that this particular search led to murder is lower, probably a lot lower.

But if data scientists could build a model that showed that the threat against a particular individual was, say, 1 in 100, we might want to do something with that information. At the least, the person under threat might have the right to be informed that there is a 1-in-100 chance she will be murdered by a particular person.

Overall, however, we have to be very cautious using search data to predict crimes at an individual level. The data clearly tells us that there are many, many horrifying searches that rarely lead to horrible actions. And there has been, as of yet, no proof that the government can predict a particular horrible action, with high probability, just from examining these searches. So we have to be really cautious about allowing the government to intervene at the individual level based on search data. This is not just for ethical or legal reasons. It's also, at least for now, for data science reasons.

CONCLUSION

▬

HOW MANY PEOPLE
FINISH BOOKS?

After signing my book contract, I had a clear vision of how the book should be structured. Near the start, you may recall, I described a scene at my family's Thanksgiving table. My family members debated my sanity and tried to figure out why I, at thirty-three, couldn't seem to find the right girl.

The conclusion to this book, then, practically wrote itself. I would meet and marry the girl. Better still, I would use Big Data to meet the right girl. Perhaps I could weave in tidbits from the courting process throughout. Then the story would all come together in the conclusion, which would describe my wedding day and double as a love letter to my new wife.

Unfortunately, life didn't match my vision. Locking myself in my apartment and avoiding the world while writing a book probably didn't help my romantic life. And I, alas, still need to find a wife. More important, I needed a new conclusion.

I pored over many of my favorite books in trying to find what makes a great conclusion. The best conclusions, I concluded, bring to the surface an important point that has been there all along, hovering just beneath the surface. For this book, that big point is this: social science is becoming a real science. And this new, real science is poised to improve our lives.

In the beginning of Part II, I discussed Karl Popper's critique of Sigmund Freud. Popper, I noted, didn't think that Freud's wacky vision of the world was scientific. But I didn't mention something about Popper's critique. It was actually far broader than just an attack on Freud. Popper didn't think *any* social scientist was particularly scientific. Popper was simply unimpressed with the rigor of what these so-called scientists were doing.

What motivated Popper's crusade? When he interacted with the best intellectuals of his day—the best physicists, the best historians, the best psychologists—Popper noted a striking difference. When the physicists talked, Popper believed in what they were doing. Sure, they sometimes made mistakes. Sure, they sometimes were fooled by their subconscious biases. But physicists were engaged in a process that was clearly finding deep truths about the world, culminating in Einstein's Theory of Relativity. When the world's most famous social scientists talked, in contrast, Popper thought he was listening to a bunch of gobbledygook.

Popper is hardly the only person to have made this distinction. Just about everybody agrees that physicists, biologists, and chemists are real scientists. They utilize rigorous experiments to find how the physical world works. In contrast, many people think that economists, sociologists, and psychologists are soft scientists who throw around meaningless jargon so they can get tenure.

To the extent this was ever true, the Big Data revolution has changed that. If Karl Popper were alive today and attended a presentation by Raj Chetty, Jesse Shapiro, Esther Duflo, or (humor me) myself, I strongly suspect he would not have the same reaction he had back then. To be honest, he might be more likely to question whether today's great string theorists are truly scientific or just engaging in self-indulgent mental gymnastics.

If a violent movie comes to a city, does crime go up or down? If more people are exposed to an ad, do more people use the product? If a baseball team wins when a boy is twenty, will he be more likely to root for them when he's forty? These are all clear questions with clear yes-or-no answers. And in the mountains of honest data, we can find them.

This is the stuff of science, not pseudoscience.

This does not mean the social science revolution will come in the form of simple, timeless laws.

Marvin Minsky, the late MIT scientist and one of the first to study the possibility of artificial intelligence, suggested that psychology got off track by trying to copy physics. Physics had success finding simple laws that held in all times and all places.

Human brains, Minsky suggested, may not be subject to such laws. The brain, instead, is likely a complex system of hacks—one part correcting mistakes in other parts. The economy and political system may be similarly complex.

For this reason, the social science revolution is unlikely to come in the form of neat formulas, such as $E = MC^2$. In fact, if someone is claiming a social science revolution based on a neat formula, you should be skeptical.

The revolution, instead, will come piecemeal, study by study, finding by finding. Slowly, we will get a better understanding of the complex systems of the human mind and society.

A proper conclusion sums up, but it also points the way to more things to come.

For this book, that's easy. The datasets I have discussed herein are revolutionary, but they have barely been explored. There is so much more to be learned. Frankly, the overwhelming majority of academics have ignored the data explosion caused by the digital age. The world's most famous sex researchers stick with the tried and true. They ask a few hundred subjects about their desires; they don't ask sites like PornHub for their data. The world's most famous linguists analyze individual texts; they largely ignore the patterns revealed in billions of books. The methodologies taught to graduate students in psychology, political science, and sociology have been, for the most part, untouched by the digital revolution. The broad, mostly unexplored terrain opened by the data explosion has been left to a small number of forward-thinking professors, rebellious grad students, and hobbyists.

That will change.

For every idea I have talked about in this book, there are a hundred ideas just as important ready to be tackled. The research discussed here is the tip of the tip of the iceberg, a scratch on the scratch of the surface.

So what else is coming?

For one, a radical expansion of the methodology that was used in one of the most successful public health studies of all time. In the mid-nineteenth century, John Snow, a British physician, was interested in what was causing a cholera outbreak in London.

His ingenious idea: he mapped every cholera case in the city. When he did this, he found the disease was largely clustered around one particular water pump. This suggested the disease spread through germ-infested water, disproving the then-conventional idea that it spread through bad air.

Big Data—and the zooming in that it allows—makes this type of study easy. For any disease, we can explore Google search data or other digital health data. We can find if there are any tiny pockets of the world where prevalence of this disease is unusually high or unusually low. Then we can see what these places have in common. Is there something in the air? The water? The social norms?

We can do this for migraines. We can do this for kidney stones. We can do this for anxiety and depression and Alzheimer's and pancreatic cancer and high blood pressure and back pain and constipation and nosebleeds. We can do this for everything. The analysis that Snow did once, we might be able to do four hundred times (something as of this writing I am already starting to work on).

We might call this—taking a simple method and utilizing Big Data to perform an analysis several hundred times in a short period of time—science at scale. Yes, the social and be-havioral sciences are most definitely going to scale. Zooming in on health conditions will help these sciences scale. Another thing that will help them scale: A/B testing. We discussed A/B testing in the context of businesses getting users to click on headlines and ads—and this has been the predominant use of the methodology. But A/B testing can be used to uncover things more fundamental—and socially valuable—than an arrow that gets people to click on an ad.

Benjamin F. Jones is an economist at Northwestern who is trying to use A/B testing to better help kids learn. He has helped create a platform, EDU STAR, which allows for schools to randomly test different lesson plans.

Many companies are in the education software business. With EDU STAR, students log in to a computer and are randomly exposed to different lesson plans. Then they take short tests to see how well they learned the material. Schools, in other words, learn what software works best for helping students grasp material.

Already, like all great A/B testing platforms, EDU STAR is yielding surprising results. One lesson plan that many educators were very excited about included software that utilized games to help teach students fractions. Certainly, if you turned math into a game, students would have more fun, learn more, and do better on tests. Right? Wrong. Students who were taught fractions via a game tested worse than those who learned fractions in a more standard way.

Getting kids to learn more is an exciting, and socially beneficial, use of the testing that Silicon Valley pioneered to get people to click on more ads. So is getting people to sleep more.

The average American gets 6.7 hours of sleep every night. Most Americans want to sleep more. But 11 P.M. rolls around, and *SportsCenter* is on or YouTube is calling. So shut-eye waits. Jawbone, a wearable-device company with hundreds of thousands of customers, performs thousands of tests to try to find interventions that help get their users to do what they want to do: go to bed earlier.

Jawbone scored a huge win using a two-pronged goal. First, ask customers to commit to a not-that-ambitious goal. Send them a message like this: "It looks like you haven't been sleeping much in the last 3 days. Why don't you aim to get to bed by 11:30 tonight? We know you normally get up at 8 A.M." Then the users will have an option to click on "I'm in."

Second, when 10:30 comes, Jawbone will send another message: "We decided you'd aim to sleep at 11:30. It's 10:30 now. Why not start now?"

Jawbone found this strategy led to twenty-three minutes of extra sleep. They didn't get customers to actually get to bed at 10:30, but they did get them to bed earlier.

Of course, every part of this strategy had to be optimized through lots of experimentation. Start the original goal too early—ask users to commit to going to bed by 11 P.M.—and few will play along. Ask users to go to bed by midnight and little will be gained.

Jawbone used A/B testing to find the sleep equivalent of Google's right-pointing arrow. But instead of getting a few more clicks for Google's ad partners, it yields a few more minutes of rest for exhausted Americans.

In fact, the whole field of psychology might utilize the tools of Silicon Valley to dramatically improve their research. I'm eagerly anticipating the first psychology paper that, instead of detailing a couple of experiments done with a few undergrads, shows the results of a thousand rapid A/B tests.

The days of academics devoting months to recruiting a small number of undergrads to perform a single test will come to an end. Instead, academics will utilize digital data to test a few hundred or a few thousand ideas in just a few seconds. We'll be able to learn a lot more in a lot less time.

Text as data is going to teach us a lot more. How do ideas spread? How do new words form? How do words disappear? How do jokes form? Why are certain words funny and others not? How do dialects develop? I bet, within twenty years, we will have profound insights on all these questions.

I think we might consider utilizing kids' online behavior— appropriately anonymized—as a supplement to traditional tests to see how they are learning and developing. How is their spelling? Are they showing signs of dyslexia? Are they developing mature, intellectual interests? Do they have friends? There are clues to all these questions in the thousands of keystrokes every child makes every day.

And there is another, not-trivial area, where plenty more insights are coming.

In the song "Shattered," by the Rolling Stones, Mick Jagger describes all that makes New York City, the Big Apple, so magical. Laughter. Joy. Loneliness. Rats. Bedbugs. Pride. Greed. People dressed in paper bags. But Jagger devotes the most words for what makes the city truly special: "sex and sex and sex and sex."

As with the Big Apple, so with Big Data. Thanks to the

digital revolution, insights are coming in health. Sleep. Learning. Psychology. Language. Plus, sex and sex and sex and sex.

One question I am currently exploring: how many dimensions of sexuality are there? We usually think of someone as gay or straight. But sexuality is clearly more complex than that. Among gay people and straight people, people have types—some men like "blondes," others "brunettes," for instance. Might these preferences be as strong as the preferences for gender? Another question I am looking into: where do sexual preferences come from? Just as we can figure out the key years that determine baseball fandom or political views, we can now find the key years that determine adult sexual preferences. To learn these answers, you will have to buy my next book, tentatively titled *Everybody (Still) Lies*.

The existence of porn—and the data that comes with it—is a revolutionary development in the science of human sexuality.

It took time for the natural sciences to begin changing our lives—to create penicillin, satellites, and computers. It may take time before Big Data leads the social and behavioral sciences to important advances in the way we love, learn, and live. But I believe such advances are coming. I hope you see at least the outlines of such developments from this book. I hope, in fact, that some of you reading this book help create such advances.

To properly write a conclusion, an author should think about why he wrote the book in the first place. What goal is he trying to achieve?

I think the largest reason I wrote this book is as a result of one of the most formative experiences of my life. You see, a little more than a decade ago, the book *Freakonomics* came out. The surprise bestseller described the research of Steven Levitt, an award-winning economist at the University of Chicago mentioned frequently in this book. Levitt was a "rogue economist" who seemed to be able to use data to answer any question his quirky mind could think to ask: Do sumo wrestlers cheat? Do contestants on game shows discriminate? Do real estate agents get you the same deals they get for themselves?

I was just out of college, having majored in philosophy, with little idea what I wanted to do with my life. After reading *Freakonomics*, I knew. I wanted to do what Steven Levitt did. I wanted to pore through mountains of data to find out how the world *really* worked. I would follow him, I decided, and get a Ph.D. in economics.

So much has changed in the intervening twelve years. A couple of Levitt's studies were found to have coding errors. Levitt said some politically incorrect things about global warming. *Freakonomics* has gone out of favor in intellectual circles.

But I think, a few mistakes aside, the years have been kind to the larger point Levitt was trying to make. Levitt was telling us that a combination of curiosity, creativity, and data could dramatically improve our understanding of the world. There were stories hidden in data that were ready to be told and this has been proven right over and over again.

And I hope this book might have the same effect on others that *Freakonomics* had on me. I hope there is some young person reading this right now who is a bit confused on what she wants to do with her life. If you have a bit of statistical skill, an abundance of creativity, and curiosity, enter the data analysis business.

This book, in fact, and if I can be so bold, may be seen as next-level *Freakonomics*. A major difference between the studies discussed in *Freakonomics* and those discussed in this book is the ambition. In the 1990s, when Levitt made his name, there wasn't that much data available. Levitt prided himself on going after quirky questions, where data did exist. He largely ignored big questions where the data did not exist. Today, however, with so much data available on just about every topic, it makes sense to go after big, profound questions that get to the core of what it means to be a human being.

The future of data analysis is bright. The next Kinsey, I strongly suspect, will be a data scientist. The next Foucault will be a data scientist. The next Freud will be a data scientist. The next Marx will be a data scientist. The next Salk might very well be a data scientist.

Anyway, those were my attempts to do some of the things that a proper conclusion does. But great conclusions, I came to realize, do a lot more. So much more. A great conclusion must be ironic. It must be moving. A great conclusion must be profound and playful. It must be deep, humorous, and sad. A great conclusion must, in one sentence or two, make a point that sums up everything that has come before, everything that is coming. It must do so with a unique, novel point—a twist. A great book must end on a smart, funny, provocative bang.

Now might be a good time to talk a bit about my writing

process. I am not a particularly verbose writer. This book is only about seventy-five thousand words, which is a bit short for a topic as rich as this one.

But what I lack in breadth, I make up in obsessiveness. I spent five months on, and wrote forty-seven drafts of, my first *New York Times* sex column, which was two thousand words. Some chapters in this book took sixty drafts. I can spend hours finding the right word for a sentence in a footnote.

I lived much of my past year as a hermit. Just me and my computer. I lived in the hippest part of New York City and went out approximately never. This is, in my opinion, my magnum opus, the best idea I will have in my life. And I was willing to sacrifice whatever it took to make it right. I wanted to be able to defend every word in this book. My phone is filled with emails I forgot to respond to, e-vites I never opened, Bumble messages I ignored.*

After thirteen months of hard work, I was finally able to send in a near-complete draft. One part, however, was missing: the conclusion.

---

* Since everybody lies, you should question much of this story. Maybe I'm not an obsessive worker. Maybe I didn't work extraordinarily hard on this book. Maybe I, like lots of people, can exaggerate just how much I work. Maybe my thirteen months of "hard work" included full months in which I did no work at all. Maybe I didn't live as a hermit. Maybe, if you checked my Facebook profile, you'd see pictures of me out with friends during this supposed hermit period. Or maybe I was a hermit, but it was not self-imposed. Maybe I spent many nights alone, unable to work, hoping in vain that someone would contact me. Maybe nobody e-vites me to anything. Maybe nobody messages me on Bumble. Everybody lies. Every narrator is unreliable.

I explained to my editor, Denise, that it could take another few months. I told her six months was my most likely guess. The conclusion is, in my opinion, the most important part of the book. And I was only beginning to learn what makes a great conclusion. Needless to say, Denise was not pleased.

Then, one day, a friend of mine emailed me a study by Jordan Ellenberg. Ellenberg, a mathematician at the University of Wisconsin, was curious about how many people actually finish books. He thought of an ingenious way to test it using Big Data. Amazon reports how many people quote various lines in books. Ellenberg realized he could compare how frequently quotes were highlighted at the beginning of the book versus the end of the book. This would give a rough guide to readers' propensity to make it to the end. By his measure, more than 90 percent of readers finished Donna Tartt's novel *The Goldfinch*. In contrast, only about 7 percent made it through Nobel Prize economist Daniel Kahneman's magnum opus, *Thinking, Fast and Slow*. Fewer than 3 percent, this rough methodology estimated, made it to the end of economist Thomas Piketty's much discussed and praised *Capital in the 21st Century*. In other words, people tend not to finish treatises by economists.

One of the points of this book is we have to follow the Big Data *wherever* it leads and act accordingly. I may hope that most readers are going to hang on my every word and try to detect patterns linking the final pages to what happened earlier. But, no matter how hard I work on polishing my prose, most people are going to read the first fifty pages, get a few points, and move on with their lives.

Thus, I conclude this book in the only appropriate way: by following the data, what people actually do, not what they say. I am going to get a beer with some friends and stop working on this damn conclusion. Too few of you, Big Data tells me, are still reading.

ACKNOWLEDGMENTS

This book was a team effort.

These ideas were developed while I was a student at Harvard, a data scientist at Google, and a writer for the *New York Times*.

Hal Varian, with whom I worked at Google, has been a major influence on the ideas of this book. As best I can tell, Hal is perpetually twenty years ahead of his time. His book *Information Rules*, written with Carl Shapiro, basically predicted the future. And his paper "Predicting the Present," with Hyunyoung Choi, largely started the Big Data revolution in the social sciences that is described in this book. He is also an amazing and kind mentor, as so many who have worked under him can attest. A classic Hal move is to do most of the work on a paper you are coauthoring with him and then insist that your name goes before his. Hal's combination of genius and generosity is something I have rarely encountered.

My writing and ideas developed under Aaron Retica, who has been my editor for every single *New York Times* column. Aaron is a polymath. He somehow knows everything about music, history, sports, politics, sociology, economics, and God only knows what else. He is responsible for a huge amount of what is good about the *Times* columns that have my name on them. Other players on the team for these columns include Bill

Marsh, whose graphics continue to blow me away, Kevin McCarthy, and Gita Daneshjoo. This book includes passages from these columns, reprinted with permission.

Steven Pinker, who kindly agreed to write the foreword, has long been a hero of mine. He has set the bar for a modern book on social science—an engaging exploration of the fundamentals of human nature, making sense of the best research from a range of disciplines. That bar is one I will be struggling to reach my entire life.

My dissertation, from which this book has grown, was written under my brilliant and patient advisers Alberto Alesina, David Cutler, Ed Glaeser, and Lawrence Katz.

Denise Oswald is an amazing editor. If you want to know how good her editing is, compare this final draft to my first draft—actually, you can't do that because I am not going to ever show anyone else that embarrassing first draft. I also thank the rest of the team at HarperCollins, including Michael Barrs, Lynn Grady, Lauren Janiec, Shelby Meizlik, and Amber Oliver.

Eric Lupfer, my agent, saw potential in this project from the beginning, was instrumental in forming the proposal, and helped carry it through.

For superb fact-checking, I thank Melvis Acosta.

Other people from whom I learned a lot in my professional and academic life include Susan Athey, Shlomo Benartzi, Jason Bordoff, Danielle Bowers, David Broockman, Bo Cowgill, Steven Delpome, John Donohue, Bill Gale, Claudia Goldin, Suzanne Greenberg, Shane Greenstein, Steve Grove, Mike Hoyt, David Laibson, A.J. Magnuson, Dana Maloney, Jeffrey Oldham, Peter Orszag, David Reiley, Jonathan Rosenberg, Michael Schwarz, Steve Scott, Rich Shavelson, Michael D. Smith, Lawrence Summers, Jon Vaver, Michael Wiggins, and Qing Wu.

I thank Tim Requarth and NeuWrite for helping me develop my writing.

For help in interpreting studies, I thank Christopher Chabris, Raj Chetty, Matt Gentzkow, Solomon Messing, and Jesse Shapiro.

I asked Emma Pierson and Katia Sobolski if they might give advice on a chapter in my book. They decided, for reasons I do not understand, to offer to read the entire book—and give wise counsel on every paragraph.

My mother, Esther Davidowitz, read the entire book on multiple occasions and helped dramatically improve it. She also taught me, by example, that I should follow my curiosity, no matter where it led. When I was interviewing for an academic job, a professor grilled me: "What does your mother think of this work you do?" The idea was that my mom might be embarrassed that I was researching sex and other taboo topics. But I always knew she was proud of me for following my curiosity, wherever it led.

Many people read sections and offered helpful comments. I thank Eduardo Acevedo, Coren Apicella, Sam Asher, David Cutler, Stephen Dubner, Christopher Glazek, Jessica Goldberg, Lauren Goldman, Amanda Gordon, Jacob Leshno, Alex Peysakhovich, Noah Popp, Ramon Roullard, Greg Sobolski, Evan Soltas, Noah Stephens-Davidowitz, Lauren Stephens-Davidowitz, and Jean Yang. Actually, Jean was basically my best friend while I wrote this, so I thank her for that, too.

For help in collecting data, I thank Brett Goldenberg, James

Rogers, and Mike Williams at MindGeek and Rob McQuown and Sam Miller at Baseball Prospectus.

I am grateful for financial support from the Alfred Sloan Foundation.

At one point, while writing this book, I was deeply stuck, lost, and close to abandoning the project. I then went to the country with my dad, Mitchell Stephens. Over the course of a week, Dad put me back together. He took me for walks in which we discussed love, death, success, happiness, and writing—and then sat me down so we could go over every sentence of the book. I could not have finished this book without him.

All remaining errors are, of course, my own.

NOTES

INTRODUCTION

2 *American voters largely did not care that Barack Obama:* Katie Fretland, "Gallup: Race Not Important to Voters," The Swamp, *Chicago Tribune,* June 2008.

2 *Berkeley pored through:* Alexandre Mas and Enrico Moretti, "Racial Bias in the 2008 Presidential Election," *American Economic Review* 99, no. 2 (2009).

2 *post-racial society:* On the November 12, 2009, episode of his show, Lou Dobbs said we lived in a "post-partisan, post-racial society." On the January 27, 2010, episode of his show, Chris Matthews said that President Obama was "post-racial by all appearances." For other examples, see Michael C. Dawson and Lawrence D. Bobo, "One Year Later and the Myth of a Post-Racial Society," *Du Bois Review: Social Science Research on Race* 6, no. 2 (2009).

5 *I analyzed data from the General Social Survey:* Details on all these calculations can be found on my website, sethsd.com, in the csv labeled "Sex Data." Data from the General Social Survey can be found at http://gss.norc.org/.

5 *fewer than 600 million condoms:* Data provided to the author.

7 *searches and sign-ups for Stormfront:* Author's analysis of Google Trends data. I also scraped data on all members of Stormfront, as discussed in Seth Stephens-Davidowitz, "The Data of Hate," *New York Times,* July 13, 2014, SR4. The relevant data can be downloaded at sethsd.com, in the data section headlined "Stormfront."

7 *more searches for "nigger president" than "first black president":* Author's analysis of Google Trends data. The states for which this is true include Kentucky, Louisiana, Arizona, and North Carolina.

9 *rejected by five academic journals:* The paper was eventually

published as Seth Stephens-Davidowitz, "The Cost of Racial Animus on a Black Candidate: Evidence Using Google Search Data," *Journal of Public Economics* 118 (2014). More details about the research can be found there. In addition, the data can be found at my website, sethsd.com, in the data section headlined "Racism."

13 *single factor that best correlated:* "Strongest correlate I've found for Trump support is Google searches for the n-word. Others have reported this too" (February 28, 2016, tweet). See also Nate Cohn, "Donald Trump's Strongest Supporters: A New Kind of Democrat," *New York Times,* December 31, 2015, A3.

13 This shows the percent of Google searches that include the word "nigger(s)." Note that, because the measure is as a percent of Google searches, it is not arbitrarily higher in places with large populations or places that make a lot of searches. Note also that some of the differences in this map and the map for Trump support have obvious explanations. Trump lost popularity in Texas and Arkansas because they were the home states of two of his opponents, Ted Cruz and Mike Huckabee.

13 This is survey data from Civis Analytics from December 2015. Actual voting data is less useful here, since it is highly influenced by when the primary took place and the voting format. The maps are reprinted with permission from the *New York Times.*

15 *2.5 million trillion bytes of data:* "Bringing Big Data to the Enterprise," IBM, https://www-01.ibm.com/software/data/bigdata/what -is-big-data.html.

17 *needle comes in an increasingly larger haystack:* Nassim M. Taleb, "Beware the Big Errors of 'Big Data,'" *Wired,* February 8, 2013, http:// www.wired.com/2013/02/big-data-means-big-errors-people.

18 *neither racist searches nor membership in Stormfront:* I examined how internet racism changed in parts of the country with high and low exposure to the Great Recession. I looked at both Google search rates for "nigger(s)" and Stormfront membership. The relevant data can be downloaded at sethsd.com, in the data sections headlined "Racial Animus" and "Stormfront."

18 *But Google searches reflecting anxiety:* Seth Stephens-Davidowitz, "Fifty States of Anxiety," *New York Times,* August 7, 2016,

SR2. Note, while the Google searches do give much bigger samples, this pattern is consistent with evidence from surveys. See, for example, William C. Reeves et al., "Mental Illness Surveillance Among Adults in the United States," *Morbidity and Mortality Weekly Report Supplement* 60, no. 3 (2011).

18 *search for jokes:* This is discussed in Seth Stephens-Davidowitz, "Why Are You Laughing?" *New York Times*, May 15, 2016, SR9. The relevant data can be downloaded at sethsd.com, in the data section headlined "Jokes."

19 *"my husband wants me to breastfeed him":* This is discussed in Seth Stephens-Davidowitz, "What Do Pregnant Women Want?" *New York Times*, May 17, 2014, SR6.

19 *porn searches for depictions of women breastfeeding men:* Author's analysis of PornHub data.

19 *Women make nearly as many:* This is discussed in Seth Stephens-Davidowitz, "Searching for Sex," *New York Times*, January 25, 2015, SR1.

20 *"poemas para mi esposa embarazada":* Stephens-Davidowitz, "What Do Pregnant Women Want?"

21 *Friedman says:* I interviewed Jerry Friedman by phone on October 27, 2015.

21 *sampling of all their data:* Hal R. Varian, "Big Data: New Tricks for Econometrics," *Journal of Economic Perspectives* 28, no. 2 (2014).

CHAPTER 1: YOUR FAULTY GUT

26 *The best data science, in fact, is surprisingly intuitive:* I am speaking about the corner of data analysis I know about—data science that tries to explain and predict human behavior. I am not speaking of artificial intelligence that tries to, say, drive a car. These methodologies, while they do utilize tools discovered from the human brain, are less easy to understand.

28 *what symptoms predict pancreatic cancer:* John Paparrizos, Ryan W. White, and Eric Horvitz, "Screening for Pancreatic Adenocarcinoma Using Signals from Web Search Logs: Feasibility Study and Results," *Journal of Oncology Practice* (2016).

31 *Winter climate swamped all the rest:* This research is discussed in

Seth Stephens-Davidowitz, "Dr. Google Will See You Now," *New York Times*, August 11, 2013, SR12.

32 *biggest dataset ever assembled on human relationships:* Lars Backstrom and Jon Kleinberg, "Romantic Partnerships and the Dispersion of Social Ties: A Network Analysis of Relationship Status on Facebook," in *Proceedings of the 17th ACM Conference on Computer Supported Cooperative Work & Social Computing* (2014).

33 *people consistently rank:* Daniel Kahneman, *Thinking, Fast and Slow* (New York: Farrar, Straus and Giroux, 2011).

33 *asthma causes about seventy times more deaths:* Between 1979 and 2010, on average, 55.81 Americans died from tornados and 4216.53 Americans died from asthma. See Annual U.S. Killer Tornado Statistics, National Weather Service, http://www.spc.noaa.gov/climo/torn/fatalmap.php and Trends in Asthma Morbidity and Mortality, American Lung Association, Epidemiology and Statistics Unit.

33 *Patrick Ewing:* My favorite Ewing videos are "Patrick Ewing's Top 10 Career Plays," YouTube video, posted September 18, 2015, https://www.youtube.com/watch?v=Y29gMuYymv8; and "Patrick Ewing Knicks Tribute," YouTube video, posted May 12, 2006, https://www.youtube.com/watch?v=8T2l5Emzu-I.

34 *"basketball as a matter of life or death":* S. L. Price, "Whatever Happened to the White Athlete?" *Sports Illustrated*, December 8, 1997.

34 *an internet survey:* This was a Google Consumer Survey I conducted on October 22, 2013. I asked, "Where would you guess that the majority of NBA players were born?" The two choices were "poor neighborhoods" and "middle-class neighborhoods"; 59.7 percent of respondents picked "poor neighborhoods."

36 *a black person's first name is an indication of his socioeconomic background:* Roland G. Fryer Jr. and Steven D. Levitt, "The Causes and Consequences of Distinctively Black Names," *Quarterly Journal of Economics* 119, no. 3 (2004).

37 *Among all African-Americans born in the 1980s:* Centers for Disease Control and Prevention, "Health, United States, 2009," Table 9, Nonmarital Childbearing, by Detailed Race and Hispanic Origin

of Mother, and Maternal Age: United States, Selected Years 1970–2006.

37 *Chris Bosh . . . Chris Paul:* "Not Just a Typical Jock: Miami Heat Forward Chris Bosh's Interests Go Well Beyond Basketball," Palm BeachPost.com, February 15, 2011, http://www.palmbeachpost .com/news/sports/basketball/not-just-a-typical-jock-miami-heat -forward-chris-b/nLp7Z/; Dave Walker, "Chris Paul's Family to Compete on 'Family Feud,' nola.com, October 31, 2011, http:// www.nola.com/tv/index.ssf/2011/10/chris_pauls_family_to_com pete.html.

38 *four inches taller:* "Why Are We Getting Taller as a Species?" *Scientific American,* http://www.scientificamerican.com/article/why -are-we-getting-taller/. Interestingly, Americans have stopped getting taller. Amanda Onion, "Why Have Americans Stopped Growing Taller?" ABC News, July 3, 2016, http://abcnews.go.com /Technology/story?id=98438&page=1. I have argued that one of the reasons there has been a huge increase in foreign-born NBA players is that other countries are catching up to the United States in height. The number of American-born seven-footers in the NBA increased sixteenfold from 1946 to 1980 as Americans grew. It has since leveled off, as Americans have stopped growing. Meanwhile, the number of seven-footers from other countries has risen substantially. The biggest increase in international players, I found, has been extremely tall men from countries, such as Turkey, Spain, and Greece, where there have been noticeable increases in childhood health and adult height in recent years.

38 *Americans from poor backgrounds:* Carmen R. Isasi et al., "Association of Childhood Economic Hardship with Adult Height and Adult Adiposity among Hispanics/Latinos: The HCHS/SOL Socio-Cultural Ancillary Study," *PloS One* 11, no. 2 (2016); Jane E. Miller and Sanders Korenman, "Poverty and Children's Nutritional Status in the United States," *American Journal of Epidemiology* 140, no. 3 (1994); Harry J. Holzer, Diane Whitmore Schanzenbach, Greg J. Duncan, and Jens Ludwig, "The Economic Costs of Childhood Poverty in the United States," *Journal of Children and Poverty* 14, no. 1 (2008).

38 *the average American man is 5'9":* Cheryl D. Fryar, Qiuping Gu, and Cynthia L. Ogden, "Anthropometric Reference Data for Children and Adults: United States, 2007–2010," *Vital and Health Statistics Series* 11, no. 252 (2012).

39 *something like one in five reach the NBA:* Pablo S. Torre, "Larger Than Real Life," *Sports Illustrated,* July 4, 2011.

39 *middle-class, two-parent families:* Tim Kautz, James J. Heckman, Ron Diris, Bas Ter Weel, and Lex Borghans, "Fostering and Measuring Skills: Improving Cognitive and Non-Cognitive Skills to Promote Lifetime Success," National Bureau of Economic Research Working Paper 20749, 2014.

39 *Wrenn jumped the highest:* Desmond Conner, "For Wrenn, Sky's the Limit," *Hartford Courant,* October 21, 1999.

39 *But Wrenn:* Doug Wrenn's story is told in Percy Allen, "Former Washington and O'Dea Star Doug Wrenn Finds Tough Times," *Seattle Times,* March 29, 2009.

40 *"Doug Wrenn is dead":* Ibid.

40 *Jordan could be a difficult kid:* Melissa Isaacson, "Portrait of a Legend," ESPN.com, September 9, 2009, http://www.espn.com/chicago/columns/story?id=4457017&columnist=isaacson_melissa. A good Jordan biography is Roland Lazenby, *Michael Jordan: The Life* (Boston: Back Bay Books, 2015).

40 *His father was:* Barry Jacobs, "High-Flying Michael Jordan Has North Carolina Cruising Toward Another NCAA Title," *People,* March 19, 1984.

40 *Jordan's life is filled with stories of his family guiding him:* Isaacson, "Portrait of a Legend."

41 *speech upon induction into the Basketball Hall of Fame:* Michael Jordan's Basketball Hall of Fame Enshrinement Speech, YouTube video, posted February 21, 2012, https://www.youtube.com/watch?v=XLzBMGXfK4c. The most interesting aspect of Jordan's speech is not that he is so effusive about his parents; it is that he still feels the need to point out slights from early in his career. Perhaps a lifelong obsession with slights is necessary to become the greatest basketball player of all time.

41 *LeBron James was interviewed:* "I'm LeBron James from Akron,

Ohio," YouTube video, posted June 20, 2013, https://www.youtube
.com/watch?v=XceMbPVAggk.

CHAPTER 2: WAS FREUD RIGHT?

47   *a food's being shaped like a phallus:* I coded foods as being shaped
as a phallus if they were significantly more long than wide and
generally round. I counted cucumbers, corn, carrots, eggplant,
squash, and bananas. The data and code can be found at sethsd.com.

48   *errors collected by Microsoft researchers:* The dataset can be
downloaded at https://www.microsoft.com/en-us/download/de
tails.aspx?id=52418. The researchers asked users of Amazon Me-
chanical Turk to describe images. They analyzed the keystroke logs
and noted any time someone corrected a word. More details can
be found in Yukino Baba and Hisami Suzuki, "How Are Spelling
Errors Generated and Corrected? A Study of Corrected and Un-
corrected Spelling Errors Using Keystroke Logs," Proceedings of
the Fiftieth Annual Meeting of the Association for Computational
Linguistics, 2012. The data, code, and a further description of this
research can be found at sethsd.com.

51   *Consider all searches of the form "I want to have sex with my":*
The full data—warning: graphic—is as follows:

"I WANT TO HAVE SEX WITH . . ."

	MONTHLY GOOGLE SEARCHES WITH THIS EXACT PHRASE
my mom	720
my son	590
my sister	590
my cousin	480
my dad	480
my boyfriend	480
my brother	320
my daughter	260
my friend	170
my girlfriend	140

52 *cartoon porn:* For example, *"porn"* is one of the most common words included in Google searches for various extremely popular animated programs, as seen below.

CARTOONS, MEET PORN
(MOST COMMON GOOGLE SEARCHES FOR VARIOUS CARTOONS)

family guy porn	watch the simpsons	**futurama porn**	scooby doo games
family guy episodes	**the simpsons porn**	futurama leela	scooby doo movie
family guy free	the simpsons online	futurama episodes	**scooby doo porn**
watch family guy	the simpsons movie	futurama online	scooby doo velma

52 *babysitters:* Based on author's calculations, these are the most popular female occupations in porn searches by men, broken down by the age of men:

OCCUPATIONS OF WOMEN IN MALE PORN SEARCHES, BY AGE OF MEN

	18-24	25-64	65+
1.	Babysitter	Babysitter	Babysitter
2.	Teacher	Yoga Instructor	Cheerleader
3.	Yoga Instructor	Teacher	Doctor
4.	Cheerleader	Cheerleader	Teacher
5.	Doctor	Real Estate Agent	Real Estate Agent
6.	Prostitute	Doctor	Nurse
7.	Real Estate Agent	Prostitute	Yoga Instructor
8.	Nurse	Secretary	Secretary
9.	Secretary	Nurse	Prostitute

CHAPTER 3: DATA REIMAGINED

56 *algorithms in place:* Matthew Leising, "HFT Treasury Trading Hurts Market When News Is Released," Bloomberg Markets,

December 16, 2014; Nathaniel Popper, "The Robots Are Coming for Wall Street," *New York Times Magazine*, February 28, 2016, MM56; Richard Finger, "High Frequency Trading: Is It a Dark Force Against Ordinary Human Traders and Investors?" *Forbes*, September 30, 2013, http://www.forbes.com/sites/richardfinger /2013/09/30/high-frequency-trading-is-it-a-dark-force-against -ordinary-human-traders-and-investors/#50875fc751a6.

56 *Alan Krueger:* I interviewed Alan Krueger by phone on May 8, 2015.

57 *important indicators of how fast the flu:* The initial paper was Jeremy Ginsberg, Matthew H. Mohebbi, Rajan S. Patel, Lynnette Brammer, Mark S. Smolinski, and Larry Brilliant, "Detecting Influenza Epidemics Using Search Engine Query Data," *Nature* 457, no. 7232 (2009). The flaws in the original model were discussed in David Lazer, Ryan Kennedy, Gary King, and Alessandro Vespignani, "The Parable of Google Flu: Traps in Big Data Analysis," *Science* 343, no. 6176 (2014). A corrected model is presented in Shihao Yang, Mauricio Santillana, and S. C. Kou, "Accurate Estimation of Influenza Epidemics Using Google Search Data Via ARGO," *Proceedings of the National Academy of Sciences* 112, no. 47 (2015).

58 *which searches most closely track housing prices:* Seth Stephens-Davidowitz and Hal Varian, "A Hands-on Guide to Google Data," mimeo, 2015. Also see Marcelle Chauvet, Stuart Gabriel, and Chandler Lutz, "Mortgage Default Risk: New Evidence from Internet Search Queries," *Journal of Urban Economics* 96 (2016).

60 *Bill Clinton:* Sergey Brin and Larry Page, "The Anatomy of a Large-Scale Hypertextual Web Search Engine," Seventh International World-Wide Web Conference, April 14–18, 1998, Brisbane, Australia.

61 *porn sites:* John Battelle, *The Search: How Google and Its Rivals Rewrote the Rules of Business and Transformed Our Culture* (New York: Penguin, 2005).

61 *crowdsource the opinions:* A good discussion of this can be found in Steven Levy, *In the Plex: How Google Thinks, Works, and Shapes Our Lives* (New York: Simon & Schuster, 2011).

64 *"Sell your house":* This quote was also included in Joe Drape,

"Ahmed Zayat's Journey: Bankruptcy and Big Bets," *New York Times,* June 5, 2015, A1. However, the article incorrectly attributes the quote to Seder. It was actually made by another member of his team.

65 *I first met up with Seder:* I interviewed Jeff Seder and Patty Murray in Ocala, Florida, from June 12, 2015, through June 14, 2015.

66 *Roughly one-third:* The reasons racehorses fail are rough estimates by Jeff Seder, based on his years in the business.

66 *hundreds of horses die:* Supplemental Tables of Equine Injury Database Statistics for Thoroughbreds, http://jockeyclub.com/pdfs/eid_7_year_tables.pdf.

66 *mostly due to broken legs:* "Postmortem Examination Program," California Animal Health and Food Laboratory System, 2013.

67 *Still, more than three-fourths do not win a major race:* Avalyn Hunter, "A Case for Full Siblings," *Bloodhorse,* April 18, 2014, http://www.bloodhorse.com/horse-racing/articles/115014/a-case-for-full-siblings.

67 *Earvin Johnson III:* Melody Chiu, "E. J. Johnson Loses 50 Lbs. Since Undergoing Gastric Sleeve Surgery," *People,* October 1, 2014.

67 *LeBron James, whose mom is 5'5":* Eli Saslow, "Lost Stories of LeBron, Part 1," ESPN.com, October 17, 2013, http://www.espn.com/nba/story/_/id/9825052/how-lebron-james-life-changed-fourth-grade-espn-magazine.

68 *The Green Monkey:* See Sherry Ross, "16 Million Dollar Baby," New York *Daily News,* March 12, 2006, and Jay Privman, "The Green Monkey, Who Sold for $16M, Retired," ESPN.com, February 12, 2008, http://www.espn.com/sports/horse/news/story?id=3242341. A video of the auction is available at "$16 Million Horse," YouTube video, posted November 1, 2008, https://www.youtube.com/watch?v=EyggMC85Zsg.

71 *weakness of Google's attempt to predict influenza:* Sharad Goel, Jake M. Hofman, Sébastien Lahaie, David M. Pennock, and Duncan J. Watts, "Predicting Consumer Behavior with Web Search," *Proceedings of the National Academy of Sciences* 107, no. 41 (2010).

72 *Strawberry Pop-Tarts:* Constance L. Hays, "What Wal-Mart Knows About Customers' Habits," *New York Times*, November 14, 2004.

74 *"It worked out great":* I interviewed Orley Ashenfelter by phone on October 27, 2016.

80 *studied hundreds of heterosexual speed daters:* Daniel A. McFarland, Dan Jurafsky, and Craig Rawlings, "Making the Connection: Social Bonding in Courtship Situations," *American Journal of Sociology* 118, no. 6 (2013).

82 *Leonard Cohen once gave his nephew the following advice for wooing women:* Jonathan Greenberg, "What I Learned From My Wise Uncle Leonard Cohen," *Huffington Post*, November 11, 2016.

83 *the words used in hundreds of thousands of Facebook:* H. Andrew Schwartz et al., "Personality, Gender, and Age in the Language of Social Media: The Open-Vocabulary Approach," *PloS One* 8, no. 9 (2013). The paper also breaks down the ways people speak based on how they score on personality tests. Here is what they found:

88 *text of thousands of books and movie scripts:* Andrew J. Reagan, Lewis Mitchell, Dilan Kiley, Christopher M. Danforth, and Peter Sheridan Dodds, "The Emotional Arcs of Stories Are Dominated by Six Basic Shapes," *EPJ Data Science* 5, no. 1 (2016).

91 *what types of stories get shared:* Jonah Berger and Katherine L. Milkman, "What Makes Online Content Viral?" *Journal of Marketing Research* 49, no. 2 (2012).

95 *why do some publications lean left:* This research is all fleshed out in Matthew Gentzkow and Jesse M. Shapiro, "What Drives Media Slant? Evidence from U.S. Daily Newspapers," *Econometrica* 78, no. 1 (2010). Although they were merely Ph.D. students when this project started, Gentzkow and Shapiro are now star economists. Gentzkow, now a professor at Stanford, won the 2014 John Bates Clark Medal, given to the top economist under the age of forty. Shapiro, now a professor at Brown, is an editor of the prestigious *Journal of Political Economy.* Their joint paper on media slant is among the most cited papers for each.

96 *Rupert Murdoch:* Murdoch's ownership of the conservative *New York Post* could be explained by the fact that New York is so big, it can support newspapers of multiple viewpoints. However, it seems pretty clear the *Post* consistently loses money. See, for example, Joe Pompeo, "How Much Does the 'New York Post' Actually Lose?" *Politico,* August 30, 2013, http://www.politico.com/media/story/2013/08/how-much-does-the-new-york-post-actually-lose-001176.

97 *Shapiro told me:* I interviewed Matt Gentzkow and Jesse Shapiro on August 16, 2015, at the Royal Sonesta Boston.

98 *scanned yearbooks from American high schools:* Kate Rakelly, Sarah Sachs, Brian Yin, and Alexei A. Efros, "A Century of Portraits: A Visual Historical Record of American High School Yearbooks," paper presented at International Conference on Computer Vision, 2015. The photos are reprinted with permission from the authors.

99 *subjects in photos copied subjects in paintings:* See, for example, Christina Kotchemidova, "Why We Say 'Cheese': Producing the Smile in Snapshot Photography," *Critical Studies in Media Communication* 22, no. 1 (2005).

100 *measure GDP based on how much light there is in these countries at night:* J. Vernon Henderson, Adam Storeygard, and David N. Weil, "Measuring Economic Growth from Outer Space," *American Economic Review* 102, no. 2 (2012).

101 *estimated GDP was now 90 percent higher:* Kathleen Caulderwood, "Nigerian GDP Jumps 89% as Economists Add in Telecoms, Nollywood," *IBTimes*, April 7, 2014, http://www.ibtimes.com /nigerian-gdp-jumps-89-economists-add-telecoms-nollywood -1568219.

101 *Reisinger said:* I interviewed Joe Reisinger by phone on June 10, 2015.

103 *$50 million:* Leena Rao, "SpaceX and Tesla Backer Just Invested $50 Million in This Startup," *Fortune*, September 24, 2015.

CHAPTER 4: DIGITAL TRUTH SERUM

106 *important paper in 1950:* Hugh J. Parry and Helen M. Crossley, "Validity of Responses to Survey Questions," *Public Opinion Quarterly* 14, 1 (1950).

106 *survey asked University of Maryland graduates:* Frauke Kreuter, Stanley Presser, and Roger Tourangeau, "Social Desirability Bias in CATI, IVR, and Web Surveys," *Public Opinion Quarterly* 72(5), 2008.

107 *failure of the polls:* For an article arguing that lying might be a problem in trying to predict support for Trump, see Thomas B. Edsall, "How Many People Support Trump but Don't Want to Admit It?" *New York Times*, May 15, 2016, SR2. But for an argument that this was not a large factor, see Andrew Gelman, "Explanations for That Shocking 2% Shift," *Statistical Modeling, Causal Inference, and Social Science*, November 9, 2016, http://andrewgelman .com/2016/11/09/explanations-shocking-2-shift/.

107 *says Tourangeau:* I interviewed Roger Tourangeau by phone on May 5, 2015.

107 *so many people say they are above average:* This is discussed in Adam Grant, *Originals: How Non-Conformists Move the World* (New York: Viking, 2016). The original source is David Dunning, Chip Heath, and Jerry M. Suls, "Flawed Self-Assessment: Impli-

cations for Health, Education, and the Workplace," *Psychological Science in the Public Interest* 5 (2004).

108 *mess with surveys:* Anya Kamenetz, " 'Mischievous Responders' Confound Research on Teens," *nprED*, May 22, 2014, http://www .npr.org/sections/ed/2014/05/22/313166161/mischievous-respond ers-confound-research-on-teens. The original research this article discusses is Joseph P. Robinson-Cimpian, "Inaccurate Estimation of Disparities Due to Mischievous Responders," *Educational Researcher* 43, no. 4 (2014).

110 *search for "porn" more than they search for "weather":* https:// www.google.com/trends/explore?date=all&geo=US&q=porn,weat her.

110 *admit they watch pornography:* Amanda Hess, "How Many Women Are Not Admitting to Pew That They Watch Porn?" *Slate*, October 11, 2013, http://www.slate.com/blogs/xx_factor /2013/10/11/pew_online_viewing_study_percentage_of_women _who_watch_online_porn_is_growing.html.

110 *"cock," "fuck," and "porn":* Nicholas Diakopoulus, "Sex, Violence, and Autocomplete Algorithms," *Slate*, August 2, 2013, http:// www.slate.com/articles/technology/future_tense/2013/08/words _banned_from_bing_and_google_s_autocomplete_algorithms .html.

111 *3.6 times more likely to tell Google they regret:* I estimate, including various phrasings, there are about 1,730 American Google searches every month explicitly saying they regret having children. There are only about 50 expressing a regret not having children. There are about 15.9 million Americans over the age of forty-five who have no children. There are about 152 million Americans who have children. This means, among the eligible population, people with children are about 3.6 times as likely to express a regret on Google than people without children. Obviously, as mentioned in the text but worth emphasizing again, these confessionals to Google are only made by a small, select number of people—presumably those feeling a strong enough regret that they momentarily forget that Google cannot help them here.

113 *highest support for gay marriage:* These estimates are from Nate

Silver, "How Opinion on Same-Sex Marriage Is Changing, and What It Means," FiveThirtyEight, March 26, 2013, http://fivethirty eight.blogs.nytimes.com/2013/03/26/how-opinion-on-same-sex -marriage-is-changing-and-what-it-means/?_r=0.

113 *About 2.5 percent of male Facebook users who list a gender of interest say they are interested in men:* Author's analysis of Facebook ads data. I do not include Facebook users who list "men and women." My analysis suggests a non-trivial percent of users who say they are interested in men and women interpret the question as interest in friendship rather than romantic interest.

115 *about 5 percent of male porn searches are for gay-male porn:* As discussed, Google Trends does not break down searches by gender. Google AdWords breaks down page views for various categories by gender. However, this data is far less precise. To estimate the searches by gender, I first use the search data to get a statewide estimate of the percent of gay porn searches by state. I then normalize this data by the Google AdWords gender data. Another way to get gender-specific data is using PornHub data. However, PornHub could be a highly selected sample, since many gay people might instead use sites focused only on gay porn. PornHub suggests that gay porn use among men is lower than Google searches would suggest. However, it confirms that there is not a strong relationship between tolerance toward homosexuality and male gay porn use. All this data and further notes are available on my website, at sethsd.com, in the section "Sex."

116 *4 percent of them are openly gay on Facebook:* Author's calculation of Facebook ads data: On February 8, 2017, roughly 300 male high school students in San Francisco-Oakland-San Jose media market on Facebook said they were interested in men. Roughly, 7,800 said they were interested in women.

119 *"In Iran we don't have homosexuals":* " 'We Don't Have Any Gays in Iran,' Iranian President Tells Ivy League Audience," Daily Mail.com, September 25, 2007, http://www.dailymail.co.uk/news /article-483746/We-dont-gays-Iran-Iranian-president-tells-Ivy -League-audience.html.

119 *"We do not have them in our city":* Brett Logiurato, "Sochi Mayor

Claims There Are No Gay People in the City," *Sports Illustrated*, January 27, 2014.

119 *internet behavior reveals significant interest in gay porn in Sochi and Iran:* According to Google AdWords, there are tens of thousands of searches every year for "гей порно" (gay porn). The percent of porn searches for gay porn is roughly similar in Sochi as in the United States. Google AdWords does not include data for Iran. PornHub also does not report data for Iran. However, PornMD studied their search data and reported that five of the top ten search terms in Iran were for gay porn. This included "daddy love" and "hotel businessman" and is reported in Joseph Patrick McCormick, "Survey Reveals Searches for Gay Porn Are Top in Countries Banning Homosexuality," *PinkNews,* http://www.pinknews .co.uk/2013/03/13/survey-reveals-searches-for-gay-porn-are-top -in-countries-banning-homosexuality/. According to Google Trends, about 2 percent of porn searches in Iran are for gay porn, which is lower than in the United States but still suggests widespread interest.

122 *When it comes to sex:* Stephens-Davidowitz, "Searching for Sex." Data for this section can be found on my website, sethsd.com, in the section "Sex."

122 *11 percent of women:* Current Contraceptive Status Among Women Aged 15–44: United States, 2011–2013, Centers for Disease Control and Prevention, http://www.cdc.gov/nchs/data/data briefs/db173_table.pdf#1.

122 *10 percent of them to become pregnant every month:* David Spiegelhalter, "Sex: What Are the Chances?" BBC News, March 15, 2012, http://www.bbc.com/future/story/20120313-sex-in-the-city-or -elsewhere.

122 *1 in 113 women of childbearing age:* There are roughly 6.6 million pregnancies every year and there are 62 million women between ages 15 and 44.

128 *performing oral sex on the opposite gender:* As mentioned, I do not know the gender of a Google searcher. I am assuming that the overwhelming majority of searches looking how to perform cunnilingus are by men and that the overwhelming majority of searches

looking how to perform fellatio are by women. This is both because the large majority of people are straight and because there might be less of a need to learn how to please a same-sex partner.

128 *top five negative words:* Author's analysis of Google AdWords data.

130 *kill them:* Evan Soltas and Seth Stephens-Davidowitz, "The Rise of Hate Search," *New York Times,* December 13, 2015, SR1. Data and more details can be found on my website, sethsd.com, in the section "Islamophobia."

132 *seventeen times more common:* Author's analysis of Google Trends data.

132 *Martin Luther King Jr. Day:* Author's analysis of Google Trends data.

133 *correlates with the black-white wage gap:* Ashwin Rode and Anand J. Shukla, "Prejudicial Attitudes and Labor Market Outcomes," mimeo, 2013.

134 *Their parents:* Seth Stephens-Davidowitz, "Google, Tell Me. Is My Son a Genius?" *New York Times,* January 19, 2014, SR6. The data for exact searches can be found using Google AdWords. Estimates can also be found with Google Trends, by comparing searches with the words "gifted" and "son" versus "gifted" and "daughter." Compare, for example, https://www.google.com/trends /explore?date=all&geo=US&q=gifted%20son,gifted%20daughter and https://www.google.com/trends/explore?date=all&geo=US &q=overweight%20son,overweight%20daughter. One exception to the general pattern that there are more questions about sons' brains and daughters' bodies is there are more searches for "fat son" than "fat daughter." This seems to be related to the popularity of incest porn discussed earlier. Roughly 20 percent of searches with the words "fat" and "son" also include the word "porn."

135 *girls are 9 percent more likely than boys to be in gifted programs:* "Gender Equity in Education: A Data Snapshot," Office for Civil Rights, U.S. Department of Education, June 2012, http://www2.ed .gov/about/offices/list/ocr/docs/gender-equity-in-education.pdf.

136 *About 28 percent of girls are overweight, while 35 percent of boys are:* Data Resource Center for Child and Adolescent Health,

http://www.childhealthdata.org/browse/survey/results?q=2415
&g=455&a=3879&r=1.

137 *Stormfront profiles:* Stephens-Davidowitz, "The Data of Hate."
The relevant data can be downloaded at sethsd.com, in the data
section headlined "Stormfront."

139 *Stormfront during Donald Trump's candidacy:* Google search interest in Stormfront was similar in October 2016 to the levels it
was during October 2015. This is in stark contrast to the situation
during Obama's first election. In October 2008, search interest in
Stormfront had risen almost 60 percent compared to the previous
October. On the day after Obama was elected, Google searches for
Stormfront had risen roughly tenfold. On the day after Trump was
elected, Stormfront searches rose about two-point-five-fold. This
was roughly equivalent to the rise the day after George W. Bush
was elected in 2004 and may largely reflect news interest among
political junkies.

141 *political segregation on the internet:* Matthew Gentzkow and
Jesse M. Shapiro, "Ideological Segregation Online and Offline,"
Quarterly Journal of Economics 126, no. 4 (2011).

144 *friends on Facebook:* Eytan Bakshy, Solomon Messing, and Lada
A. Adamic, "Exposure to Ideologically Diverse News and Opinion on Facebook," *Science* 348, no. 6239 (2015). They found that,
among the 9 percent of active Facebook users who declare their
ideology, about 23 percent of their friends who also declare an ideology have the opposite ideology and 28.5 percent of the news they
see on Facebook is from the opposite ideology. These numbers are
not directly comparable with other numbers on segregation because they only include the small sample of Facebook users who
declare their ideology. Presumably, these users are much more
likely to be politically active and associate with other politically
active users with the same ideology. If this is correct, the diversity
among all users will be much greater.

144 *one crucial reason that Facebook:* Another factor that makes social
media surprisingly diverse is that it gives a big bonus to extremely
popular and widely shared articles, no matter their political slant.
See Solomon Messing and Sean Westwood, "Selective Exposure

in the Age of Social Media: Endorsements Trump Partisan Source Affiliation When Selecting News Online," 2014.

144 *more friends on Facebook than they do offline:* See Ben Quinn, "Social Network Users Have Twice as Many Friends Online as in Real Life," *Guardian*, May 8, 2011. This article discusses a 2011 study by the Cystic Fibrosis Trust, which found that the average social network user has 121 online friends compared with 55 physical friends. According to a 2014 Pew Research study, the average Facebook user had more than 300 friends. See Aaron Smith, "6 New Facts About Facebook," February 3, 2014, http://www.pewresearch.org/fact-tank/2014/02/03/6-new-facts-about-facebook/.

144 *weak ties:* Eytan Bakshy, Itamar Rosenn, Cameron Marlow, and Lada Adamic, "The Role of Social Networks in Information Diffusion," *Proceedings of the 21st International Conference on World Wide Web*, 2012.

145 *"doom-and-gloom predictions haven't come true":* "Study: Child Abuse on Decline in U.S.," Associated Press, December 12, 2011.

146 *did child abuse really drop:* See Seth Stephens-Davidowitz, "How Googling Unmasks Child Abuse," *New York Times*, July 14, 2013, SR5, and Seth Stephens-Davidowitz, "Unreported Victims of an Economic Downturn," mimeo, 2013.

146 *facing long wait times and giving up:* "Stopping Child Abuse: It Begins With You," *The Arizona Republic*, March 26, 2016.

147 *off-the-books ways to terminate a pregnancy:* Seth Stephens-Davidowitz, "The Return of the D.I.Y. Abortion," *New York Times*, March 6, 2016, SR2. Data and more details can be found on my website, sethsd.com, in the section "Self-Induced Abortion."

150 *similar average circulations:* Alliance for Audited Media, Consumer Magazines, http://abcas3.auditedmedia.com/ecirc/magtitlesearch.asp.

151 *On Facebook:* Author's calculations, on October 4, 2016, using Facebook's Ads Manager.

151 *top ten most visited websites:* "List of Most Popular Websites," Wikipedia. According to Alexa, which tracks browsing behavior, as of September 4, 2016, the most popular porn site was XVideos, and this was the 57th-most-popular website. According to SimilarWeb,

as of September 4, 2016, the most popular porn site was XVideos, and this was the 17th-most-popular website. The top ten, according to Alexa, are Google, YouTube, Facebook, Baidu, Yahoo!, Amazon, Wikipedia, Tencent QQ, Google India, and Twitter.

153 *In the early morning of September 5, 2006:* This story is from David Kirkpatrick, *The Facebook Effect: The Inside Story of the Company That Is Connecting the World* (New York: Simon & Schuster, 2010).

155 *great businesses are built on secrets:* Peter Thiel and Blake Masters, *Zero to One: Notes on Startups, or How to Build the Future* (New York: The Crown Publishing Group, 2014).

157 *says Xavier Amatriain:* I interviewed Xavier Amatriain by phone on May 5, 2015.

159 *top questions Americans had during Obama's 2014:* Author's analysis of Google Trends data.

162 *this time at a mosque:* "The President Speaks at the Islamic Society of Baltimore," YouTube video, posted February 3, 2016, https://www.youtube.com/watch?v=LRRVdVqAjdw.

163 *hateful, rageful searches against Muslims dropped in the hours after the president's address:* Author's analysis of Google Trends data. Searches for "kill Muslims" were lower than the comparable period a week before. In addition, searches that included "Muslims" and one of the top five negative words about this group were lower.

CHAPTER 5: ZOOMING IN

166 *how childhood experiences influence which baseball team you support:* Seth Stephens-Davidowitz, "They Hook You When You're Young," *New York Times*, April 20, 2014, SR5. Data and code for this study can be found on my website, sethsd.com, in the section "Baseball."

170 *the single most important year:* Yair Ghitza and Andrew Gelman, "The Great Society, Reagan's Revolution, and Generations of Presidential Voting," unpublished manuscript.

173 *Chetty explains:* I interviewed Raj Chetty by phone on July 30, 2015.

176 *escape the grim reaper:* Raj Chetty et al., "The Association Be-

tween Income and Life Expectancy in the United States, 2001–2014," *JAMA* 315, no. 16 (2016).

178 *Contagious behavior may be driving some of this:* Julia Belluz, "Income Inequality Is Chipping Away at Americans' Life Expectancy," vox.com, April 11, 2016.

178 *why some people cheat on their taxes:* Raj Chetty, John Friedman, and Emmanuel Saez, "Using Differences in Knowledge Across Neighborhoods to Uncover the Impacts of the EITC on Earnings," *American Economic Review* 103, no. 7 (2013).

180 *I decided to download Wikipedia:* This is from Seth Stephens-Davidowitz, "The Geography of Fame," *New York Times*, March 23, 2014, SR6. Data can be found on my website, sethsd.com, in the section "Wikipedia Birth Rate, by County." For help downloading and coding county of birth of every Wikipedia entrant, I thank Noah Stephens-Davidowitz.

183 *a big city:* For more evidence on the value of cities, see Ed Glaeser, *Triumph of the City* (New York: Penguin, 2011). (Glaeser was my advisor in graduate school.)

191 *many examples of real life imitating art:* David Levinson, ed., *Encyclopedia of Crime and Punishment* (Thousand Oaks, CA: SAGE, 2002).

191 *subjects exposed to a violent film will report more anger and hostility:* Craig Anderson et al., "The Influence of Media Violence on Youth," *Psychological Science in the Public Interest* 4 (2003).

192 *On weekends with a popular violent movie:* Gordon Dahl and Stefano DellaVigna, "Does Movie Violence Increase Violent Crime?" *Quarterly Journal of Economics* 124, no. 2 (2009).

195 *Google searches can also be broken down by the minute:* Seth Stephens-Davidowitz, "Days of Our Digital Lives," *New York Times*, July 5, 2015, SR4.

196 *alcohol is a major contributor to crime:* Anna Richardson and Tracey Budd, "Young Adults, Alcohol, Crime and Disorder," *Criminal Behaviour and Mental Health* 13, no. 1 (2003); Richard A. Scribner, David P. MacKinnon, and James H. Dwyer, "The Risk of Assaultive Violence and Alcohol Availability in Los Angeles County," *American Journal of Public Health* 85, no. 3 (1995);

Dennis M. Gorman, Paul W. Speer, Paul J. Gruenewald, and Erich W. Labouvie, "Spatial Dynamics of Alcohol Availability, Neighborhood Structure and Violent Crime," *Journal of Studies on Alcohol* 62, no. 5 (2001); Tony H. Grubesic, William Alex Pridemore, Dominique A. Williams, and Loni Philip-Tabb, "Alcohol Outlet Density and Violence: The Role of Risky Retailers and Alcohol-Related Expenditures," *Alcohol and Alcoholism* 48, no. 5 (2013).

196 *letting all four of his sons play football:* "Ed McCaffrey Knew Christian McCaffrey Would Be Good from the Start—'The Herd,'" YouTube video, posted December 3, 2015, https://www.youtube.com/watch?v=boHMmp7DpX0.

197 *analyzing piles of data:* Researchers have found more from utilizing this crime data broken down into small time increments. One example? Domestic violence complaints rise immediately after a city's football team loses a game it was expected to win. See David Card and Gordon B. Dahl, "Family Violence and Football: The Effect of Unexpected Emotional Cues on Violent Behavior," *Quarterly Journal of Economics* 126, no. 1 (2011).

197 *Here's how Bill Simmons:* Bill Simmons, "It's Hard to Say Goodbye to David Ortiz," ESPN.com, June 2, 2009, http://www.espn.com/espnmag/story?id=4223584.

198 *how can we predict how a baseball player will perform in the future:* This is discussed in Nate Silver, *The Signal and the Noise: Why So Many Predictions Fail—But Some Don't* (New York: Penguin, 2012).

199 *"beefy sluggers" indeed do, on average, peak early:* Ryan Campbell, "How Will Prince Fielder Age?" October 28, 2011, http://www.fangraphs.com/blogs/how-will-prince-fielder-age/.

199 *Ortiz's doppelgangers':* This data was kindly provided to me by Rob McQuown of Baseball Prospectus.

204 *Kohane asks:* I interviewed Isaac Kohane by phone on June 15, 2015.

205 *James Heywood is an entrepreneur:* I interviewed James Heywood by phone on August 17, 2015.

CHAPTER 6: ALL THE WORLD'S A LAB

207 *February 27, 2000:* This story is discussed, among other places, in Brian Christian, "The A/B Test: Inside the Technology That's Changing the Rules of Business," *Wired*, April 25, 2012, http://www.wired.com/2012/04/ff_abtesting/.

209 *When teachers were paid, teacher absenteeism dropped:* Esther Duflo, Rema Hanna, and Stephen P. Ryan, "Incentives Work: Getting Teachers to Come to School," *American Economic Review* 102, no. 4 (2012).

209 *when Bill Gates learned of Duflo's work:* Ian Parker, "The Poverty Lab," *New Yorker*, May 17, 2010.

211 *Google engineers ran seven thousand A/B tests:* Christian, "The A/B Test."

211 *forty-one marginally different shades of blue:* Douglas Bowman, "Goodbye, Google," stopdesign, March 20, 2009, http://stopdesign.com/archive/2009/03/20/goodbye-google.html.

211 *Facebook now runs:* Eytan Bakshy, "Big Experiments: Big Data's Friend for Making Decisions," April 3, 2014, https://www.facebook.com/notes/facebook-data-science/big-experiments-big-datas-friend-for-making-decisions/10152160441298859/. Sources for information on pharmaceutical studies can be found at "How many clinical trials are started each year?" Quora post, https://www.quora.com/How-many-clinical-trials-are-started-each-year.

211 *Optimizely:* I interviewed Dan Siroker by phone on April 29, 2015.

214 *netting the campaign roughly $60 million:* Dan Siroker, "How Obama Raised $60 Million by Running a Simple Experiment," Optimizely blog, November 29, 2010, https://blog.optimizely.com/2010/11/29/how-obama-raised-60-million-by-running-a-simple-experiment/.

214 *The* Boston Globe *A/B-tests headlines:* The *Boston Globe* A/B tests and results were provided to the author. Some details about the *Globe's* testing can be found at "The Boston Globe: Discovering and Optimizing a Value Proposition for Content," Marketing Sherpa Video Archive, https://www.marketingsherpa.com/video/boston-globe-optimization-summit2. This includes a recorded

conversation between Peter Doucette of the *Globe* and Pamela Markey at MECLABS.

217 *Benson says:* I interviewed Clark Benson by phone on July 23, 2015.

217 *added a rightward-pointing arrow surrounded by a square:* "Enhancing Text Ads on the Google Display Network," Inside AdSense, December 3, 2012, https://adsense.googleblog.com/2012 /12/enhancing-text-ads-on-google-display.html.

218 *Google customers were critical:* See, for example, "Large arrows appearing in google ads—please remove," DoubleClick Publisher Help Forum, https://productforums.google.com/forum/#!topic/dfp /p_TRMqWUF9s.

219 *the rise of behavioral addictions in contemporary society:* Adam Alter, *Irresistible: The Rise of Addictive Technology and the Business of Keeping Us Hooked* (New York: Penguin, 2017).

219 *Top addictions reported to Google:* Author's analysis of Google Trends data.

222 *says Levitt in a lecture:* This is discussed in a video currently featured on the Freakonomics page of the Harry Walker Speakers Bureau, http://www.harrywalker.com/speakers/authors-of-freako nomics/.

225 *beer and soft drink ads run during the Super Bowl:* Wesley R. Hartmann and Daniel Klapper, "Super Bowl Ads," unpublished manuscript, 2014.

226 *a pimply kid in his underwear:* For the strong case that we likely are living in a computer simulation, see Nick Bostrom, "Are We Living in a Computer Simulation?" *Philosophical Quarterly* 53, no. 211 (2003).

227 *Of forty-three American presidents:* Los Angeles Times staff, "U.S. Presidential Assassinations and Attempts," *Los Angeles Times*, January 22, 2012, http://timelines.latimes.com/us-presi dential-assassinations-and-attempts/.

227 *Compare John F. Kennedy and Ronald Reagan:* Benjamin F. Jones and Benjamin A. Olken, "Do Assassins Really Change History?" *New York Times*, April 12, 2015, SR12.

227 *Kadyrov died:* A disturbing video of the attack can be seen at "Pa-

rade surprise (Chechnya 2004)," YouTube video, posted March 31, 2009, https://www.youtube.com/watch?v=fHWhs5QkfuY.

227 *Hitler had changed his schedule:* This story is also discussed in Jones and Olken, "Do Assassins Really Change History?"

228 *the effect of having your leader murdered:* Benjamin F. Jones and Benjamin A. Olken, "Hit or Miss? The Effect of Assassinations on Institutions and War," *American Economic Journal: Macroeconomics* 1, no. 2 (2009).

229 *winning the lottery does not:* This point is made in John Tierney, "How to Win the Lottery (Happily)," *New York Times*, May 27, 2014, D5. Tierney's piece discusses the following studies: Bénédicte Apouey and Andrew E. Clark, "Winning Big but Feeling No Better? The Effect of Lottery Prizes on Physical and Mental Health," *Health Economics* 24, no. 5 (2015); Jonathan Gardner and Andrew J. Oswald, "Money and Mental Wellbeing: A Longitudinal Study of Medium-Sized Lottery Wins," *Journal of Health Economics* 26, no. 1 (2007); and Anna Hedenus, "At the End of the Rainbow: Post-Winning Life Among Swedish Lottery Winners," unpublished manuscript, 2011. Tierney's piece also points out that the famous 1978 study—Philip Brickman, Dan Coates, and Ronnie Janoff-Bulman, "Lottery Winners and Accident Victims: Is Happiness Relative?" *Journal of Personality and Social Psychology* 36, no. 8 (1978)—which found that winning the lottery does not make you happy was based on a tiny sample.

229 *your neighbor winning the lottery:* See Peter Kuhn, Peter Kooreman, Adriaan Soetevent, and Arie Kapteyn, "The Effects of Lottery Prizes on Winners and Their Neighbors: Evidence from the Dutch Postcode Lottery," *American Economic Review* 101, no. 5 (2011), and Sumit Agarwal, Vyacheslav Mikhed, and Barry Scholnick, "Does Inequality Cause Financial Distress? Evidence from Lottery Winners and Neighboring Bankruptcies," working paper, 2016.

229 *neighbors of lottery winners:* Agarwal, Mikhed, and Scholnick, "Does Inequality Cause Financial Distress?"

230 *doctors can be motivated by monetary incentives:* Jeffrey Clemens and Joshua D. Gottlieb, "Do Physicians' Financial Incentives Affect Medical Treatment and Patient Health?" *American Eco-*

nomic Review 104, no. 4 (2014). Note that these results do not mean that doctors are evil. In fact, the results might be more troubling if the extra procedures doctors ordered when they were paid more to order them actually saved lives. If this were the case, it would mean that doctors needed to be paid enough to order life-saving treatments. Clemens and Gottlieb's results suggest, instead, that doctors will order lifesaving treatments no matter how much money they are given to order them. For procedures that don't help all that much, doctors must be paid enough to order them. Another way to say this: doctors don't pay too much attention to monetary incentives for life-threatening stuff; they pay a ton of attention to monetary incentives for unimportant stuff.

231 *$150 million:* Robert D. McFadden and Eben Shapiro, "Finally, a Face to Fit Stuyvesant: A High School of High Achievers Gets a High-Priced Home," *New York Times,* September 8, 1992.

231 *It offers:* Course offerings are available on Stuy's website, http://stuy.enschool.org/index.jsp.

231 *one-quarter of its graduates are accepted:* Anna Bahr, "When the College Admissions Battle Starts at Age 3," *New York Times,* July 29, 2014, http://www.nytimes.com/2014/07/30/upshot/when -the-college-admissions-battle-starts-at-age-3.html.

231 *Stuyvesant trained:* Sewell Chan, "The Obama Team's New York Ties," *New York Times,* November 25, 2008; Evan T. R. Rosenman, "Class of 1984: Lisa Randall," *Harvard Crimson,* June 2, 2009; "Gary Shteyngart on Stuyvesant High School: My New York," YouTube video, posted August 4, 2010, https://www.youtube.com /watch?v=NQ_phGkC-Tk; Candace Amos, "30 Stars Who Attended NYC Public Schools," New York *Daily News,* May 29, 2015.

231 *Its commencement speakers have included:* Carl Campanile, "Kids Stuy High Over Bubba: He'll Address Ground Zero School's Graduation," *New York Post,* March 22, 2002; United Nations Press Release, "Stuyvesant High School's 'Multicultural Tapestry' Eloquent Response to Hatred, Says Secretary-General in Graduation Address," June 23, 2004; "Conan O'Brien's Speech at Stuyvesant's Class of 2006 Graduation in Lincoln Center," YouTube video, posted May 6, 2012, https://www.youtube.com/watch?v=zAMkUE9Oxnc.

231 *Stuy ranked number one:* See https://k12.niche.com/rankings /public-high-schools/best-overall/.

232 *Fewer than 5 percent:* Pamela Wheaton, "8th-Graders Get High School Admissions Results," *Insideschools,* March 4, 2016, http:// insideschools.org/blog/item/1001064-8th-graders-get-high -school-admissions-results.

235 *prisoners assigned to harsher conditions:* M. Keith Chen and Jesse M. Shapiro, "Do Harsher Prison Conditions Reduce Recidivism? A Discontinuity-Based Approach," *American Law and Economics Review* 9, no. 1 (2007).

236 *The effects of Stuyvesant High School?* Atila Abdulkadiroğlu, Joshua Angrist, and Parag Pathak, "The Elite Illusion: Achievement Effects at Boston and New York Exam Schools," *Econometrica* 82, no. 1 (2014). The same null result was independently found by Will Dobbie and Roland G. Fryer Jr., "The Impact of Attending a School with High-Achieving Peers: Evidence from the New York City Exam Schools," *American Economic Journal: Applied Economics* 6, no. 3 (2014).

238 *average graduate of Harvard makes:* See http://www.payscale .com/college-salary-report/bachelors.

238 *similar students accepted to similarly prestigious schools who choose to attend different schools end up in about the same place:* Stacy Berg Dale and Alan B. Krueger, "Estimating the Payoff to Attending a More Selective College: An Application of Selection on Observables and Unobservables," *Quarterly Journal of Economics* 117, no. 4 (2002).

239 *Warren Buffett:* Alice Schroeder, *The Snowball: Warren Buffett and the Business of Life* (New York: Bantam, 2008).

CHAPTER 7: BIG DATA, BIG SCHMATA? WHAT IT CANNOT DO

247 *claimed they could predict which way:* Johan Bollen, Huina Mao, and Xiaojun Zeng, "Twitter Mood Predicts the Stock Market," *Journal of Computational Science* 2, no. 1 (2011).

248 *The tweet-based hedge fund was shut down:* James Mackintosh, "Hedge Fund That Traded Based on Social Media Signals Didn't Work Out," *Financial Times,* May 25, 2012.

250 *could not reproduce the correlation:* Christopher F. Chabris et al., "Most Reported Genetic Associations with General Intelligence Are Probably False Positives," *Psychological Science* (2012).

252 *Zoë Chance:* This story is discussed in TEDx Talks, "How to Make a Behavior Addictive: Zoë Chance at TEDx Mill River," YouTube video, posted May 14, 2013, https://www.youtube.com /watch?v=AHfiKav9fcQ. Some details of the story, such as the color of the pedometer, were fleshed out in interviews. I interviewed Chance by phone on April 20, 2015, and by email on July 11, 2016, and September 8, 2016.

253 *Numbers can be seductive:* This section is from Alex Peysakhovich and Seth Stephens-Davidowitz, "How Not to Drown in Numbers," *New York Times,* May 3, 2015, SR6.

254 *cheated outright in administering those tests:* Brian A. Jacob and Steven D. Levitt, "Rotten Apples: An Investigation of the Prevalence and Predictors of Teacher Cheating," *Quarterly Journal of Economics* 118, no. 3 (2003).

255 *says Thomas Kane:* I interviewed Thomas Kane by phone on April 22, 2015.

256 *"Each measure adds something of value":* Bill and Melinda Gates Foundation, "Ensuring Fair and Reliable Measures of Effective Teaching," http://k12education.gatesfoundation.org/wp-content/up loads/2015/05/MET_Ensuring_Fair_and_Reliable_Measures_Prac titioner_Brief.pdf.

CHAPTER 8: MO DATA, MO PROBLEMS?
WHAT WE SHOULDN'T DO

257 *Recently, three economists:* Oded Netzer, Alain Lemaire, and Michal Herzenstein, "When Words Sweat: Identifying Signals for Loan Default in the Text of Loan Applications," 2016.

258 *about 13 percent of borrowers:* Peter Renton, "Another Analysis of Default Rates at Lending Club and Prosper," October 25, 2012, http://www.lendacademy.com/lending-club-prosper-default -rates/.

261 *Facebook likes are frequently correlated:* Michal Kosinski, David Stillwell, and Thore Graepel, "Private Traits and Attributes Are

Predictable from Digital Records of Human Behavior," *PNAS* 110, no. 15 (2013).

265 *businesses are at the mercy of Yelp reviews:* Michael Luca, "Reviews, Reputation, and Revenue: The Case of Yelp," unpublished manuscript, 2011.

266 *Google searches related to suicide:* Christine Ma-Kellams, Flora Or, Ji Hyun Baek, and Ichiro Kawachi, "Rethinking Suicide Surveillance: Google Search Data and Self-Reported Suicidality Differentially Estimate Completed Suicide Risk," *Clinical Psychological Science* 4, no. 3 (2016).

267 *3.5 million Google searches:* This uses a methodology discussed on my website in the notes on self-induced abortion. I compare searches in the Google category "suicide" to searches for "how to tie a tie." There were 6.6 million Google searches for "how to tie a tie" in 2015. There were 6.5 times more searches in the category suicide. 6.5*6.6/12 » 3.5.

268 *12 murders of Muslims reported as hate crimes:* Bridge Initiative Team, "When Islamophobia Turns Violent: The 2016 U.S. Presidential Election," May 2, 2016, available at http://bridge.georgetown .edu/when-islamophobia-turns-violent-the-2016-u-s-presidential -elections/.

CONCLUSION

272 *What motivated Popper's crusade?:* Karl Popper, *Conjectures and Refutations* (London: Routledge & Kegan Paul, 1963).

275 *mapped every cholera case in the city:* Simon Rogers, "John Snow's Data Journalism: The Cholera Map That Changed the World," *Guardian*, March 15, 2013.

276 *Benjamin F. Jones:* I interviewed Benjamin Jones by phone on June 1, 2015. This work is also discussed in Aaron Chatterji and Benjamin Jones, "Harnessing Technology to Improve K–12 Education," Hamilton Project Discussion Paper, 2012.

283 *people tend not to finish treatises by economists:* Jordan Ellenberg, "The Summer's Most Unread Book Is . . . ," *Wall Street Journal*, July 3, 2014.

INDEX